The Yukon Queen

A Record-breaking Journey and the Story of an Amazing Car

One Englishman, one Dutch woman and two clapped-out Citroen 2CVs set out on an incredible journey of do-daring and fortitude and other very macho things - je ne regrette rien

Rob Godfrey

The Yukon Queen
Spiderbomb Publishing 2005
Version CS102
Copyright © Rob Godfrey 2005 – 2013

Contents

Prologue - 3
1) The Marie Anne - 6
2) Into The Arms Of America - 51
3) The Wild West - 77
4) The Arctic - 128
5) Wilderness Blues - 165
6) Lotus Land - 205
7) A Retreat In The Snow - 234
Epilogue - 250

Authors Note: *The Yukon Queen* was originally published as two e-books: *I've just had a brilliant idea!*, which was about the 2CV Alaska Challenge (the Prologue and Chapters 1 to 4 in this book), and *Down and out in Duncan and Port Hardy*, which was about the aftermath of the Alaska Challenge (Chapters 5 to 7 and the Epilogue in this book). Both e-books sold reasonably well. However, some readers didn't like the fact that what is really one continuous story had been split into two parts. Hence I'm now publishing *The Yukon Queen* in its entirety, both as a paperback and an e-book (the e-book contains a large number of photographs).

Prologue
Vancouver, October 1990

Caligula was in fine form. He delivered the punch line to a long, complicated joke about a hockey player with a lisp who went looking for a puck. Julius Caesar burst into laughter. I laughed too, even though I didn't really understand the joke. The bar heaved with Romans. It was noisy and hot and I began to feel tired. I finished my glass of Rickards Red and figured I'd head for the sack. My two companions had other ideas.

"Hey, Rob, there's someone I want you to meet". Caligula had to almost shout to make himself heard above the noise in the bar. He disappeared into the crowd in search of ' someone'. Caesar began telling me how much of a struggle it was to pay the rent each month. His sing-song voice melted into the general hubbub and I found myself only half listening to what he was saying.

We were in a neighbourhood pub in Kitslano, a trendy district on the west side of Vancouver. It was Halloween and the pub was packed with students from the University of British Columbia. The students were going to a fancy dress party later that evening. Everyone came dressed as an ancient Roman, except for me. I spoke with a London accent, and, in my mid twenties, I was a little bit older than the rest of the people crowded around the bar. Perhaps this had aroused Caligula and Caesar's curiosity. They came over and introduced themselves and we got talking. I'd had a late one the previous night and popped into the pub just for a quick drink. I now found myself on my third pint of Rickards Red.

Caligula returned:
"Rob, Rob, you'll never guess who this is!"Behind Caligula stood a smallish man with long hair. The long hair partially obscured his face, making it difficult to distinguish his features. An array of bracelets and beads hung from his body. A red silk shirt was

complimented by green corduroy trousers and a pair of dirty trainers. Nicotine stained fingers with long nails clutched a French cigarette. He had a lop-sided laurel leaf array on his head. Caligula steered the man towards me:

"This is Ringo Starr's brother. He's a fellow Brit."

Ringo Starr's brother let out a long chuckle and I could hear his beads and bracelets rattling above the general din.

"Pleased to meet you," I said, "what's your name?" My question was met with more chuckles.

"His name's Zak," put in Caesar, "he lives on a houseboat down at the harbour. He's a painter; well known in Vancouver."

Ringo Starr's brother stayed with us for about twenty minutes. I noticed that during this time he never actually said anything. Instead, he chuckled continuously and threw back gin like there was no tomorrow. Finally a Roman Empress took charge of him and I heard his chuckles die away as he was led across the room to meet Nero. It appeared that being Ringo Starr's brother was a full time job. I wondered just how he had ended-up in Vancouver.

And you may be wondering just how I ended-up in Vancouver. Well, during the winter of 1987/88 I'd been living in Calgary, trying to salvage a failed relationship with a woman. The summer of 1988 found me in San Francisco with the beautiful people, trying to forget the aforementioned woman. During these trips, Vancouver had been on my list of 'things to do', but I never got round to it. After San Francisco I spent nearly two years working back in London. Then I just took off on my own for Vancouver, but not before the Inland Revenue had relieved me of most of the money I had saved for the trip.

So, there I am in Vancouver, autumn 1990. I had hardly any money and did not have a permit to work in Canada. Not that there was much work anyway, since the world was going through a bad recession at the time. Sounds pretty dumb, huh? but I often do things without really understanding why I'm doing them. It's only years later, as your life starts to unravel a bit more, that you realise there's some kind of rhyme or reason to what has gone before, however tenuous.

But at the time there didn't appear to be much rhyme or reason in trying to find a job that just didn't exist, or writing reams of bad poetry, or regularly getting soaked from rain that fell like stair rods from the tempestuous sky. Yes, the monsoon season had arrived in Vancouver, Canada's main western port and gateway to the Pacific, and a continuous flow of churning blue/black clouds rolled down off the surrounding mountains. In these circumstances it is perhaps not surprising that I spent a lot of my time getting drunk in the neighbourhood pub.

Julius Caesar thrust another pint of Rickards Red into my hand and started telling me about the vacation he and Caligula had taken that summer, when they drove an old, beat- up VW camper van all the way along the Alaska Highway and up to Fairbanks, in the Alaskan interior. Now, I felt very tired that evening in the pub but their enthusiasm about the trip got me hooked and I was soon listening with rapt attention. I'd been vaguely aware of the Alaska Highway and knew that it was a very long road that went to, well, Alaska. But I didn't know much else about it. I now heard tales of a 1500 mile dirt and rock road that ran through a vast wilderness, a wilderness patrolled by bears, wolves and eagles. A road that threw up rock slides and floods and mountain precipices. A road where you could drive for days and never see another human being. A road where danger lay around every bend. Hey, this sounded like fun, so I pumped Caligula and Julius Caesar for more information. I suppose it was at that moment that I resolved that one day I, too, would drive the Alaska Highway.

I had no idea that the seed planted in my mind on that rainy evening in Vancouver would take nine years to germinate. I also had no idea of the drama that would ensue during my own trip to Alaska.

Chapter 1. The Marie Anne

We left London on Tuesday evening, 29th June 1999. A small group of friends and neighbours gathered outside my house to see us off. They clapped and cheered as our little convoy pulled away. I drove the No.1 car, Jose drove the No.2 car. The rush hour was just coming to an end and we had a clear run down to my parent's place in Kent, where we all had a meal in a nearby pub and toasted the success of the 2CV Alaska Challenge. I felt somewhat dazed. After all the years of research and planning it was finally happening. From here on in all the cares and worries of everyday existence had ceased. Life had now taken on the dimensions of a big adventure. Each day would bring a different horizon. Everything would be new. It made me feel both excited and apprehensive.

Jose was a bit more grounded than me. It would be another week or so before she left her job and flew over to Savannah to meet the *Marie Anne*, for the start of the road journey across North America. Waving off me and the cars in Rotterdam was a mini-holiday for her. In fact, Jose did seem more relaxed than I'd seen her in a long time. Our heated exchanges the previous week seemed to have cleared the air between us. Or maybe Jose's good mood was because I was about to go off on an ocean voyage, and she would be rid of me for the best part of two weeks.

We got down to Dover at half past eleven. The night was clear and warm and the man at the embarkation barrier would not let us through. He wore thick pebble glasses which made his eyes look like two moons. The moons studied the B70 customs forms I'd handed over. He told us the cars were freight and could not go on a passenger ferry. I tried to explain that the cars were actually being exported from Rotterdam, not Dover, and until they were loaded in Rotterdam they were still just ordinary cars. He wouldn't have it though, and steadfastly refused to let us through. We were confronting a case of 'jobsworth', and I don't think he really understood the B70 customs forms. Mind you, he wasn't the only one.

The B70 form is required when you are exporting goods from the European Union, and that includes cars. The B70 is about twelve pages long and a degree in quantum mechanics is required in order to understand it. It left me totally baffled, so back in May I took the B70 forms to the main UK Customs Office at Heathrow Airport. A customs officer called Mr Jackson was most helpful and showed me how to fill in the B70s correctly. Mr Jackson told me that he often had intrepid adventurers showing up at his office, waving B70 forms - his last case had been a Landrover that was going to be driven across Asia. This was the first time, though, that he had come across Citroen 2CVs that were being taken on an adventure journey. I gave Mr Jackson some of our publicity blurbs and he wished us the best of luck.

So, I knew the B70 forms had been filled out correctly and everything was in order; but Moon Eyes didn't know the paperwork. Of course, it would have been simpler to have not revealed the B70 forms and to have driven on the ferry as ordinary passengers. Thing is, those forms needed to have all the correct stamps on them, for when they were inspected by customs in Rotterdam and Savannah. The cars came from the UK, therefore there had to be a stamp somewhere on the B70s showing that the cars had left the UK. I know, bureaucracy is so idiotic, isn't it, and it's what led me to Dover Customs Office in the wee hours of the morning, where I had to stand in line with east European lorry drivers for the best part of an hour. When I did finally reach the front of the queue I discovered that the pleasant lady customs officer also had B70itis: she didn't have a clue what the forms were about. Fortunately her supervisor had a degree in quantum mechanics. The supervisor looked through the B70s, asked me a few questions then authorised our onward journey. The lady customs officer put the all important stamp on the forms and wished us luck on our journey. I gave out some of our publicity blurbs. Other customs officers came over to wish us good luck. It was all rather jolly, although I'm not quite sure what the east European lorry drivers made of it all.

This time we got through the embarkation barrier without any problems. Our intended ferry had sailed long ago, but the ferries ran at frequent intervals and we didn't have to wait long for the next one. At 2.00am we watched the lights of Dover receding behind us. As far as I was concerned they couldn't recede fast enough: the constant stream of 'good lucks' and 'bon voyages' we'd received had me fired-up and itching to get on with the journey.

No one checked our documents in Calais at 4am as we drove off the ferry. In Calais it's but a short drive from the ferry ramps to the motorway system and soon we were bowling along across northern France. Dawn began to break as we crossed into Belgium. This country gets a bad press, yet it gave birth to Margrette, Simone, Georges Remy (aka Hergé) and Jacques Brel, so it's all right by me. We stopped at a service station for breakfast, then snatched an hours sleep in the cars before continuing the journey. We finally arrived in Rotterdam mid morning, Wednesday 30th June.

Rotterdam is located in the south-western Netherlands, in Zuid-Holland. It lies at the heart of a maze of rivers and artificial waterways which form the seaward outlet of the rivers Rhine and Maas. This area has more than 70 harbours and is called Europoort. It is by far the largest port in the world. The city of Rotterdam is just one part of Europoort, which goes to show just how big and how confusing Europoort is.

Yes, very confusing. The shipping agent told us we would find the *Marie Anne* at Berth No.232, in Vlissengen. Vlissengen is some miles to the south of Rotterdam and we drove around for hours looking for Berth No.232. Martinet Shipping Line vessels have very distinctive white funnels. On the side of the funnel is the 'MSL' logo, which has a cane with a sea serpent wrapped around it. I spotted the funnel above the top of the warehouses. We turned around and drove back to the harbour entrance. A bored guy at the security barrier waved us through. The docks were decrepit and looked abandoned. Every metal surface was stained with rust. Every piece of wood was rotting. Rubbish lay strewn all over the place. The air smelt of oil and sewage. The only sign of activity was on the far side of the harbour, where the *Marie Anne* strained at her moorings like a reluctant mare tethered to a post. We drove round to the other side of the quay, careful to avoid lumps of scrap iron that were liberally scattered across the cobbles, and pulled up beside the stern of the ship.

The *Marie Anne* is a very big vessel. I felt reassured. She's a bulk carrier and has seven giant holds that run along the length of the ship. Spaced equally along the cargo deck there's four cranes, painted bright yellow. At the rear of the ship is the superstructure. This rises up five decks and contains the crew's living quarters, galleys, workshops and at the very top the Bridge. Beneath the superstructure, and below the main deck, is the giant engine room. All in all, she looked very impressive, even in these dreary surroundings.

One of the cranes near the front of the ship was in use. The crane's claw held a thick, quivering pipeline which came from a steel gantry that ran along the quay. A white powder-like substance spewed from the end of the pipe, down into one of the holds. Three men in boiler suits lounged around and watched with boredom. During the loading operation a layer of white dust coated both the ship and the quay. Precipitation had turned this dust into a white slime that adhered to the underside of your shoes and found its way everywhere, including the interior of the ship. A trail of white footprints marked our tour around the *Marie Anne.*

This white powder was kaolin, a form of china clay. Kaolin is used mostly in the paper industry. Global demand for kaolin is around $3.7 billion a year. The USA and UK are the world's top exporters. White kaolin is found mainly in Europe. Black kaolin is found mainly in North America. Both are in equal demand. The *Marie Anne* carried the white stuff over from Europe to the USA, and returned with the black stuff. This trans Atlantic ping-pong satisfied both markets and made the owners of Martinet Shipping Line very rich and very happy.

The Master of the *Marie Anne* was not happy when Jose and I appeared at his cabin door. Captain Nikola Markiewicz was a solid looking man in his late fifties. He had greying hair and a pair of horn-rimmed glasses. The eyes looked at us curiously: what kind of nutters cross the Atlantic by cargo ship? Passengers were a nuisance to him, but orders from Head Office had to be obeyed. He rose from the desk and put his cap on. I thought perhaps that we should salute him. He brushed aside my feeble attempt at a salute and told us to follow him.

The Captain led us along dark wood panelled corridors. The inside of the ship smelt of oil and boiled cabbage. We climbed a flight of stairs and came out on a narrow deck. Another flight of steep steps took us to a deck high up on the superstructure, where a small swimming pool lay empty and stained with rust. Captain Markiewicz told us that the cars would be placed here, either side of the swimming pool, for the duration of the voyage. The cars would be loaded the following day, Thursday 1st July, which was *Marie Anne*'s scheduled sailing date. With a wave of his hand the Captain left us to it. Jose and I leaned on the railings and looked around the decrepit harbour. It did not seem like a very glamorous start to the 2CV Alaska Challenge. Just to emphasise this a large seagull swooped overhead and covered us in runny, white excrement.

The next morning we returned to the harbour, where kaolin still spewed from the quivering pipeline. However, this time there was more activity on the decks and the *Marie Anne* looked like a ship on the eve of departure. We found Captain Markiewicz in the lounge adjoining his cabin. This area was used as a passenger's day lounge when the ship was at sea. While in port it became an office where all the ship's business was conducted. The lounge lived high up on the superstructure, just below the Bridge, and had four windows that looked directly out along the cargo deck. A large table covered in green beize held piles of paperwork, cups of coffee, cartons of cigarettes, ash trays and a bottle of whisky. The main cast were assembled around this table: Captain Markiewicz, the Chief (aka 1st Mate), the Chief Engineer, an official from the Port Authority and a young man from the MSL head office in Hamburg. The young man introduced himself as Karl. He was a troubleshooter for the company and travelled all over the world shooting trouble on behalf of MSL. Ships carry an enormous amount of machinery, everything from the huge cargo cranes to the hot water system to the toaster in the galley. It was Karl's job to draw up a manifest, outlining what needed fixing, what spare parts were required, how much fuel the ship required, etc. It was very apparent that he loved his job.

Captain Markiewicz informed us that the ship would sail with one hold empty, and so he had decided to put the cars there for the duration of the voyage (we later discovered that the crane at the aft of the ship was broken, and so the cars could not be hoisted up to the swimming pool deck). Captain Markiewicz also informed us that the ship would not be sailing for the open sea that day. Instead she would move round to another part of Rotterdam to load more cargo. I had my bags with me, ready to become one of the cast and crew of the *Marie Anne*. However, the Captain told me that passengers could only join the ship on the day of sailing. Karl suggested that I could join the *Marie Anne* that day as a guest of the Captain. The Captain said no. Karl winked at us: we'd give the Captain more time to mull over the idea. In the meantime, the cars needed to be loaded. I handed over the dreaded B70 forms to the Captain, then Jose and I followed the Chief down to the quay, where some of the crewmen were waiting. The officers and crew of the *Marie Anne* were all Croatian, most of them from Dubrovnik. This worked out cheaper for the shipping line than west European officers and crew, who would demand west European wages.

The Chief was a large, muscular man whose bald head glistened with beads of sweat. He directed operations as four grappling hooks were lowered on to the quayside. Each hook was then placed around each wheel of the No.1 car. A problem arose: the wings of a 2CV stick out further than on most cars. As the crane raised the ropes they taunted and began crunching into the wings of the car. The Chief and his crew had to wedge pieces of timber between the wheels and the face of the grappling hooks to prevent any further damage being done. Eventually the No.1 car was hoisted far up into the air. I couldn't watch. There was so much weight in the car that it looked like it was going to break in half. But it didn't break in half and disappeared below the hatches of No.7 hold and into the bowels of the ship. The No.2 car followed and once again I found myself unable to look.

With the loading operation completed, Jose and I stood beside the hatch covers and looked at the two toy cars in the giant hold. The Chief came over and told us an interesting piece of news: apparently the ship was going to call at New York first, before continuing on down to Savannah, in the southern states of America. Marvelous; New York was much nearer to the Canadian border than Savannah; unloading the cars in the Big Apple would save us more than 1500 miles. The way things kept changing in cargo ship land should have been a warning that it might not be quite as simple as this. At the time, though, we were still getting acquainted with the vagaries and frustrations of cargo ship travel.

Jose had to fly back to London that evening, and I didn't want to kick my heels in a hotel room, so we continued badgering the Captain to see if he would allow me to join the ship as his guest. With Karl's help the Captain finally gave in. He asked to see my ticket and passport. He enquired if I was in good health. I replied that I was and felt a little bit guilty because it wasn't quite true. With this little white lie the Captain admitted me on board the *Marie Anne*.

I carried a rucksack with my personal belongings and a shoulder bag with all my paperwork and money. Jose and I said our goodbyes at the top of the gangway. I felt a bit like Long John Silver, minus the parrot and wooden leg. In nine days time Jose and I would meet again in New York. In nine days time the road journey across North America would begin. You have to be optimistic, don't you.

The Captain summoned Barry, the Chief Steward. Barry's handlebar moustache and hangdog expression told you straight away that he came from the Balkans. He was a slim man in his early forties with thinning brown hair. He took my rucksack and led me down to the deck below. He unlocked the door of a single cabin next to the Officer's Mess. The *Marie Anne* carried a maximum of 12 passengers. On this trip she was only carrying 2 passengers. I'd been told that I could have a double cabin. Barry explained that I would be moved to the double cabin after the ship left port. I asked him exactly when that would be and he shrugged: 'tomorrow, the day after, who knows'. It was another example of the fact that cargo ships don't run to fixed schedules, as I found out to my cost just a week or so previously back in London

The last week of June had just arrived when I got a call from our shipping agent. The agent told me that the *Marie Anne* was now sailing on the 1st of July, not the 14th of July as originally planned. Oh, great. I was still absorbing this rather alarming piece of news when, half an hour later, the telephone rang again. I found myself talking to Jose and before I could tell her about the altered sailing dates she told me that she was dropping out from The 2CV Alaska Challenge. I put the phone down for a moment. Hmm, I now had just one week, instead of three, before the *Marie Anne* sailed from

Rotterdam, and my partner on the trip had decided to do something else instead.

Jose came round to see me and we had a long chat. She was irritated and annoyed by me. Thing is, I'd been planning the Alaska trip for years and Jose had only come on to the scene in the final stages. It was my baby and she felt left out of it. She said I didn't consult her. I didn't consider her feelings. It was all emotional stuff that women are driven by and men find hard to grasp; but Jose had a point, and it resembled a scene from an Eisenstein movie as we thrashed things out in my hot office. Eventually we came to a compromise: Jose would do the trip after all, but only as far as Winnipeg, where we had a buyer for the No.2 car. This meant that I wouldn't be left completely in the lurch: there would be two drivers for the two cars, and after the No.2 car was left in Winnipeg, Jose could fly back home and I would continue west in the No.1 car. Phew! this problem had now been resolved, but there was nothing I could do about the earlier sailing date of the *Marie Anne*. We now had only one week before our date with destiny in Rotterdam. Those final seven days were a mad rush to get work commitments tied up and everything ready for the Alaska trip.

That evening I was the only person in the Officer's Mess for dinner. Everyone else was either working or ashore. The Officer's Mess lay on the starboard (right hand) side of the superstructure. It was divided into two halves by a trelliswork screen; one half containing a sofa, armchairs, stereo, tv and chess table, the other half occupied entirely by a long oval-shaped table around which were 14 chairs. Barry fussed over me. He asked me what I thought of the food. It was good; better than I'd expected it to be.

After dinner I went back to my small cabin and felt depressed. I shrugged it off with the notion that I would only be spending a night or two here before moving to the larger double cabin. I turned in early and slept like the proverbial log.

Overnight the *Marie Anne* moved to Dordrecht, which is about 5 miles from Vlissengen. In the early hours I'd been vaguely aware of the ship moving, but the sound of the ventilators and a soft throbbing of machinery sent me back to sleep. In the morning I went to the cabin window and found myself staring at a big pile of scrap metal. Further down the quay sat an even bigger mountain of kaolin. I went up on deck to see the loading operation. For half an hour I watched two of the ship's cranes attacking the kaolin mountain with enormous grabbers. It soon became obvious that the loading operation wouldn't be finished in one day. I asked Captain Markiewicz if I could go ashore. He granted my request with a nod and a dismissive wave of his hand.

The centre of Dordrecht was more than 3 miles from the dock. A bus service ran from the Harbour Office. I didn't have much Dutch currency on me and so I walked. Dordrecht appeared similar to many other towns in the Netherlands. It's outlaying areas were a collection of industry and ugly modern buildings, and yes, grotty docks. The centre, though, was a delight, with a network of canals, cobbled streets, quaint houses, old churches and beautiful little squares. The town was crowded with Friday afternoon shoppers who were out enjoying the summer sunshine. Long John Silver was in 'last mode': I went into a European bank for the last time; had my last meal in a European restaurant; and went into a European supermarket for the last time, where I had a brief conversation with a bored European check-out girl for the last time and paid for lots of chocolate bars and packets of crisps and a case of beer. Sweat dripped off me as I struggled back to the dock with my shopping.

As I approached the ship someone called out to me. A man ran awkwardly down the gangway. He seemed excited. I thought he was going to embrace me. 'You are Rube?' The man spoke with a heavy Germanic accent. He was small and very old, with a large nose and sunken eyes. His parchment-like skin gave some indication of just how ancient he was. He wore a captain's hat on his head, the sort you buy in seaside shops. The old man pumped my hand enthusiastically and offered to carry my shopping, although it was obvious he wasn't strong enough.

I didn't know at the time that I'd just met a living legend. However, I did figure out that this old man was the only other passenger on the *Marie Anne*'s July sailing to America. He'd joined the ship while I was in town shopping. Barry the Chief Steward knew all the ship's business and later he told me something of my fellow passenger: his name was Kurt Benz and he was an amazing 91-years-old. For such an age he was very agile, both mentally and physically. He came from Hamburg and had spent his working life at sea. Kurt had crossed the Atlantic Ocean 143 times and made his first visit to New York in 1924, when he was just fifteen years old. The previous year, 1923, he'd sailed on a tea clipper to South Africa. The man had sea water running through his veins.

During the 30 years of his retirement, Kurt had travelled all over the world as a passenger on cargo ships. It was as though he were unable to break his strong bond with the sea. This was his tenth voyage on the *Marie Anne* and he was well known to everyone at Martinet Shipping Line. There was no getting away from his great age, though, and every time Kurt travelled with them, Martinet Shipping Line demanded a $6000 insurance bond in case he fell ill and the ship had to be diverted. Captain Markiewicz became most upset about having to carry Kurt on this sailing. Passengers were a nuisance. Ninety-one-year-old passengers were not only a nuisance they were also a big risk.

At dinner that evening I had some company. Captain Markiewicz sat at the head of the table. To the right of the Captain sat the Chief, then the 2nd Mate, then the 3rd Mate. To the left of the Captain sat the Chief Engineer, 2nd Engineer, 3rd Engineer and 4th Engineer. It was a hierarchical seating arrangement and Kurt and I were at the bottom end of the table.

The shipping line have a policy of rotating crews on a regular basis. Presumably so that their employees would not have to see the same old faces month after month, thus reducing the risk of murder and mayhem at sea. Captain Markiewicz had been Master of the *Marie Anne* for just four weeks. Most of his officers had also joined the ship only recently. Dinner was not a gathering of friends and colleagues, but of new acquaintances and it made for an awkward atmosphere.

Barry the Chief Steward hovered around the table. The polite conversation was a mixture of English and Croatian. The Captain and officers ignored us, the passengers, and so me and Kurt tried to talk amongst ourselves. I can't speak German very well and I soon discovered that's Kurt's English was also somewhat limited. He had a stock of English phrases that he spoke excellently but beyond that it was very difficult to communicate with him; not helped by the fact that he was a bit hard of hearing. This first gathering of the cast of the good ship *Marie Anne* showed what an ordeal mealtimes were going to be.

The shipping line gave all passengers a welcome pack. This consisted of a canvas holdall with the MSL logo on it, a sewing kit, a pair of white shorts, also with the MSL logo, and a small basket of chocolate eggs. These gifts seemed like the sort of things that would come in handy in a lifeboat. There was also a welcome letter, part of which said:

The freighter you are riding is a working place first of all. The crew's duty is the handling of cargo and sometimes this can be a tough job. Therefore we ask for your understanding if you may have the feeling that crew or Officers are not as communicative as you wish them to be. They are hard working people who in the first instance have to handle their jobs on deck or in the engine room.

It didn't take me long to discover that the officers and crew of the *Marie Anne* were a nice bunch of people. The awkward atmosphere at mealtimes was largely due to the authoritarian presence of the Captain.

The next morning, Saturday, I went up on deck. The mountain of kaolin had now been reduced to a small hill. The cargo deck and the wharf were a flurry of activity as the crew worked to complete the loading operation. Barry told me that the Captain wanted to sail on the evening tide. Time is money and if they didn't make this deadline the ship would be delayed for 24 hours until the next high tide. Barry tutted. He had seen these rushed loading operations before: 'ees money, money, all they care bout ees making money'.

At midday they tested the ship's engines. During the three days I'd been onboard, the ship had been a quiet place. Now every rivet, every plate, every fixture, every fitting vibrated and shook as the scream of the engines echoed through the ship's corridors. The *Marie Anne* strained at her moorings. Water churned and rolled away from her stern. A huge cloud of black smoke billowed up from her chimney. It was all rather alarming; however it did show that the Captain intended to make the evening tide.

By early evening the hill of kaolin had been swallowed by No.5 hold. There was some last minute toing and froing by customs officers and shipping line officials. The Pilot came on board. Then, at 7pm, with a toot on her horn the *Marie Anne* cast off her moorings. Kurt and I stood out on poop deck. Kurt moved from one side of the ship to the other as he watched the tugs manoeuvring: ' ist very good, ya', he was smiling and happy now that things had taken a more nautical turn.

The *Marie Anne* weighs 27,000 tons when laden. The tugs had to turn her around 180 degrees so that she could proceed up the channel. The ship is more than 650 feet / 200 metres long and as she turned her bow and stern came within feet of the wharfs on either side of the channel. It was a hair-raising operation to watch. If a mistake were made those 27,000 tons could not be stopped quickly; but the tug men and the *Marie Anne*'s crew were highly skilled at their job and within 15 minutes she was pointing in the right direction. Then, another toot on the ships horn and we proceeded up the waterway and very soon Dordrecht became a memory.

As we made our way back towards the city of Rotterdam two large waves acted as escort, racing along each bank, snapping branches and flooding lowland. Regardless of this, the *Marie Anne* progressed up the narrow channel, her engines fighting against the strong current, her funnel ejecting steam that condensed and formed rainbows in her wake.

Of all the departures I've experienced, in ports, railway stations and airports, this one seemed the most poignant, perhaps because it was such a drawn-out process. Europoort is huge and it can take hours to wind through its waterways to the open sea. At many points along the banks there are parks and on a typical summer's evening there were lots of people out enjoying the sunshine. Many of them waved at us as we slowly went by. Kurt and I and the crewmen returned these greetings. The Captain, standing on the Bridge Deck, looked gruff and kept his hands on the rail. I did notice, though, that when he thought the rest of us weren't looking he coyly return some of the waves from the people.

This dream-like departure continued until 10pm, when we reached the ugly industrial heart of Rotterdam. At this point things turned sour. The *Marie Anne* developed engine problems and had to be helped into a dock by two tugs. We spent the night there, between a rubbish incineration plant and the inevitable piles of scrap metal.

The engineers worked all night and at lunchtime, Sunday 4th July, the ships engines came to life again. We all felt like cheering as tugs helped the *Marie Anne* from her dock. The engines powered up and the ship began shaking and vibrating as we progressed up the Niuwe Maas under our own steam. We passed oil refineries on the port side and pretty little fishing villages on the starboard side. The wind picked up as we reached the Hook of Holland. I could see the Harwich ferry there. I'd taken that ferry many times myself and it always seemed like a large ship. Now, though, it was dwarfed by the *Marie Anne*.

We dropped the Pilot. A small boat came alongside. It was painted bright yellow, with 'Rotterdam Port Authority' written in large letters on its side. We could hear the throb of its powerful engines as it maintained station beside the ship. The Pilot dangled on the end of a rope ladder. The Port Authority boat rode up and down on the waves. The Pilot waited until it reached the top of a wave trough and jumped. He timed it perfectly, landed on the deck and grabbed hold of a handrail. It was the sort of thing you'd pay money to see in a stunt circus. The Pilots did it all the time and without a second thought.

Out in the North Sea we jostled for position amongst scores of other ships and headed south for the English Channel. Our crossing time to New York would be nine days. The QE2 goes from Southampton to

New York in six days. The QE2 can afford to rev up its engines and burn fuel. Martinet Shipping Line cannot. The first scheduled passenger service across the Atlantic began in 1816. In that year the Black Ball Line started a regular Liverpool to New York run. These sailing ships took an average of 23 days to cross the Atlantic from west to east, and 40 days going in the opposite direction. This difference in sailing time was due to the winds and currents.

Now that the *Marie Anne* had finally got underway the first order of business was to clean the ship. The white kaolin powder coated every surface and had congealed into lumps. Captain Markiewicz stood on the Bridge and watched his crew using pressure hoses to clear the kaolin. It took them most of the afternoon and at the end of it the ship was gleaming. Once the outside of the ship had been taken care of, attention then turned to the inside. While in port, cardboard mats were placed along the corridors to try and contain the mess that people brought in on their shoes. These mats were now removed and every surface received a polish. In the upper part of the superstructure, where the officers and passengers were quartered, Barry carried out this cleaning, and it was thorough. You could see your face in the polished walls and floors. When he wasn't presiding over mealtimes, Barry spent most of his time in an endless round of polishing. He wore a red bandana around his head to prevent drips of sweat from ruining his work. When making your way around inside the superstructure, if Barry was wearing his red bandana you had to be careful not to slip and break your neck.

On the morning of the second day at sea, Barry knocked on my cabin door: 'you ees moving todair'. True to his word, the Captain was letting me have a double cabin. Barry led me up to the deck above, where I was surprised to discover that my new quarters were in the owner's cabin, the biggest on the ship. The only other cabins up on this deck were the Captain's and Chief Engineer's. The owner's cabin consisted of a bedroom with a double bed and adjoining bathroom, and a large sitting room with two sofas, a low table and a huge porthole. The sitting room also had a desk. Perfect for writing bad poetry and the Alaska Challenge bulletins.

Once settled in my new quarters I sought out the Chief and asked him if I could get some of my stuff from the cars in No.7 hold. The 'stuff' included my typewriter and office equipment. The only access to No.7 hold was via a hatch on the cargo deck. A steel ladder ran down the side of the cavernous hold, 50 feet to the bottom. They told me that on a pitching, rolling ship it was too dangerous for a passenger to climb down that ladder. One of the crewmen would go down and get the things for me. The problem being, the cars contained so much gear that the crewman would never be able to find what I wanted. The Chief and some of the crew gathered around the hatch and I explained this to them. In the end they agreed to let me go down, but only with a rope tied around me. Two of the crewman held on to the rope while I carefully made my way down the ladder. They were right, it was dangerous. The sea was quite calm but the ship still moved around a lot and at times I had to halt my descent and cling on to the ladder for dear life. Eventually I made it to the bottom of the hold, where the two Citroen 2CVs had been out of sight and out of mind for the last five days. Seeing them again reminded me that this ocean voyage was just the start of an even bigger adventure. As I stood there alone at the bottom of the hold it felt strange, it felt exciting.

At the end of that second day at sea we left the English Channel and headed out into the Atlantic Ocean. A family of dolphins began following us. The sea was calm. The weather good. I stood on deck and gazed around: no land, no other ships, no nothing except the deep, swelling ocean. Gulp. I experienced a terrible anxiety as it hit home that I would be on this ship, on this ocean for eight more days with no escape, in the hands of fate and its servant, the cruel sea. I became acutely aware that the little white lie I'd told the Captain might well come back to haunt me.

For some months I'd been experiencing an uncomfortable feeling in my lower right abdomen. Not a pain exactly, just something which made me aware that things were amiss. I put it down to my lifestyle: cigarettes, booze, burning the candle at both ends, and all that malarky. However, knowing that I was soon to cross the Atlantic on a cargo ship I thought it would be prudent to go along and see my doctor. The doctor told me to stop smoking and then felt and prodded my stomach. He said that my appendix seemed ok, in that it wasn't about to burst. The doc then jammed his fingers up under my rib cage for a feel of my liver, which he said wasn't swollen. The doc thought I should have tests, though, and sent me along to my local hospital. The hospital appointment was due nine days before the *Marie Anne*'s original sailing date of 14th July; but of course, the sailing date was brought forward by two weeks and so I never went for those tests.

Unlike cruise ships, most cargo ships do not have a doctor on board. For this reason passengers are asked pretty vigorous questions about their health before they are allowed to travel on a cargo ship. Pregnant women aren't allowed to travel, nor are very old people (except for living legends like Kurt Benz). If you get something seriously wrong with you in mid ocean you are in big trouble. All that stuff about passing warships, with surgeons and operating theatres on board, is fallacy. If you fall ill in the middle of an ocean the chance of a big warship being nearby is pretty remote. All you can do is prey.

During those final weeks in London I became hardly aware of the thingy in my lower right abdomen, occupied as I was by other matters. It was still there, though, but travelling on a cargo ship had been a longtime dream of mine and I didn't want to miss out on the chance just because of a 'thingy', so I decided to take a risk and go ahead with the voyage on the *Marie Anne*.

Life at sea soon settled into a routine which centred largely around mealtimes: breakfast 7.30 to 8.30, lunch 12.00 to 1.00 and dinner 5.30 to 6.30. Breakfast wasn't too bad, because it was usually just me and Kurt, joined occasionally by the 3rd Mate before he went on watch. Lunch and dinner, however, I found to be a daily ordeal that I came to dread, so much so that on one occasion I asked Barry if I could take sandwiches in my cabin instead of going to the Officer's Mess. The Chief Steward was most offended by this idea and treated me to one of his more theatrical displays of temperament. After that I didn't broach the subject again.

Barry was the star at mealtimes and he didn't want to lose a member of his audience. His pantry adjoined the Officer's Mess and these two areas were the stages on which he performed. He always attended to the Captain first, followed by the two Chiefs and then us passengers. The lower ranking mates and engineers were served last. It was supposedly silver service, until something went wrong, as it quite often did. When these little crisis occurred we could hear Barry in his pantry, shouting down the dumb waiter to Maladen, the Cook, in the galley below. A string of heated, echoing Croatian could be heard as the steward and cook exchanged verbal blows. We all sat there at the table and acted as though nothing was happening, our silence punctuated only by the Captain as he chewed noisily on a bread roll. Barry would then come out of the pantry holding two plates of steaming Croatian cuisine, calm, collected, as though all were normal. His red face the only sign that things weren't running smoothly.

During these meals, Kurt and I would hold excruciating conversations in mangled English and mangled German. My fellow passenger was delighted when he discovered I was on my way to Alaska and Prudhoe Bay, on the shores of the Arctic Ocean. Kurt, of course, had been everywhere and done everything. This included driving up the Dalton Highway to Prudhoe Bay. He last made the trip at the tender age of 89, when he used the *Marie Anne* to ship over a camper van to Savannah before driving it to Alaska. In previous years he and his wife and their friends had come over in groups, sometimes with as many as four camper vans, and toured around North America. As Kurt tried to explain all this to me I caught the Captain's eye and sensed some grudging respect for the old man.

At 6am every morning you would find Kurt jogging around the cargo deck; well, it amounted to more of a shuffle than a proper jog, but heck, he was 91-years-old. One complete circuit amounted to approximately one third of a mile. We all used to watch Kurt in amazement. After finishing his jog he'd climb up the five decks of the superstructure and stand for hours on the Bridge Deck, gazing out over the ocean. Seeing Kurt standing there, stripped to the waist, his parchment-like skin soaking up the rays of the sun, you soon realised it was the sea that had kept him alive and healthy for so long.

Kurt's wife died some years previously and he had never got over it. He referred to her as 'my dear wife' and talked about her constantly. Despite this terrible loss, Kurt's spirit was still alive. At ninety one years of age each new day was a blessing and when talking about future events he always said, 'God willing'. The precarious nature of

Kurt's great age became most apparent during mealtimes. For such a small fellow, Kurt ate and drank a large amount. However, his tubes were quite congested and sometimes things got stuck in his throat. This first happened during lunch on our second day at sea. The old man was shovelling lettuce into his mouth and a piece of it got stuck in his throat. He immediately began choking and spluttering. His face went red. His eyes streamed with water. The cutlery rattled. The Captain and officers ignored the little drama that was going on at the bottom end of the table. I tried patting Kurt on the back, but he waved me away, got up and staggered into the other part of the Officer's Mess, where he collapsed on to one of the sofas. This left me in a bit of a quandary, since no one else was taking a blind bit of notice of Kurt, who appeared to be choking to death. Hmm, Kurt was a regular passenger with Martinet Shipping Line and I figured that by now the MSL crews would be quite familiar with his quirks: it couldn't be anything serious or else they would have gone to his aid. For the next five minutes Kurt continued coughing and spluttering, then we heard huge draughts of air being drawn into his lungs. Finally, he came back to the table and carried on as though nothing had happened. I was beginning to learn that this 'carry on as if nothing unusual was happening' attitude was part of life at sea. Whether it was a UFO landing on the cargo deck, or Jesus walking across the waves, one never showed any outward reaction.

Sometimes I was late for lunch or dinner. Kurt was always early and I could tell if there had been another choking incident by the atmosphere in the mess and Kurt's streaming eyes. The choking fits were a regular thing and it got to the stage where I was afraid to engage Kurt in conversation in case it provoked another one. I later learned that the crew were taking bets as to whether Kurt would actually make it to New York. The Captain was irritated by it all and spent the voyage composing a letter to his masters in Hamburg, explaining just why he shouldn't be made to carry passengers on his ship. I spent the voyage composing a letter to Hamburg, explaining just why they shouldn't carry Captains on their ships.

The Captain's cabin adjoined mine. My bathroom wall was also his bathroom wall. My neighbour never got out of bed before 10am, so the early part of the morning was the best time to avoid him. Before lunch he would prowl silently around the ship, loud bursts of

Croatian signalling when he had found something to his displeasure. If you were unfortunate enough to bump into him during one of these tours he would give you one of his strange stares, then he'd continue on his way as if you didn't exist. I once found him sitting quite still in one of the lifeboats. He seemed to be in some kind of reverie. Another time I went down to the Officer's Mess to make myself a cup of coffee. I discovered the Captain on his hands and knees. He was carefully wiping a dirty rag over one of the air conditioning units. When he noticed me watching him he looked guilty.

Captain Markiewicz came across as somewhat shy and retiring, yet he was also the boss, a figure of authority, and this put everyone ill at ease. This was most striking in the Officer's Mess. After woofing down his food the Captain would often turn his chair around and sit with his back to the rest of us, while picking his teeth and ignoring anyone who tried to speak to him. Occasionally he would belch and this normally signalled the start of a voluble argument with one of his officers. He would turn his chair back round and stare at the person in question, then the argument would start. I don't understand Croatian, and so have no idea of what these arguments were about, but they always ended with the Captain giving a dismissive wave of his hand and leaving the mess. The Captain struck me as a kindly man, but his job always put him in conflict with the crew, and the passengers.

Apart from mealtimes, the Alaska Challenge bulletins were the only other kind of routine I had on the *Marie Anne*. Even back in 1999, travelogues on the internet were nothing new. There were quite a few 'ongoing travel adventures', with bulletins and pictures posted to a web site. I found with a lot of them, though, the latest bulletins were often weeks or even months old. It was yesterday's news, and it was mostly very boring news. I wanted be more up to date with our own trip progress. The 2CV Alaska Challenge bulletins would be posted every 2 or 3 days (back then, before the widespread use of the Net, finding internet connection while on the road became a major part of the Alaska Challenge). If you were looking at the latest Alaska Challenge bulletin the text and photographs would be about events that happened within the last few days, or even the last few hours: 'almost live' reportage. I designed each bulletin to contain around 400 words and at least two photographs. When I came up with this idea I didn't realise the work it would involve. I also didn't even consider if anyone would be remotely interested in yet another load of holiday snaps posted on the internet.

The 2CV Alaska Challenge web site didn't have the audience of the Jerry Springer show, yet there were quite a lot of people all around the world following our journey. It was my mission to keep posting bulletins to the web site on a regular basis, even from the middle of the Atlantic Ocean. This was achieved by means of faxing the bulletins through to Jose on the ship's satellite telephone link. She would then e-mail them to Tony Carr in Canada, who was doing the web site for us. The satellite link was expensive, $20USD per minute, but I didn't mind paying this. I sent the first Atlantic bulletin when the ship was approximately 500 miles south west of Ireland. It seemed strange that within a short time people would be reading it on the web site. It helped ease my sense of isolation.

Before I left the UK people asked me: what on earth are you going to write about an ocean voyage on a cargo ship? I wasn't short of material, the trouble was I had to censor it. I typed out the bulletins on my old Imperial 80, sitting at the desk in my cabin. I'd then take a finished bulletin up to the Bridge, where the satellite station lurked. The satellite station consisted of an ancient computer terminal which had a curtain you could pull around it so that sunlight wouldn't obscure the screen. The officers on duty on the Bridge had it all set-up for me, so that all I had to do was retype my words into the computer, press a button and bingo, it was faxed via the satellite link. But Captain Markiewicz would stand behind me and look over my shoulder and read every single word I typed. For reasons unbeknown to me the Captain had got the wrong end of the stick and thought that I was a correspondent from the *Daily Telegraph*. As Master of the *Marie Anne*, Captain Markiewicz had the power of life and death over everyone aboard, so I tried to avoid upsetting him too much, especially at twenty dollars a minute.

Eating meals, writing and sending bulletins and avoiding the Captain were not exactly strenuous yet time did not hang heavy on the *Marie Anne*, particularly for the crew, who were always busy. This surprised me. I thought that once a ship left port there wasn't much for the crew to do, apart from keeping the engines running. This proved wrong: a ship is heavy industry on the waves and there's a multitude of machinery and systems that enable it to operate, such as the fresh water supply, ventilation and air conditioning, refrigeration system, ballast and drain system, bilge water collection pumps, electricity generators and a whole host of hoists, winches, cranes and other bits of machinery. All of this had to be maintained and kept running by just 18 crewman and 7 Officers.

Some of this work looked highly dangerous. Three days out from Rotterdam the Captain ordered that the cargo cranes be repainted. The four cranes ran along the length of the cargo deck. They were bright yellow and higher than the ship's superstructure. The crewmen looked like ants as they crawled over the cranes. Each crewman had a paint pot dangling between his legs and a brush tied to the end of a long stick. They wore safety harnesses but it was still terrifying to watch them working, 50 feet above the cargo deck on that gently rolling ship.

I watched them from the Bridge. When at sea there was only one person on duty on the Bridge. The three Mates shared this duty between them in four hour shifts. The Third Mate did 8.00am to midday. The Second Mate did midday to 4pm. The Chief did 4pm till 8pm, and so on until the 24 hours had been completed and the cycle repeated itself again. The Mates sat on a high stool in front of a large table that held the radar screen. There was no spoked steering wheel, much to the disappointment of Long John Silver. Navigation was done automatically using global satellite positioning technology. The ship had very powerful radar which could pick up objects many miles away. It seemed strange to me that this huge vessel was in the hands of one bored Mate on the Bridge, reading a comic, playing games on a laptop computer or cutting his toenails. I asked Zelko the 2nd Mate about the possibility of collisions. He told me that the radar gave plenty of warning of approaching vessels. The biggest headache on Atlantic crossings were the record breakers. From the way Zelko said this it appeared that there must be an army of people setting out in canoes, inflatables, rafts, and the like, all trying to get into the record books. These record breakers often did not understand the movements of large ships. The fact that the *Marie Anne* could sometimes be thrown into a state of emergency just because of an eccentric trying to cross the Atlantic in a bath tub was annoying to say the least.

We had perfect summer weather. The sky was always a deep, deep blue during the day and jet black at night, with wispy galaxies and bright burning stars - the night sky over the ocean has a clarity you never get on land. On the starboard side of the Boat Deck there was a large wooden decked pontoon sitting on blocks. This pontoon became my sunbathing spot. I was rarely disturbed by anyone and spent hours sitting there, just gazing out at the ocean. The deep ocean has a blue/black translucence to it that's hard to describe in words. It has a shine, a vitality. It's alive. It's appealing. It's inviting... on the fifth day at sea I went up to the Bridge and asked if we could stop the ship and go swimming. The thought of stopping a massive cargo ship just to go swimming appealed to me. The Chief liked the idea as well, and said that the crew sometimes did this during the warmer months, if the Captain was in a good mood. However, he explained that at this time of year there were sharks in these particular waters and it was too dangerous to go in.

I felt the pull of the ocean but could not dive into its cool depths. Instead I sat on the pontoon, soaked up the sunshine, drank bottled water and watched the family of dolphins, who were still keeping company with us. The best time to see the dolphins was just after dawn, but they were also visible during the afternoon. I counted three adults and at least five baby ones. The dolphins had absolutely no fear and seemed to be eternally having fun. I envied them. The baby dolphins were particularly playful and zipped up out of the waves, cartwheeling before falling back into the water. After witnessing this display many times I began to wonder if they had escaped from a marine park.

If you see a picture of the open ocean it looks rather lifeless. When you're actually on it you realise this is not the case. The ocean is teeming with life and gives an ever changing panorama. As well as the dolphins I saw sea turtles, so slow and cumbersome it's a miracle that evolution has allowed them to survive, a sword fish, seriously weird flying fish, jelly fish, and just about every other kind of fish, but none of the sharks that the Chief had warned me of. There was also a large amount of junk floating about, including a fridge door, some hair rollers caught up in a fishing net, a sofa, a shopping basket, a suitcase and a French no entry road sign. None of it surprised me. A big poster had been tacked on the wall of the corridor leading to the Officer's Mess. This cartoon- style poster warned of the dangers of polluting the ocean. Nevertheless, all garbage on the *Marie Anne* got thrown over the side. Old paint tins, oil cans, the rubbish from the Galley, redundant pieces of machinery, and, on occasion, dead bodies, it all went into the ocean without a second thought.

There's nothing surprising about human nature, yet I also saw some mysterious things while crossing the ocean. There were jets of water that suddenly shot up 6ft above the waves. You soon become familiar with the wildlife in this environment and I knew these water jets were not caused by animals. Also, during one sunset I saw a pure white bubble/ ball that travelled very quickly just above the tops of the waves. It's journey lasted less than a minute until it kind of evaporated. And perhaps strangest of all, a huge dark shadow that passed beneath the ship. It looked at least as big as the ship's five deck high superstructure. I've no idea if the shadow was some kind of reflection caused by the water or indeed a relative of Moby Dick.

I was travelling on such a large ship that I didn't lose much sleep over the dangers of the ocean and its inhabitants. The *Marie Anne* smashes through the waves like a giant fist, creating hissing bubbles as the oxygenated water passes along her sides. She maintains a speed of 13.5 knots and averages 350 nautical miles a day. 150 metric tons of fuel are burned each day to achieve those 350 nautical miles. To keep the ship running each day, 425 filter cigarettes, 68 cups of coffee and 15 litres of wine are required. The dolphins who accompany the ship run on pure sea water and have no known vices apart from being annoyingly happy.

On that fifth day of the voyage we reached mid ocean. We were now thousands of miles from anywhere. It was a lonely place to be but our little community of 27 souls - twenty five Croatians, one German and one Englishman - continued to function as before. The weather continued to be glorious, with blue skies and a blazing sun beating down on boiling mercury. There was a light sea swell. Small waves smashed into the side of the ship and turned into dancing foam snakes. The dolphins played in the wash from the ships propellers. It was all so relaxed, so peaceful, just like they'd told me it would be: 'the Atlantic is never rough in the summer'. Oh yes? The Captain and the Chief now had a serious look on their faces. The maritime forecast said there were very rough seas ahead. Ships are the same as aircraft, in that they try to go around bad weather. We diverted south to avoid the storm.

The ocean seemed pretty annoyed about something and as we sailed along the southern edge of the storm we still felt its anger. The charging waves grew higher and the ship began lurching and bucking like a geriatric broncho. The wind bitched and moaned. The engines, which had given us so much trouble in Rotterdam, roared and whined as they drove the ship onwards through the storm tossed waves.

The waves were running to between 40ft and 50ft. Now, instead of slicing through the ocean the *Marie Anne* was being tossed around by it. I ventured out on to the poop deck, which in the space of seconds was rising and falling fifty feet. Wow! I clutched on to the hand rail in an attempt to steady myself. Whoosh! the spray from a big wave soaked me. I returned to my cabin. Everything that I had arranged on my desk, and on the cabinet in the corner, was scattered across the floor. My heavy typewriter, though, still sat on the desk, but was nearing the edge so I lifted it off and put it on the floor. My whisky bottle, which had been on the top shelf of the cabinet, had also fallen to the floor. It was unbroken so I poured myself a shot. It was my first drink for eight days.

Due to that 'thingy' in my lower right abdomen, since first boarding the ship I had been on a bit of a health kick. I didn't drink any alcohol, smoked hardly any cigarettes and ate as healthily as possible. I didn't find this monastic lifestyle easy. For starters, there was alcohol everywhere on board the ship. At each meal sitting, including breakfast, there were three very large jugs of wine on the table. You could freely help yourself to this wine. Duty Free was also available on board. Barry held the key. A carton of 200 cigarettes cost $10. A crate of beer cost $10; in fact, everything seemed to cost ten bucks. If that was your thing, you could smoke and drink to your hearts content and it would cost next to nothing. Most of the crew smoked and cigarettes were handed around at every occasion. Likewise with bottles of beer. A cargo ship is not the best place for monks.

But I had done it and resisted temptation for eight days. That was while we were heading out into the ocean. Now we had reached the half way point I decided that drinking and smoking would become a part of my life again. We were no longer moving away from a land mass, we were now moving towards one and every day brought us closer to civilisation; and medical help, if required.

At dinner that evening I surprised everyone by helping myself to a large glass of wine. I suppose they all thought the stormy weather was making me hit the booze. Barry came out of his pantry. He carried the Captain's dinner. The plate was balanced on the palm of his hand. He moved forward, but instead of stopping beside the Captain he carried on going along what was now a sloping deck. He managed to bring himself to a halt in the other half of the Mess. Miraculously, the Captain's dinner remained intact. Every time the *Marie Anne* crashed into a wave trough an almighty shudder ran through the ship. We all had to quickly grab our plates and glasses to stop them moving. Barry spent most of the meal chasing boiled potatoes and vegetables around the table. The Third Mate got a plate of soup in his lap. The philosophy was maintained: everyone carried on as though nothing unusual was happening.

After a day or so the ocean became less petulant and you were able to venture out on deck without being simultaneously washed and blow dried. Rather like the aftermath of a storm on land, the sea storm had left everything cleaner, fresher, with a rich salty smell emanating from the ocean. The dolphins had scarpered and I was surprised to see birds hovering above the waves. I don't know enough about our feathered friends to tell you what sort of birds they were, but since they were thousands of miles from the nearest land the word 'dumb' springs to mind.

The weather became glorious again. On the Sunday, which was our eighth day at sea, a barbeque was held on the aft deck. Preparations began early in the morning. An oil drum which had been cut in half was used as the barbeque. They used a blow torch to get it going. A rich smell of burning wood and charcoal wafted around the ship. An entire lamb was placed on the barbeque and left to cook. Tables were placed together to form one long table. Croatian music played on the ship's tannoy. Bunting was hung from the back of the superstructure. It was all very festive, a bit like the Five Year Plan celebrations in Magnitogorsk.

Captain Markiewicz still had the wrong end of the stick and still thought I was a journalist from the *Daily Telegraph*. He began a process of explaining everything to me, as all good Captains should do when they have a journalist on board. At midday we all sat down at the table. For hours now the smell of barbequed lamb had been permeating the ship. Everyone felt ravenous. Captain Markiewicz explained to me, quite unnecessarily, that we were now going to eat. As the representative of the *Daily Telegraph* I was given pride of place at the top of the table, next to the Captain – poor old Kurt had been placed much further down the table. Captain Markiewicz explained that MSL was the only shipping company that allowed its crews to have a Sunday barbeque. The ordinary ratings and officers all sat down and ate together. Each man received four complimentary bottles of beer, courtesy of the shipping company. The crew were allowed to relax and enjoy themselves. In essence they were given a day off with pay. This is most unusual in the world of cargo ships.

Having felt he'd done his duty by explaining things to me, Captain Markiewicz proceeded to woof down his barbequed lamb. It took him just over a minute to clear his plate. He then got up and without a word to anyone he went back to his cabin. The rest of us continued eating and drinking. Kurt got a bit drunk on Becks beer. He stood up and did a little jig to the Croatian music: 'ist sailors life, ist gut, ya'. Everyone was relaxed. Some of the crew took turns to dance with the effeminate crewman. Others strolled around the deck. Empty beer bottles were chucked over the side. The leftovers from the barbeque were chucked over the side. Everything got chucked over the side. Barry told me about a barbeque he'd attended on another shipping line. It was a wet day and the 3rd Engineer tried to get the barbeque going with a petrol can. The petrol reacted with the charcoal and caused a huge flare-up. Two of the crewmen were badly burnt. One died in hospital. Filled with remorse, the 3rd Engineer later threw himself over the aft rail, where he plunged into the depths below and was cut to pieces by the ship's propeller. Barry said that they never did find all the pieces of his body.

Every morning Barry came to my cabin to make my bed and tidy up. On the morning after the barbeque he looked hung over. He told me that at midday the ship's general alarm would be sounded. We were having a lifeboat drill. When the alarm sounded I must put on my lifejacket and go to the Boat Deck as quickly as possible. The Captain put Barry in charge of Kurt for the duration of the lifeboat drill. It would be his job to get Kurt into a lifejacket and up to the Boat Deck. Barry cursed his luck.

Sure enough, at midday the ship's alarm sounded. I grabbed my lifejacket and wrapped it around me. I couldn't figure out how the straps connected together and so I just let them hang loose. Up on the Boat Deck most of the crew were already assembled. The lifeboat drill had been no secret and everyone wanted to get it over and done with as soon as possible. Captain Markiewicz held a stopwatch in his hand. He explained the safety regulations to me and took me through what was happening. First of all we gathered around the port lifeboat. It was painted bright orange. Five of the crew jumped inside and the lifeboat was lowered off its derrick. It hung there, gently swaying in the breeze. The five crewmen began peddling furiously. We could see the propeller whizzing round. Captain Markiewicz explained, quite unnecessarily, that this lifeboat was driven by peddle power.

Next we all went over to the starboard lifeboat. This was driven by a petrol motor. Two of the crewmen jumped inside. The winch was started and we could hear a grating, grinding noise. The lifeboat remained on the derrick. The engineers fiddled around with the winch but the lifeboat still wouldn't budge. The Chief went off to get a crowbar. Barry told me about a lifeboat drill he'd been involved in while crossing the Pacific Ocean. A big wave had landed on the deck and swept three crewman overboard. Barry said that the Pacific rollers were the biggest in the world. The three crewman were never seen again.

The Chief returned with a crowbar and did some violence to the winch. Still the lifeboat wouldn't budge. In the end we all got fed up with it and called it a day. So ended the lifeboat drill. If the *Marie*

Anne ever ran into difficulties only half the crew would be able to get off, and they would be the fittest ship wreck survivors ever found.

For more than a week the radio bands had been awash with static. On the morning of 14th July they came alive again: Dunkin Donuts, Dodge dealerships and Dolly Parton announced the lurking presence of America. Small, colourful fishing boats began to dot the ocean and jet planes arcing high up into the sky left vapour trails that looked like giant party streamers. The loneliness of the open ocean was coming to an end. Civilisation called out to us... Hilary Clinton was on Long Island, canvassing support against the gun lobby, and Whitney Houstin was singing in Madison Square Garden that evening. God bless America.

Late on the afternoon of the 14th we sighted land, the eastern end of Long Island, which points like a giant finger towards New York City. The last land I'd seen was Lizard Point, in Cornwall, England. That was eight days previously as we were making our way down the English Channel. Once out on the Atlantic Ocean it felt like you were in another world, another time, another dimension. Sighting land again produced a peculiar surge of both excitement and depression. The distant coastline of Long Island looked unreal, almost like an alien planet.

The ship followed that coastline for a few hours before the twin towers of the World Trade Centre peeped at us from over the horizon. During the next hour the rest of the New York skyline slid coyly into view. The depression now went and a wave of excitement ran through the ship. Even far out at sea you could still sense the energy and vibrancy of New York City. I planned to check into the Waldorf Hotel. I planned to soak in a hot bath for two hours. I planned to have cocktails in Manhattan. It was all there for the taking. The Big Apple shimmered on the horizon and the *Marie Anne* strained to reach it before sunset.

Ah, the romance, the adventure, the telex that came from the shipping company... Captain Markiewicz was ordered to heave to. The *Marie Anne* was to stay for four days at open anchorage off Ocean Beach, Long Island. You could almost hear a groan run through the ship.

How could the shipping line guys back in Germany be so cruel?

We were the victims of world trade. The *Marie Anne* carried kaolin, a valuable commodity. The commodity markets change hourly. The trading never stops. The London Stock Exchange takes over from Tokyo, then Wall Street takes over from London, and so it goes on, 24 hours a day. When the *Marie Anne* left Rotterdam her cargo was going to be sold for X amount of money in Y place. But during the nine days of her voyage the markets were constantly fluctuating. This meant that at any time the ship could be diverted or deliberately delayed in order to gain maximum profit from her cargo. For example, when we were one third of the way across the Atlantic the Captain received a telex on the satellite link saying that our first port of call might be Searsport, in Maine. The shipping line guys eventually dropped this idea and we continued on to New York. This glorious uncertainty is a part of cargo ship travel. If you need to get somewhere by a certain date, or are in a hurry, don't take a cargo ship. Kurt told me that on one of his previous trips from Rotterdam to Savannah the ship was diverted mid ocean and they went down to South America. They finally got to Savannah six weeks after leaving Rotterdam.

Economics also came into the order to heave to in open anchorage. There was no reason why the *Marie Anne* could not have docked in New York harbour and then delay unloading her cargo until the price was right, except that the shipping line would have to pay port charges. Open anchorage was free; and so we came to a grinding halt five miles off Long Island.

Time hung heavy during this period. The crew were ready for port cargo operations. Most of the ships maintenance work had been carried out during the Atlantic crossing and there wasn't much left to do; but a Captain can always find something to occupy his crew and he had them painting the decks. To make matters worse, New York was suffering from a heat wave and the temperature rose above 100F. Kurt couldn't handle this heat and stayed in his cabin most of the time. I wandered around the sweltering ship, my eyes forever drawn to the distant New York skyline. On the second day at open anchorage I went up to the Bridge. Zelko the Second Mate was on watch. He showed me the chart for the approaches to New York and pointed at our position. We were in a hatched area that said: 'DANGER, MINES' in big red letters (the approaches to New York harbour were heavily mined during World War Two and even today large areas remain uncleared). I expressed my concern but Zelko did not seem worried about high explosives. There were three other cargo ships anchored nearby us, and they hadn't blown up yet, so I carried on as though mines were nothing unusual.

By the third day at open anchorage there still appeared to be no sign that we would be moving anytime soon. You could no longer see the NY skyline because of a heat haze. The humidity was very high and everyone dripped with sweat. The Captain gave the crew a break and they were relieved of deck painting duty. Most of them stayed in their cabins and turned the air conditioning up full blast. Everything was still. The sea was dead calm and a pea soup colour. Whisps of vapour rose from it. Due to the bizarre movements of world trade we had to languish out here, on this sweating, heaving sea. Oh how I wished I was a fish, and during the blistering heat of the day I dreamed of a cold beer while at night, Gotham City twinkled in the distance with the lights of aircraft buzzing like fireflies in the sky.

Cold beer was needed in these circumstances. Problem was, we were in US territorial waters and strictly speaking duty free could not be sold. Barry told me of a similar situation, when his ship had run out of booze in the South China Sea. The Third Engineer was a roaring alcoholic and had resorted to drinking acid from the ships batteries. He died writhing in agony on the floor of his cabin.

By the end of that third day at open anchorage it appeared that we might be there for some time. Captain Markiewicz made a wise decision and with a wink and a nod sanctioned the duty free to be opened for essential items only. The essential items were beer and cigarettes. I managed to get a crate of Grolsch and 200 Marlboro. Everyone else on board was granted a similar amount. In temperatures of 100F, and with nothing much else to do, the beer was consumed fast. The empty bottles were thrown out of the ship's portholes and because the sea was so calm these bottles lingered and congregated at the ship's stern. After a while Captain Markiewicz ordered the engines to be turned on for a short time so that the wash from the propellers would drive the bottles away.

On the evening of Monday 19th July, our fifth day at open anchorage, the *Marie Anne* started shaking and vibrating. Another bottle clearing operation? No, a boat came alongside and the New York Harbour Pilot jumped on board. For five days it had felt like we were living in a pot of boiling glue. Now this feeling dispelled itself. It was still hot, but we were on the move again. We had purpose.

The ship slowly made its way down the Ambrose Channel. It was dusk and the pearly necklace of the Verazzono Narrows Bridge passed overhead. We were now in New York Harbour after 15 days at sea. To the left was the Statue of Liberty, but this was dwarfed by the buildings of Manhattan on the right, a gigantum wall of glowing, twinkling lights that reached for the sky. It looked unreal, like something out of *Star Wars*, but it confirmed that we really were in New York, at long last.

In 1624 the Dutch West India Company established the settlement of New Amsterdam on Manhattan Island. They bought Manhattan from the Indians for $24 worth of beads and trinkets. The British kicked the Dutch out in 1664 and renamed the town in honor of the Duke of York, thereby giving the world a legend: *New Amsterdam, New Amsterdam, it's a wonderful town, the Bronx is up and the Battery's down...* doesn't work, does it.

The entire crew came out on deck as we sailed into New York harbour. Even these hardened sailors were filled with awe every time they arrived in New York. The sheer scale of the place left you breathless. We were even more breathless when we realised the ship's engines were still driving her along. What was going on..? another telex from the shipping company was going on. The Captain had been ordered to dock not in New York, but in Ravena, 150 miles further up the Hudson River. Our mouths hung open as NY City was left glittering in the ships wake.

When I awoke the next morning I noticed something different: the ship was no longer rolling and pitching. This motion, produced by the waves and tide, had become a familiar sensation. Now we were on the Hudson River, which comparatively speaking was as flat as a mill pond.

The cruise up the Hudson from New York to Ravena took 14 hours. Ravena is ten miles south of Albany, in upstate New York. I was surprised that we could travel that far inland. The Hudson is a big river but we were on an equally big ship and it seemed like we were making our way up a small stream. The New York Pilot had been replaced by the Hudson Pilots. Yes, there were two of them, such was the difficulty of navigating large ocean- going vessels that far up the river. The Pilots were immaculately dressed in casual ware. They both wore dark shades. Their skin and teeth were perfect. They looked like they were made of plastic. Captain Markiewicz did not like the Pilots. No Captain likes having his Bridge invaded by complete strangers, especially strangers who are giving orders.

The heat eased-up and things became a bit more bearable. Kurt came out of his cabin. We stood on deck and watched the beautiful scenery of Hudson valley go slowly by. Kurt had been nearly everywhere and seen just about everything. However, this was the first time he'd been up the Hudson River on a huge cargo ship. He was excited by it all. So was I. We passed places called Bear Mountain, Cornwall, Fishkill and Poughkeepsie. There were eccentric houses built on tiny river islands, pretty little farms with white picket fences, mansions built by New York's wealthy, and in the distance the Catskill Mountains.

The river got its name from an Englishman called Henry Hudson. In 1609 he was looking for a quick passage to China. Perhaps he had been on the rum, because he entered New York bay and followed the river for 150 miles to what is now Albany, before realising that it did not go to China. In those days the Hudson valley was viewed as inhospitable, with wild animals, poisonous snakes, mountains and thick forests too dense to traverse. The river itself was seen as treacherous, especially in the stretch known as the Hudson Highlands. Here the hills rise up more than 1,000 feet along either shore and fierce currents and strong winds made sailing extremely difficult and dangerous. Areas of the river here were dubbed World's End and Devil's Horse Race by the early sailors.

Today, the Hudson River is navigable by ocean-going vessels as far as Albany. Here, cargo can continue its journey on the New York State Barge Canal, which goes west to the Great Lakes via the Erie

Canal. After completion of the Erie Canal in 1825, the Hudson River became one of the North America's main arteries of trade, opening a gateway to the west and prompting a period of major economic and industrial expansion in the area. Henry Hudson never did find a quick route to China yet his discovery of the river which bears his name was of great benefit to everyone.

The disappointment caused by not docking in New York harbour soon dispelled when I began to study my maps. Ravena is less than 100 miles from the Canadian border. Savannah is 1500 miles from the Canadian border. If we offloaded the cars at Ravena we could get The 2CV Alaska Challenge back on schedule - the delays crossing the Atlantic had made our itinerary nearly one week late. We now had the opportunity to claw back this time.

At midday on Tuesday 20th July the *Marie Anne* arrived in Ravena. You couldn't see much of the town from the river except for a marina and small cluster of houses on the hillside. Half a mile upriver from the marina a narrow jetty ran parallel to the river bank. The *Marie Anne* slowly manoeuvred towards it. There were people waiting for us on the jetty but we were still too far away to see who they were. I felt a sense of anticipation. Would Jose be there to meet me?

Jose and I hadn't known each other long. We'd met the previous summer on a blind date, only to discover that we were both just not that blind. However, although we didn't click in the romance department we did remain friends. Throughout those final months of 1998 I'd been boring Jose with news of the forthcoming Alaska trip, which I was doing with my cousin Andre. The only problem was that my co-driver didn't have a driving licence, so I started giving him lessons. Thing is, 2CVs are not the best cars to learn to drive in. For a start, the gear lever on the dashboard takes some getting used to, and then there's the car itself: you don't drive a 2CV, you operate it. You have to keep your foot hard on the accelerator nearly all the time to get every ounce of power out of that 602cc engine. You have to really work the gear lever to make best use of that power. To ventilate the car you turn a big wheel under the dash that slowly opens a flap below the windscreen. The windscreen wash is a button that you have to keep pumping with your finger to keep the water coming. The only windows that can be opened on a 2CV are on the front doors. The lower half of the window hinges up like a flap and has to be secured to a clip at the top of the door. The headlight switch has two positions and is in French, 'V' for ville, and 'R' for autoroute, dipped headlights or full beam. There's a big knob just beneath the steering column, which you must not touch under any circumstances, because it makes the headlights go up and down and adjusts the length of the beam. On the primitive dashboard there's a very inviting button with a light. No one is quite sure what this button does, but legend has it that it's a brake fluid level warning system. Some people are surprised when you tell them that the 2CV has excellent brakes. Occupied as you are, turning knobs and wheels, pressing buttons and coaxing every ounce of power out of the engine, you need to be able to stop fast.

Some people are born never to drive and the lessons were not going very well. During the first week of January 1999, Andre bowed out from the Alaska trip. I was now stuck without a co-driver and asked Jose if she'd be interested in the job. She jumped at the chance; thing is, Jose had never done a big adventure journey, let alone one that was raising money for charity and had media attention.

One week before we left London, Jose made her doubts about the Alaska trip all too apparent. Jose said she was only coming as far as Winnipeg, so that I wouldn't be lumbered in North America with two cars. I'd had no contact with Jose since our farewell in Rotterdam, three weeks previously, and no news as to whether she did actually leave her job and fly over to New York. I didn't know if she'd e-mailed my Atlantic bulletins on to Tony Carr or if she'd been able to keep track of the unscheduled movements of the *Marie Anne*. As the ship moved slowly towards that jetty in Ravena I was about to find out the answers to these questions.

Dockhands caught ropes thrown from the ship. The *Marie Anne* let out a toot on her horn and shuddered slightly as she met the jetty. Jose waved at me. I waved back. Jose looked fit and tanned. A woman with blonde hair was standing beside her. The relief at seeing Jose standing there was almost as great as my relief that we had finally made landfall in America. I went back to my cabin and poured a celebratory shot of whisky. I don't particularly like whisky. It just seemed the sort of booze one should drink on a ship. Perhaps I'd read one too many Tintin books?

Jose appeared in the cabin doorway. We greeted each other. It was an emotional moment, or maybe it was the whisky. Jose had a good look round my cabin while I told her something of what life on the ocean wave had been like. I could see that Jose now regretted missing out on the ocean voyage, because the original plan was that she'd accompany me on the *Marie Anne*.

The voyage cost £800 per person and £500 per car. I found a lot of people were surprised when I told them how much it cost for this one-way voyage. You can get a return air ticket across the Atlantic for around two hundred quid. Point is, the fare on a cargo ship includes 3 meals a day with wine, a high standard of accommodation and your own steward. It's like staying in a hotel. How much would it cost to stay in a good hotel for ten days? and this hotel is moving you thousands of miles from one continent to another. Looked at this way, cargo ships are perhaps not so expensive.

But Jose had other ideas, because sailors have a reputation for drinking, fighting and whoring. She felt a little bit nervous about being the only woman amongst such company, and who can blame her? Jose decided that she'd had enough of being an intrepid adventurer and announced that she didn't want to cross the Atlantic on the *Marie Anne*. Salty sea dogs, flagons of rum and pirates on the port bow did not appeal to her. I wasn't too happy with her decision, since the golden rule when travelling is always stick together, but Jose had made up her mind and that was that - Jose bowing out from the ocean voyage cost us an £800 cancellation fee,but what could I say: she'd got most of the sponsorship money.

Now that we were in port the passenger's day cabin was once again turned into the ship's office. The blonde woman who'd been standing on the jetty with Jose was the shipping agent in Albany who took care of MSL business. Her name was Diane and she seemed pleasant enough. Also present were two US Customs and Immigration Officers. The entire crew were summoned to the day cabin and one by one their passports were examined and stamped. Then came the turn of the passengers. Captain Markiewicz seemed irritated by it all, especially when it became known that there was a problem with Kurt's passport. Kurt didn't have a US visa. The Customs Officers could not understand what Kurt was trying to tell them. Jose spoke excellent German and translated into English what the old man was saying. Kurt was a German national but it turned out that years previously he had been made an honorary citizen of the United States. He didn't need a visa. There was an ageing stamp at the back of his passport which showed his US citizenship. The Customs Officers had never come across anything like this before and were unsure what to do. Eventually they phoned their head office and it was soon sorted out. Kurt was telling the truth and had a genuine stamp of citizenship in the back of his passport. I never did find out just what heroic deed Kurt had done to cause the American Government to bestow honorary citizenship on him. I suppose it's all part of being a living legend.

For the last two days, Jose had been staying at a hotel in Albany. She got a lift down to Ravena with Diane the shipping agent, who would now be making daily visits to the ship. Jose and I agreed that she should go back to Albany while I spent that night on board ship. This gave me a chance to get all my things packed. Tomorrow, Jose would return to the ship to see the cars offloaded and then we'd be on the road to Alaska, at long last.

I climbed down the gang ladder with Jose and Diane and then watched them drive off. It felt very strange to be standing on dry land again. I looked around. The dock area consisted of a small crane and a conveyor belt that ran from the jetty to a clearing. All around was thick forest. A dirt road led away from the clearing and up the hillside. The air was clean and fresh. The only sound came from birds twittering in the trees. Quite a difference from Rotterdam.

That dirt road looked too inviting and so later in the afternoon I set off for Ravena. Kurt wanted to come with me. This wasn't possible. For a start, we all doubted if he would be able to climb down the gang ladder, and even if he managed it he'd never make it up that steep hill. The old man of the sea would have to remain onboard ship.

By the time I got to the top of the dirt road I was puffing and panting and dripping with sweat. It was a very hot afternoon and I cursed myself for not bringing a water bottle with me. I was standing beside a tarmac road. It had a yellow line down the middle. Yup, this was America all right. The sound of the conveyor belt echoed up from the riverbank. They were unloading the cargo. All I could see from the road was the top of the ship's cranes. Everything else was obscured by trees.

There was no traffic. I set off down the road. Within five minutes I reached the first houses. Ravena is a small place yet it sprawls over a wide area. Its main claim to fame is that it sits at an important railway junction. It took me another 30 minutes to reach the centre of town, where there was a main highway and a car dealership and a supermarket. None of it looked very pretty. There'd been a settlement here for well over 100 years but few of the older buildings remained. They'd all been torn down in the name of progress. I dined on roast beef and mashed potato in the local restaurant then did a bit of shopping in the supermarket. Overall I felt let down by Ravena.

On the way back to the ship I stopped at a bar for a glass of cool beer. I sat by the window and gazed out at the dreary street. It looked dreary even in the bright summer sunshine. God knows what it was like when it was overcast and rainy. I got to wondering about the suicide rate in Ravena. Then a big American came into the bar: HI THERE GUY, HOWYA DOING. I jumped and almost spilt my beer. I'd forgotten how loud Americans could be.

The marina sounded more promising. I walked down a steep hill towards the river. There wasn't much sign of life and a bored dog trailed me. The marina looked deserted. There was a small wooden jetty by the public launch ramp. I could see the *Marie Anne* further up the river and I felt homesick for her.

The marina was the original settlement here. It was called Coeymans Landing and had a brisk traffic of steamships serving the Hudson River. When they built the railway further up the hill in the late 19th century the settlement that grew up around it became known as Coeymans Junction. Later the two were incorporated into one town. It was named after a popular brand of flour called 'Raven'. No one knows why the 'a' was added to it. No one particularly cares.

The next day Captain Markiewicz gave us the bad news. The cars had been hoisted out of No.7 hold and were now sitting on its hatch covers. They looked very impressive. We weren't impressed when the Captain told us that the cars couldn't be offloaded onto the jetty because it was too narrow. This was due to the way the ship had berthed. The superstructure was adjacent to the widest point of the jetty, the part that attached to the river bank. If the ship could just be backed-up 40 feet, so that the cargo deck was adjacent to the widest point of the jetty, it wouldn't be a problem... No, they were unloading cargo and nothing was allowed to interfere with that. What about when they finished unloading the cargo..? No, as soon as the cargo was offloaded the ship would get under way. Howabout if we got a mobile crane to the riverbank and tried to get the cars off with that? The Captain shrugged: 'that's up to you', he said. Jose and I decided to think over the idea. We had plenty of time. It was going to take them at least three days to unload the cargo.

I left the ship and became a landlubber again. Jose and I got a lift from Diana, who took us back to Jose's hotel in Albany. I didn't like the hotel much. It was the sort of place where business people stay; in otherwords, lifeless. Our room was spacious, though, and it didn't rock and sway like my cabin on the ship: time to get used to the real world again. The real world included an annoyed Dutch girl, annoyed at all the delays, annoyed at an Englishman who kept moaning about the hotel. We had our first row in North America. It frightened the pigeons who were nesting on the window ledge. Jose went off for a long walk. When she got back I suggested that we hire a car. I thought it might cheer her up a bit. It seemed ironic that we had our own two cars back on the ship.

We drove through the immaculate streets of Albany to find an internet café. I wanted to send the latest Alaska Challenge bulletin. Jose wanted to check her e-mails. Afterwards I rang my Mother to let her know I had landed safely in America. Mother had followed my progress across the Atlantic via the bulletins I sent from the *Marie Anne*. This was another handy thing about having the web site. Jose's family, too, followed our progress on the internet.

My Mother asked me about Albany. Hmm, Albany is the capital of the State of New York. It's a large city that has an almost identical history to New York City. The Dutch got there first in the early 15th century and called it Fort Orange. Fifty years later the Brits turned up and kicked the Dutch out, renaming the place Albany after the Duke of York, who was also the Duke of Albany. Potato chips were first invented in Albany, as were detachable collars and paperclips, which is handy stuff to know if you take part in pub quizes.

The next day we drove down to Ravena. It seemed that the mobile crane idea was a no-no. A very large crane would be needed to span the distance between the river bank and the ship. Such a large crane would never be able to get down the dirt track to the jetty. We were determined to get the cars off the ship somehow, so the next idea was to use a barge crane. The owner of the marina told us that a guy called Jim owned a barge crane which could do the job. However, Jim was working up in Albany and wouldn't be back till later. The marina owner took our hotel telephone number and said he'd ask Jim to call us. We then went to the small wooden jetty by the launch ramp and swam in the Hudson River.

Getting the cars off the ship now seemed to be possible, but there was nothing else we could do for the moment and so after our swim we drove down to Woodstock, in the Catskill Mountains. Woodstock, of course, was the site of the famous 1969 music festival. Well, that's actually not quite true; as is so often the case, history tends to get distorted: the people of Woodstock objected to having the festival on their doorstep and so it took place at Max Yasgurs' farm, near Bethel in neighbouring Sullivan county.

The promoters billed Woodstock as "Three Days of Peace and Music" and hoped to draw a crowd of 150,000 for a celebration of the communal spirit and to hear some of the most popular rock acts of the day. The festival started on Friday, August 15, 1969, and the crowds quickly grew to number over 450,000, causing massive traffic jams, logistical nightmares, shortages of food and medical supplies, and potential problems of crowd control. On Saturday, the gates were opened to accommodate the many thousands who arrived without tickets. The music was almost nonstop, the rains came, drug use was widespread, sanitary conditions were primitive, bad acid trips were a constant problem... and the Woodstock festival passed into legend.

I had expected the town of Woodstock to be a garish tourist trap. However, when Jose and I arrived there I was pleasantly surprised. It looked a very pretty place, and a real community. Sure, there were some tourist traps peddling on the 1969 festival, but they were few and far between. Woodstock began embracing the alternative lifestyle and peace and love long, long before the 1960s and the flower children arrived on the scene. In 1902, Ralph Radcliffe Whitehead, the heir to a Yorkshire textile fortune, set up an arts colony in Woodstock. His idea was to promote a wholesome return to nature and to provide a refuge against the Industrial Revolution. Whitehead and his partner, an art professor called Bolton Brown, spent years searching America for a suitable spot for the colony. Brown climbed Overlook Mountain above Woodstock and saw "an earthly paradise". Whitehead disliked the Catskill Mountains because they were "full of Jews", but Brown and the spectacular scenery persuaded Whitehead to form the colony there.

In the hundred years since then, Woodstock has been a magnet for those seeking creativity in the open air. There have been successive waves of artists, writers, craftspeople, dancers, musicians, urban drop outs and those seeking a green lifestyle. Bob Dylan moved to Woodstock in 1965, and at the time of the 1969 festival living in and around Woodstock there were also The Band, Van Morrison, Frank Zappa and the Mothers of Invention, Tim Hardin and a host of others.

Woodstock also attracted the occasional intrepid adventurer. Jose and I wandered down the main street amid the ever growing numbers of flower children and beautiful people. The third Woodstock Music Festival was due to take place that very weekend (the second Woodstock Music Festival had taken place in 1994). The karma felt right for our road journey across North America. That evening we went to an Irish pub in Albany. A live band played Irish music very badly. We ate chicken wings and drank beer. The atmosphere between us became more relaxed. It was all coming together nicely.

The next morning, Friday, found us once again in Ravena. Diana the shipping agent took us to one side. She was angry. Jim the barge crane man had come on board the *Marie Anne* the previous afternoon to look at the job we were asking him to do. Diana told us in no uncertain terms that the unloading of the ship's cargo was a commercial operation and we were out of bounds to start our own private operation to get the cars off the ship. Diana had obviously been to business school. I had never been to any kind of school much and told her that the cars were on their way to Alaska and all these delays were costing us money. Captain Markiewicz didn't seem too fussed about it all. No doubt he found it an amusing distraction from the usual routine of offloading kaolin, which had once again coated most of the ship. However, this run-in with the shipping agent did not help us when it came to the next phase of the journey.

Jim told us that he could easily get the cars off the ship with his crane barge. Problem was, the barge was presently up in Albany, and so to make the journey down to Ravena it would have to be hired for a full day to get the job done. This would cost almost $6000. Jose and I had discussed costs between ourselves beforehand. We would only go to a maximum of $2000 to get the cars offloaded. This would make a severe dent in our budget, but it was worth it: we'd save money in the long run by getting The 2CV Alaska Challenge back on schedule. $6000 was way, way too expensive for us and thus the idea of the crane barge was left with the pixies.

So, the cars would have to stay onboard ship and be taken down to Savannah, where we knew they could be offloaded without difficulty. Jose wanted a taste of life at sea and said that she'd join me on the *Marie Anne* for the last leg down to Savannah. Diana told us this was not possible because of something called the Jones Law. Civilians were not allowed to board cargo ships for coastal journeys in the US. Ok then, I would stay with Jose and we'd both drive down to Savannah in the hire car to meet the ship. Mr Jones and his law came into play again: passengers with cars had to stay with them until the final port of embarkation. I was no stranger here. I'd been with the Captain and crew of the *Marie Anne* for many weeks. We had a good relationship. Jose was also known to the crew of the *Marie Anne*. The law could have been bent a little bit on this one. However, because of our run in with Diana she was in no mood to do us any favours. The

Jones Law was being strictly interpreted.

And so me and the *Marie Anne* were going to remain entwined for the four day voyage down to Savannah. What should have been a nine day Atlantic crossing had now turned into a month long marathon. Jose was driving to Savannah in the hire car. I was not happy about this and wanted her to fly down, since a woman driving a car on her own across thousands of miles could easily run into trouble. But Jose, being Dutch, had made up her mind and that was the end of the argument. As well as the frustrations in Ravena I was now left with worrying about Jose's safety. On the Saturday afternoon we said goodbye to Albany. Jose dropped me off at the ship and then headed for the southern states. She promised me that she was going to drive at a fast pace, so it would only take her two days to get down to Savannah.

Back in my cabin I slumped down at my desk and looked at the familiar surroundings. Days previously I had left this cabin, I thought for the last time. Now I was back again. The bond that I'd developed with the *Marie Anne* had dissipated during our stay in New York State. I still felt affection for the ship, but now I wanted to be elsewhere. Dinner in the Officer's Mess that evening was more of an ordeal than usual.

On Sunday morning the unloading operation was completed. A mountain of white kaolin now took pride of place in the forest clearing. We had to wait for the high tide and it wasn't until the afternoon that two tugs came down from Albany to help us leave. I'd seen the *Marie Anne* making tight turns in Rotterdam. We were facing upstream and I knew the ship couldn't turn around in this narrow river. This proved correct. The tugs accompanied us along the ten miles up to Albany, where the river had been widened and the ship had just about enough room to turn round. The plastic Pilots came on board and we headed back down the river to New York and the open sea.

The ship passed through New York harbour in the early hours of Monday morning. I was asleep and didn't see it this time round. We then made our way down the eastern seaboard of the US, south towards Savannah. The days dragged by. It was the first time I felt bored on board ship. I hoped Jose had made it down to Savannah safely. There was no way of finding out until I arrived there myself; and so the clock ticked sluggishly on.

The two cars were still on the hatch cover of No.7 Hold. The No.2 car did not carry the banners of our company sponsors. There just wasn't time to get it done during the final mad rush in London, so I brought the banners along with me and now occupied myself by sticking them on the No.2 car.

At the start of 1999 we had only £500 of company sponsorship in the pot and it seemed like we would be paying for most of the trip from our own pockets. How much was the 2CV Alaska Challenge going to cost..? How long is a piece of string. There were fixed costs, like our fares across the Atlantic, the cost of buying and shipping the car, the amount of petrol you have to put in the tank to travel 7000 miles, but everything else was somewhat fluid. The amount of money you burn depends almost entirely on the way you live. Neither Jose nor I wanted to rough it in North America and I calculated that an absolute minimum of £2000 each would be required – in the event, I widely underestimated this budget.

Then there was the question of how long we would take to reach Alaska. Obviously, the longer we took to cross North America the more it would cost in hotels, food, etc. I had plans to stay on in Alaska and so favoured a fast (ie, cheaper) drive, taking just three weeks. Jose wanted to do a slow journey to Alaska. In the end we compromised and settled on a four week road journey.

Back in Holland, Jose had worked as a PA for a big multinational corporation. Her boss was moved to the UK office and Jose went along with him. That's how she came to be living in England, and that's how it happened, in the space of two weeks during late January/early February 1999. Jose did brilliantly. She asked one of the company bigshots for sponsorship for the 2CV Alaska Challenge: Yes. The multinational had divisions and subsidiaries all around the world. Jose pestered more of the big shots. Australia: Yes. Canada: Yes. USA: Yes. It was like when you win the jackpot on a fruit machine and the coins just keep on tumbling into the tray. At the end of those amazing two weeks we had 12 company sponsors and found ourselves sitting on thousands and thousand of pounds of sponsorship money. Whoopee!

We were both somewhat dazed by this sudden turn of good fortune, yet it didn't change our plans radically. It was still going to be a four week road journey. However, we did decide to bring over a second 2CV. This car would be for Tony, and we'd let him have it at cost price by way of a thank you for doing the web site. The 2CV that was going all the way to Alaska became known as the No.1 car, Tony's 2CV, which would be going only as far as Winnipeg, became known as the No.2 car.

A sea breeze was whipping around the deck and I made a pretty bad job of sticking on the banners. Some of the crew gathered to watch and clapped each time I completed a banner. Once finished, I stood back to have a look at my handiwork. The banners didn't look too bad from a distance. Besides, it didn't matter too much because the No.2 car was only going as far as Winnipeg, which was two weeks drive from Savannah. On the otherhand, the banners carried by the No.1 car had been put on by a professional firm in London. I was confident these banners would stand up to the pounding the car would take on the long journey to the Arctic Ocean.

The Arctic Ocean seemed like a strange concept at that moment. On day four of our journey down the east coast we entered the mouth of the Savannah River. The temperature was in the 100s again and the humidity was very high. Barry told me that it was always this hot in Savannah, even during the winter months. He carried on with a story about someone who had been driven insane by the heat, but I managed stop him before he came to the usual grizzly conclusion.

The Savannah River is very broad. At its mouth there are many islands, including Salt Spring Island, where a lot of millionaires have houses with big walls. Dolphins became part of the landscape again. The mouth of the Savannah River is famous for its dolphins and sightseeing boats regularly take people out to see them. We soon left the dolphins to the sightseers and passed by the old part of Savannah. It looked very nice. We then passed under a very high concrete road bridge, which didn't look very nice. On the other side of the bridge there was an industrial area, which is part of the Port of Savannah. This was the first time we'd made landfall without the help of pilots. Savannah is the *Marie Anne*'s main port of call in the US and her crew could bring the ship in with their eyes shut.

Two tugs pushed the reluctant *Marie Anne* into dock at 2.30pm on Wednesday 28th July, exactly four weeks after the cars were loaded in Rotterdam. Jose was waiting on the quayside. I had already cleared customs and immigration in Ravena so all that remained to do was to clear the cars through customs. Within 30 minutes of docking the two Citroen 2CVs were hoisted on to the quayside. I had already packed my things into the cars. I sought out Captain Markiewicz, shook his hand and thanked him for a safe voyage. As I got to the top of the gangway someone called out my name: 'Rube, Rube!' Kurt jumped up and gave me a hug. He didn't let go of me for some time. It was quite embarrassing. I promised to send him a postcard from Prudhoe Bay and wished him bon voyage. Kurt was in possession of a roundtrip ticket. He was going back to Rotterdam on the *Marie Anne*. There were no other passengers on the voyage back. I didn't envy Kurt.

Two portly black ladies from US Customs took ages to go through the paperwork. They said they would love to own a 2CV, just like ours. Finally, they were satisfied that everything was correct; and the big question was, after 4 weeks at sea, with the damp, with the corrosive salt, would the cars start..? Yes, at the first attempt both 600cc engines roared into life. The crew of the *Marie Anne* gave a cheer. After all the frustrations, after all the delays, this was it. I took the wheel of the No.1 car, Jose took the wheel of the No.2 car and we drove away from the *Marie Anne*, into the arms of America... the road journey to Alaska was underway, two weeks behind schedule.

Chapter 2. Into The Arms Of America

Savannah was established in 1733. The city is planned around a system of wonderfully green squares which are surrounded with Georgian Colonial and Greek Revival buildings. Jose and I bombed around these squares in the 2CVs. We had the car roofs rolled back. Citroen 2CVs are rarer than snow in these parts. Our ones had British number plates, the steering wheels were on the wrong side and each car was plastered with the banners of our company sponsors. People stood and stared in amazement. We drove fast. It reminded me of that film, *The Italian Job*, with Michael Caine and the Mini Coopers bombing around an Italian city: *This is the self preservation society...*

But we hadn't just robbed a bank, we were on our way to Jose's motel, and strictly speaking we shouldn't have driven the cars from the ship to the motel because we had no insurance cover. Strictly speaking, we shouldn't have driven through Savannah like bats out of hell. It was just that after all the frustrations and delays on the Atlantic crossing it felt wonderful to be on the road at long last. I don't think Savannah's finest saw it that way and they weren't too pleased to have us in their city. We soon discovered, though, that we could get away with minor traffic offences because A) the cars carried foreign license plates, and B) the traffic cops had never encountered a Citroen 2CV before. The cops would pull us over and start writing out a ticket but confronted with the aforementioned things they'd give up and let us go. It was too much of a headache for them. A pity, really, since for years I've been trying to get a speeding ticket in a 2CV. Savannah was my big chance.

The motel had been surrounded by shopping malls and fast food joints yet hadn't surrendered and was pleasant enough. Jose arrived in Savannah two days previously and she'd already done the tourist bit. I couldn't face being a tourist, it was just *too* hot, so we made a beeline for the hotel pool. A retired US Army Colonel splashed around in the water with us. He kept impersonating slitty-eyed Asians. The Colonel was receiving treatment at a nearby veteran's hospital. Savannah has a large military presence and is home to the 165th Airlift Wing and the 3rd Infantry, amongst others.

The Colonel told us that he served in Vietnam during 1969 and was wounded in the Tet Offensive. Thirty years later he was still being treated for those wounds, both physically and mentally. He felt no bitterness towards his country and still hated Asians. This meeting with the Colonel was in strong contrast to our visit to Woodstock the previous week. It seemed amazing that a country could produce such extremes.

It would have been nice to spend all day at the swimming pool. However, we needed to get road insurance for the cars. It proved impossible to get insurance cover before we got to America, because you have to give the insurance agency an address in the US as your place of residence. Fortunately, we had a contact in Savannah. Her name was Claire, one of numerous contacts in North America that we'd made via the internet. Jose spent her first night in Savannah staying with Claire and now Claire agreed to let us use her address for insurance purposes. These southerners are such friendly people.

The price wasn't very friendly, though, at a little agency just round the corner from the motel. Problem was, the insurance agent couldn't find the Citroen 2CV listed in any of his books (because the car was never sold in North America) so he whacked us into the highest insurance category, made worse by the fact that we were driving two of the damn things. We spun a yarn about how we had just moved to Savannah because we loved the food and the dolphins, and would be living here for quite some time and could we please have the cost of the insurance paid-off in lots and lots of little installments, the more the merrier. Yes, very friendly: we walked away with both cars insured for just over one hundred bucks, the first month's installment. That's all we needed to drive legally during our time in America. The rest of the installments were never paid of course. The next morning, Friday 30th July, we said goodbye to sweltering Savannah and set out on the road journey to Canada. Our original plan was to follow the coast north via Washington DC and New York, which would provide some great photo opportunities with the cars in front of the White

House, the Statue Of Liberty, etc. However, both Jose and I felt a need to get away from the hustle and bustle of the big population centres so we decided to drive up to Canada via the inland route, on Interstate Highways 26 and 77, up through the Carolinas and on to the back roads of West Virginia.

We were insured for the road. We'd stocked up with cheap cigarettes and filled the cars with the cheapest petrol in America. We were taking part in a road movie and the cars were the stars. We got just twenty miles from Savannah and then the No.1 car developed engine problems. I contacted Jose on the walkie-talkie:

'This is yellow duck calling green duck, can you give me a big ten four, over.'
'What?!.'
'Er, green duck, I'm having problems with yellow duck, do you copy?'
'Oh fuck off'
'Green duck, yellow duck has engine problems, over.'
'Bloody ducks'
'Suggest we pull off the freeway at the next gas station, copy green duck.'
'Copy what?!'

A car followed us off the freeway and on to the gas station forecourt. The driver was a young man who introduced himself as Billy. Billy wanted to video us and the 2CVs and kept saying 'Wow!' He asked us to wave at the camera and say hi to Hank. It was Hank's birthday. We tried to be polite to Billy but in that sweltering heat, and nursing a car with mechanical problems, we were polite behind gritted teeth. Despite all the 'No Smoking' signs, Jose lit-up a cigarette and spoke to Billy. Fortunately, Billy couldn't understand Dutch.

Ever since driving away from the *Marie Anne* a steady stream of people had been filming and photographing the cars. It was nice that people took an interest in us but at times it got a tad annoying. We were somewhat surprised at the reaction to the cars. People would toot at us, wave at us, give us the thumbs up. Mostly, though, they wanted to film and photograph the cars... Billy sensed the tension in the air and didn't linger long. He told us that Hank would be thrilled when he saw the video and thanked us profusely before driving off, leaving us to figure out what was wrong with the No.1 car.

It didn't take long to figure it out. Whenever I eased off on the No.1 car's accelerator the engine started spluttering. When the revs dropped down to tick over speed the engine cut out completely. The engine could be restarted without difficulty, but would only keep going if high revs were maintained. Easy. Now all we had to do was figure out how to fix it. Hmm...

Jose poured a bottle of water over her head in an attempt to cool down. I watched the cars go by on the freeway. Ten minutes elapsed. We looked at the No.1 car, but it was still not working properly. We spotted some people who were about to pounce on us with their cameras and decided to push on, since I had no desire to start working on the engine in that heat – yep, I was the mechanic on this little jaunt across North America. Jose still hadn't figured out how to open the bonnet on a 2CV. The trouble was, I didn't know much about fixing cars either. I know how an internal combustion engine works yet the finer points of what goes on under the bonnet have never interested me. That is what car mechanics are for: 'Ah, you'll be alright', said Chris and John, my mechanics in London. It's the sort of thing people say to you before you go into hospital for an operation. Chris and John weren't in America, where a 600cc air cooled French car designed in the 1940s belongs only in a Disney cartoon, where the name 'Citroen' has never been heard of, where a 2CV is looked upon as an alien apparition. That's right, if you break down in a Citroen 2CV in the USA you're in *big* trouble.

However, our Citroen 2CV could still be driven, just. It involved a juggling act with the accelerator, clutch and brake pedals. If my foot strayed away from the accelerator pedal for more than a few seconds the engine cut out. Ho hum what fun.

By early afternoon we reached Charlotte in North Carolina. Charlotte was named after the wife of George III, which is handy to know. In the 1700s the town became a gold rush centre. It's now the largest city in North Carolina. It also has the largest traffic jams. Buckets of sweat ran off me as I struggled in the heat to keep the No.1 car going.

'This is Yellow Duck calling Green Duck, do you copy?'
'You almost ran into the back of that truck.'
'Yeah, big buddy, it was a five nine, over.'
'Five what?'
'Come on in there green duck, the bears are smoking and there's alligator bait in the granny lane, over'
'What?'
'I said, I've had enough of trying to keep this pile of shite going in this traffic, over.'
'Let's keep going for a few more hours.'
'Got ya, green duck, it's a ten one and cruising.'
'Ten what?'
'I said, ok then.

Our small convoy got as far as Mount Airy, which nestles in the foothills of the Blue Ridge Mountains. We'd had enough of the heat, the traffic, the problems with the No.1 car and checked into a Best Western Hotel just outside town. A swimming pool beckoned and we wasted no time in making use of it. My ears were ringing from the No.1 car's roaring engine. I was drenched in sweat. My muscles were aching. Our first day on the road had been a bit of a disaster. However, due to the fact that even with serious mechanical problems a 2CV's engine will keep running and running we managed to cover a fair amount of mileage and were still just about on schedule.

I spent the evening studying a battered Haynes workshop manual. By next morning I'd come to the conclusion that the problem with the No.1 car was that it didn't work properly. At that moment, for want of any better ideas, I had a flash of inspiration and deduced that it must be the points that were causing the trouble. On the front of a 2CV's engine there is a big fan which draws in air to cool the engine. The points lay behind this fan and it needed to be removed to get at them. This is achieved by undoing a big bolt at the centre of the fan. The bolt was hidden within the fan shaft. Not only did you need a socket wrench to fit the bolt, you also needed the socket to be thin enough to fit within the fan shaft. We'd brought a huge array of tools with us. I turned the heavy tool box upside down and emptied it on to the ground. There were four chisels of varying size, snips for cutting sheet metal, an electrical screwdriver, a mallet, some levers for removing bicycle tyres, and a whole host of other things that were equally useless. There was even a socket, which, according to the workshop manual, was the right size for the fan bolt.Trouble was, it wouldn't fit inside the fan shaft. Perhaps you can see now why I've never had the time nor patience for mucking around with cars. On that hot morning in North Carolina I didn't have much choice, though, especially since Jose had locked me out of the hotel room.

When it became apparent that I was never going to fix the yellow duck in the hotel car park, Jose suggested that we drive into Mount Airy to try and find someone who could fix the bloody thing. We were in luck: there was a garage just on the outskirts of town, and it was open on a Saturday morning.

The two mechanics were called Billy and Billy Boy and their features looked remarkably similar. They both wore dungarees which stopped three inches short of their ankles. When they saw the 2CVs, Billy chuckled and Billy Boy guffawled. Oh well, it looked like the No.1 car's engine problems would remain unfixed. However, the two Billys' did have a correct size socket that fitted within the fan shaft and so I bought it off them for ten bucks. Chickens scattered as we drove back on to the road and into the centre of town.

Internet access is free in all public libraries in North America. We parked-up outside the Mount Airy Public Library. I needed to send the latest Alaska Challenge Bulletin. I also took a quick look at our web site and noticed that Tony hadn't put up the charity sponsorship form. I sent Tony an e-mail reminding him to do this.

Although still mid morning the temperature was already in the 80s and sweat dripped off me as I went to work on the No.1 car in the library car park. Jose watched from under the shade of a nearby tree. My efforts lasted for just five minutes. The fan bolt would not move, no matter how hard I tried to turn it. I tried whacking the end of the socket wrench with a hammer. The bolt didn't budge. I used a short piece of scaffold tube as extra leverage on the socket wrench. The fan bolt remained stubborn. Ah, sod it: I sat down on the hot tarmac and lit-up a cigarette.

Mount Airy looked like a nice place. The picturesque streets gave off a relaxed atmosphere and in the distance you could see the town's namesake. It's the shape of a mound and has a smaller granite mound at the top, making it look like a huge breast with a taut nipple. In 1996, Mount Airy was placed at number 36 in a list of America's 100 Best Small Towns, which kind of surprised me, since I felt that it should have been at least number 35. Mount Airy's one claim to fame is that it is the birthplace of the American television personality, Andy Griffith (don't worry, I've never heard of him either). Mount Airy plays heavily on this fact and Griffith memorabilia can be seen all around town. You can even stay in Andy Griffith's childhood home, if you have nothing better to do.

"Pardon me Sir, Maam, may I ask you what you are doing?"

Travis was a short 18-years-old, with spectacles and cropped fair hair. He looked remarkably like the two Billys' and wore knee length shorts, boots and a baggy t-shirt. He carried books under his arm and told us he was a poet. Travis hated Mount Airy and said that he wanted to escape the narrow-minded and dull life there. He was thinking of going to Europe and asked us about life there. He'd never been outside of North Carolina and was hesitant about making such a big step. We urged him to go for it.

Travis asked us if there were many black people in Europe. At this point my alarm bells started ringing. Then Travis went on to say that he had no problem with black people and had a friend who was black. This caused him a lot of grief with his family and white friends. Travis didn't understand why people hated each other so much. Jose and I were told that recently a black man had been murdered in the area by three white men. No one had yet been arrested for the crime, despite the fact that everyone seemed to know who the white men were. It all sounded like something from a suspense novel, although on the way up from Savannah we had seen a number of big, white wooden crosses in fields beside the highway. Pious farmers? or maybe those jolly chaps from the Klan were making their presence known to any black folks who might be driving by.

We took a photo of Travis standing beside the No.1 car and wished him luck – coming from Mount Airy, we thought he'd need it. The No.1 car refused to be fixed and so we pushed on with the journey. We left Interstate 77 and pushed on to the small roads, into the mountains. This was a bad move because the sharp gradients and hairpin bends were a tad difficult when driving a car whose engine could only run at high revs. Ever tried driving along steep, winding mountain roads when you have to use the brake, the clutch, and at the same time keep your foot jammed down on the accelerator pedal? Jose and the No.2 car very wisely kept well clear of me for most of the time.

On the plus side, the mountain scenery was beautiful, the heat no longer oppressive and because we were in a remote area there was very little other traffic on the road. I didn't make it round one particularly sharp bend and shot off down a side road. Jose followed and we found ourselves on the banks of a mountain river; don't ask me where, except that it was somewhere in the Blue Ridge Mountains where we went for a lovely cool swim. There was even a little beach which enabled me to take the No.1 car for a swim as well; or at least, to drive the front of it into the river in order to cool down its overheated and tortured engine.

You may well ask why the Citroen 2CV was the car of choice for the Alaska trip? Well, that was my doing, because I didn't see much of a challenge in driving a sturdy, comfortable car that will get you sturdily and comfortably from A to B. I'd driven 2CVs on and off for a number of years and knew it was the car for the trip to Alaska. Things got a bit complicated, though, because the 2CV was never sold in North America and the only ones you do find out there are usually collectors cars and sell for mega bucks. It would work out far cheaper to buy the cars in the UK and ship them across the Atlantic. This is how we ended up hitting the roads of North America on the east coast. What started as a 1500 mile drive up the Alaska Highway had now turned into a 7000 mile trans-continental jaunt.

The idea of doing this in a 2CV kinda appealed to me. With its canvas roof and curved lines, the 2CV has a resemblance to the wagons the pioneers used to drive west. The only question was, could a 2CV survive the rigours of the trail?

The Citroën 2CV was first presented to the world at the Paris Motor Show in 1948. The appearance of the car has changed little since then. The original designs were made by an architect and the car was aimed mainly at the rural population of France. It had to be cheap. It had to be economical to run. It had to be capable of taking the family, including Grandma, on a day trip to Clermont Ferrand. It needed to be able to drive across a ploughed field with a basket of eggs on the back seat without breaking a single egg. It had to be capable of carrying livestock or large loads or drunken peasants. Due to these design criteria it became known as "the French farmer's car".

The modern derivative of the 2CV has a 602cc twin cylinder engine that is air-cooled and very economical (the car is called the Deaux Chevaux in French, meaning 'two horses'). It has independent suspension on all four wheels and gives a smooth ride – although with its peculiar rolling motion some people say that sitting in a 2CV is like being on a boat. It has a back seat that is easily removed and a canvas roof that rolls right back, exposing a surprising amount of load space.

Citroen must have had a hard job marketing the 2CV, which it's often said looks like a corrugated iron shed on wheels. Some people call them tin snails, or upturned prams, or ducks, or other equally derogatory remarks. Yet the 2CV was one of Citroen's biggest selling cars and even though they stopped manufacture years ago (in 1990) you still see many of them on the roads of Europe. If you drive a 2CV it says that you don't care what other people think. You don't have to prove something. You have no need to impress. You are at ease with yourself and don't suffer from insecurities. If you drive a 2CV it could also say that you are poor and/or you have no taste. The debate rages on.

In West Virginia, Jose got drunk. After our second day on the road we hadn't got very far. 'Hadn't got very far' was a small town in West Virginia whose name I cannot recall. It was a real touristy place surrounded by the mountains. We checked into an ersatz Swiss motel and had a drink in the cellar bar. I think Jose and I were both now resigned to the fact that we had a knackered 2CV on our hands and as a result we relaxed a bit. With a glass of cool beer in my hand I said that I'd have a go at fixing the No.1 car 'later'. Jose had a glass of dry white wine and said that she loved West Virginia, even though we'd only been in the state for an hour or so. An English ex-pat came into the bar and got talking to us. His name was John, but things didn't get much further than that because Jose was now on her second glass of wine and suddenly started finding everything very funny. Perhaps she had a point.

After a third glass of wine, Jose grew very confused and wandered off. When she didn't return I thought that I'd better go find her. I found her out in the hotel car park, sitting on the ground in front of the No.1 car and talking to it in Dutch. I helped her back to our room, where she fell on to the bed in an uncoordinated state, giggling, talking nonsense. Drunk on just three glasses of wine?! Jose was a continental and thus well used to drinking wine. Three glasses of white were usually nothing to her, so why the drunkenness? Was it the heat? Was it the excitement? Was she unwell? The mystery was never solved.

After making sure that Jose was ok, I went back down to the bar, where I discovered that John the ex-pat had left Britain in the 1970s, he said to get away from the strikes and industrial unrest. He now considered the USA his home and ran a small building company. Like most ex-pats there were little things he missed, certain brands of tea, biscuits and jam, and so forth, but he said he'd never move back to the UK. He returned every three years or so to visit his relatives and always found himself hating the place. West Virginia was John's paradise. I think he'd been hooked by the song, which I'm sure must have been a Number One hit in Holland at some stage.

'I'm bundled out Green Duck, there's a City Kitty on my tail, give me a big ten four, over'
'What?'
'How's the motion lotion, Green Duck?'
'Lotion, what lotion?'
'Gouge on it and watch our for road pizza on the big slab.'
'Er, no, I don't feel hungry yet.'
'There's swamp donkeys so get out of the big hole, Green Duck, ten five coming at yur, Yellow Duck out.'

The next day we left the hill country behind and crossed into the little state of Maryland. Maryland was very pretty, with orchards and fields of corn and little houses with white picket fences. The countryside had a manicured look and gave the impression of a film set. It's the most aptly named state that I've ever encountered; and yes, it was named after Mary, who was the wife of... ah, ok, you really don't want to know, do you.

Maryland may be small, and may or may not be named after someone's wife, yet it's played a large part in the history of America, mostly because it has the nation's capital, Washington (which sits in its own 'District of Columbia'), but also because Maryland has always been the hinge between the North and South (the famous Mason-Dixon Line runs through Maryland), and during the American Civil War it was torn between the Unionists and the Confederates. The causes of conflicts are always complex, yet the American Civil War was quite a straightforward case: it was all about keeping the feldgling Union together and the issue of slavery.

In 1850, America had a population of 23 million people in a union comprising of 31 states. The North, embodied by New England and the Middle Atlantic states, was the main center of manufacturing, commerce and finance. The South had an economy centered on agriculture. In 1850, the American South grew more than 80 percent of the world's cotton. Slaves were used to cultivate the cotton. It was slavery which exacerbated the regional and economic differences between North and South. The vast majority of Northerners thought that slavery was repulsive, while most Southerners regarded slavery as essential to their economy. The argument grew worse as the American West was won and the new territories had to decide whether to be slave-states or free-soil states.

Abraham Lincoln had long regarded slavery as an evil. In a speech in Illinois in 1854, he declared that all national legislation should be framed on the principle that slavery was to be restricted and eventually abolished. When Abe was sworn in as president of the United States in March 1861, it was too much for the South to stomach. On April 12 1861, Confederate guns opened fire on the federal troops stationed at Fort Sumter in South Carolina; the first shots of the American Civil War. The war came to Maryland shortly after, on April 19th, when a bunch of Southerners and Northerners started fighting on a train; which is rather like what happens in Britain every Saturday afternoon during the football season.

The American Civil War lasted for four years and it is estimated that 620,000 people were killed during the conflict. Most of the destruction took place in the south, where many of the large cities lay in ruins and the countryside was ravaged. The North, with it's bigger population and greater wealth, won the war of course. The 13th Amendment, which abolished slavery in the entire United States, was ratified by the legislature in December 1865, and it would be nice to say that black Americans lived happily ever after. Alas...

We'd been following Highway 219. However, we were told that on the trip up through Pennsylvania, 219 got lost in the hills and we were advised to switch across to Highway 220. Highway 220 was similar to 219, in that it was a very small road that meandered along, but apparently it did go somewhere, eventually. That somewhere was Somerset, PA, where we spent our third night on the road. By now I'd given up trying to fix the No.1 car. This could wait until we got to Canada, where I knew we could get help, and also get the car fixed.

"Whoowe, there's a Countie Mountie sniffin round the dog. The bear's gonna bite that ballet dancer. Copy me Green Duck"
"Hmm, yes, so."
"I'm breaking wind and there's a bear in the air, give me a big ten four."
"..."
"Have you got your ears switched on, Green Duck?"

Pennsylvania is big and has lots of forests and produces more potato chips than any other state in America. The name 'Pennsylvania' means Penn's woods, after Admiral Sir William Penn. Back in 17th century England, Admiral Penn had loaned £16,000 to King Charles II and after the Admiral's death this money was owed to his son, William Penn. Penn junior had shocked his upper-class associates by his conversion to the beliefs of the Society of Friends, otherwise known as Quakers, who at that time were a very persecuted sect. Seeking a haven in the New World for persecuted Friends, Penn junior asked the King to pay back the sixteen grand by way of granting him land in the territory between Lord Baltimore's province of Maryland and the Duke of York's province of New York. The

King signed the Charter of Pennsylvania on March 4, 1681, and named the new colony in honor of his old mucker, Admiral Penn.

A large number of Quakers came to Penn junior's not-so-small haven in the New World and they became the first group to express organized opposition to slavery. Slavery slowly disappeared in Pennsylvania under the state's Gradual Emancipation Act of 1780. However, nationally the issue of slavery became acute after 1820, and in particular the new Fugitive Slave Law deeply offended those in the North. Many Pennsylvanians were averse to the return of fugitive slaves to their masters. In fact, the Quaker led antislavery movement helped slaves escape to safe refuges in the North or over the border into Canada. These escape routes were known as the "Underground Railroad" and became firmly established in the early 1800s in all parts of the North.

In 1852, Harriet Beecher Stowe published *Uncle Tom's Cabin*, a novel inspired by the passage of the Fugitive Slave Law. The book is a damning indictment of slavery (and now the book is damned by the PC brigade). More than 300,000 copies were sold in the first year and presses ran day and night to keep up with the demand. *Uncle Tom's Cabin* played a major part in promoting the antislavery movement, a movement that almost a decade later became one of the major factors in the American Civil War.

After our fourth day on the road, mostly on the back roads of Pennsylvania, we crossed the state line and spent the night in a small town in upstate New York. Not so many miles to the east of us lay Albany and Ravena, where the *Marie Anne* had docked two weeks previously. A stinking cold had docked in my system and I was coughing and spluttering. This was going to be our last night in America. We wouldn't be making her acquaintance again until we reached Alaska.

We went for dinner at a restaurant next to the hotel, where Jose gave me the good news: instead of flying back to London from Winnipeg she had now decided to accompany me all the way to Alaska. This surprised me somewhat, since thus far our road journey had not been exactly trouble free. I wheezed my thanks. The wave of political correctness which was sweeping across North America at that time had swept up this little town whose name I can not remember. A total smoking ban was going to be enforced in the morning. The locals had defiantly gathered in the restaurant to chain-smoke cigarettes. You could have cut the resulting fug with a knife. Jose coughed a reply to me. Perhaps she still felt drunk, or perhaps the adventure of it all was sweeping her along. The call of the open road is hard to resist.

Or maybe not so hard to resist: the next morning the No.2 car was very reluctant to get going. The weather had turned cold and damp and the No.2 car's engine turned over and over and refused to start. Jose got out of the car and rather violently slammed the door shut. Rust fell from the bodywork. I had a go at starting the car, without any luck. Oh gawd, it now looked like we had two knackered 2CVs on our hands, and we hadn't even got to Canada yet. Eventually we got the No.2 car going by means of towing it with the No.1 car in order to get a bump start. The No.1 car could still only be driven in high revs. Its engine screamed and smoke poured from the clutch as it pulled along the No.2 car.

We were still on Highway 220, which had now grown-up and become a big road for the drive into Buffalo. Buffalo sits at the eastern end of Lake Erie. It has a population of around one million and in 1996 it was selected as an All America City and Community, which is very interesting. Buffalo marks the start of the Niagara River, which is 36 miles long and drains four of the Great Lakes into Lake Ontario. The Niagara River is the border between the USA and Canada. Half way along its course the swift waters of the Niagara River surge forward and plunge over high cliffs, so making Niagara Falls one of the top tourist attractions in North America.

Just north of the Falls is the Rainbow Bridge, which joins the USA and Canada. At lunchtime on Tuesday 3rd August, two Citroen 2CVs trundled across the Rainbow Bridge into Canada. It had taken us five days to drive the 1500 miles up from Savannah. At the border post we were told to pull over at the Customs Office. Jose and Rob and the cars were closely inspected by Erin and Harry, Canadian Customs and Immigration Officers. The prognosis was good. We took a picture of Erin and Harry standing by the cars. Erin gave Jose and I a Maple Leaf badge each. Welcome to Canada. We thanked the two of them and then made to drive away. The No.2 car wouldn't start. Jose kept turning the ignition key but the engine wouldn't fire. An embarrassing moment as Erin and Harry grew tired of waving at us. We let the No.2 car sit for a while and tried starting it again. With much spluttering and coughing the engine finally fired into life and we were on our way.

"We're on the way to Hog Town, Green Duck, and I'm smoking the brakes comin' off the Cabbage"
"..."
"Did you eye that Crotch Rocket at the cash register?"
"..."
"It's a ten nine. Buddy's after those Lot Lizards but there's a smokin' scooter taking pictures."
"Oh for christsake, SHUT UP!"

Niagara Falls consists of two cataracts. The Horseshoe, or Canadian Falls, and the American Falls. Every second, more than half a million gallons of water dive into the wide canyon and explode on the rocks below; although lord knows how they calculate these things. At night the falls are lit up and the churning waters tumble dramatically into blackness, while in winter the whole scene changes as the falls freeze to form gigantic razor-tipped icicles which give statisticians multiple orgasms.

Niagara Falls is up there with, say, the Taj Mahal or The Great Wall of China. It's one of the world's top tourist attractions and no commercial opening has been left unexploited. The Canadian side of the Falls affords the most spectacular view. Here, hotels and apartment blocks have sprung up beside the canyon like giant steel and concrete weeds. There's a *Hard Rock Cafe* and a casino, a plague of gift shops, and to make it even easier to part with your money a variety of methods have been laid on to help you get closer to the Falls: boats, catwalks, observation towers and helicopters all push as near to the curtain of falling water as they dare. Even one hundred years ago, Oscar Wilde found the tourist operation at the Falls tacky. Oscar quipped that he would have been more impressed if the falls ran upwards.

We'd missed out on photo opportunities with the cars at the White

House and Statue Of Liberty, so I wanted to make sure that we took some pics at Niagara Falls. Easier said than done: the promenade above the canyon was jammed solid with vehicles and people. A small road ran along the promenade before doubling back on itself. The road had been made one-way and an endless procession of big tour coaches and cars slowly trundled along it. There were no-parking signs everywhere. Traffic wardens swarmed. An army of Marshals kept things on the move. Where the hell could we photograph the cars here?

The car parks at Niagara Falls are full by early morning. We drove into one by the loop of the small road. The car park occupied higher ground and we might just get the shot of the cars there. The guy at the barrier told us the car park was full. I told him we were from the press and wanted to do a quick photo shoot. He spoke to his supervisor before waving us through. He still charged us a five dollar parking fee. We managed to get a shot of the No.2 car with Niagara Falls in the background. It wasn't a particularly good shot, but it was the best we could get on an August afternoon at one of the world's top tourist attractions. Some tourists began photographing me photographing the cars. Then Jose started photographing the tourists who were photographing me photographing the cars. A crew from the local tv station began filming us all and things got a little confusing.

Queen Elizabeth II Way follows the curve of the western end of Lake Ontario, 100 miles up to Toronto, on the north shore of the lake. Toronto is Canada's largest metropolis and is the economic and cultural focus of English-speaking Canada. In the past the city somehow gained a reputation for greed and mediocrity, hence unflattering soubriquets such as "Hogtown". In recent years, Toronto's had a bit of a make-over, with glitzy architecture, an excellent public transport system and the reclamation and development of the lake front. For some, modern day Toronto is a bit too brash and exact and stage- managed, hence it's sometimes said that the city is "New York run by the Swiss".

I rather liked Toronto, that is until the No.2 car stalled in a rough part of the downtown area. I got out of the No.1 car and greeted the street people who were gathering round. One guy was more out of his head than the rest and started becoming very agitated. Mind you, I suppose our yellow and green ducks were a bit like a bad acid trip. Jose kept turning over the engine of the No.2 car but it refused to fire. The street people began running their hands over the two cars: 'Hey man, cool.' 'Whereya heading, Man?' 'Gotta cigarette?' I got behind the wheel of the No.2 car and willed it to start. The druggy guy began haranguing Jose. Another guy tried to open the boot of the No.1 car. I glanced around: where were the cops when you needed them? I could see that the street people were paying a lot of attention to Jose's shoulder bag. Thankfully, at that moment the No.2 car's stubborn engine fired into life. I revved it and the street people stood back a step, surprised by the noise. Jose took the wheel again and burnt rubber. I followed soon after with the No.1 car and its high revving engine. This little incident reminded us to keep on guard. All the way up from Savannah we had been on back roads, and passed through small towns. Middle-of-Nowhere-Ville. Toronto was the first big city we encountered on the road journey, and as we all know, cities can be dangerous places.

We limped into Toronto with two very sick ducks, but as in the movies, the 7th Cavalry arrived in the form of John Pengelly and Doug Long, members of the Toronto Citroen Club. I'd been e-mailing with John before we left London and he was one of a number of Citroen contacts we had across Canada, Citroen contacts who knew how to fix knackered cars. We rang John and he told us to come over to his place. Rain fell gently from the sky. We had trouble finding John's house. The No.2 car stalled again, this time in a more pleasant part of town. Jose started crying. I started pushing the car in an attempt to bump start it. It remained stubborn. A chap who was passing by came over to help. The chap told us that he knew John Pengelly and had gone to school with him. He gave us directions to the house. It was nearby, just three blocks away. Me and the chap gave the car another push and this time our combined brute strength managed to bump start it. Jose wiped the tears from her cheeks, or maybe it was the rain.

John Pengelly owned a beautiful mansion in a leafy part of downtown Toronto. The man was seriously rich. His fortune had been made on the internet. I never discovered exactly how he found his millions on the internet, but did know that he had the rich man's hobby of collecting classic cars and loved Citroens. The Deaux Chevaux he owned was in absolutely immaculate condition. Our 2CVs looked like rust buckets in comparison; but that's probably because they were rust buckets.

John gave us a spot of lunch. I thought the woman fussing about in the kitchen was John's wife and spoke to her as such. It was an awkward faux pas because she was in fact one of his domestics. I was saved when Doug Long appeared. Doug was a young, chubby man with glasses and short sandy hair. He was also a mechanical genius. Well, anyone was a mechanical genius compared to Jose and I.

Our two sick ducks were stretchered into John's spacious garage. The garage was immaculate. Everything was tidy. There wasn't a speck of dirt anywhere. You could have eaten off the floor. Doug began exploratory surgery on the No.1 car in an attempt to find out the problem. Jose and I paced nervously outside the garage door. The tense silence was broken only when Doctor Doug dropped a tool or let out a muffled cough.

Doctor Doug fiddled around inside the engine compartment. He took bits off the engine, mucked around with a screwdriver and gave light taps with his hammer. Jose and I moved into the garage and stroked our sick duck while Doug continued to operate. The tension was broken when Doug noticed that something was missing from the carburettor. The carburettor on a 2CV has a number of screws that can be turned to adjust the fuel and air mixture. The slow running jet screw was conspicuous by its absence. Brilliant, Watson! without a slow running jet screw you don't get any slow running. It seems that we had been very, very unlucky, because the No.1 car's slow running screw had somehow worked loose and dropped out the carburettor, hence she could only run at high revs. This was an extremely rare occurrence on a 2CV. However, thinking about it, the car had spent one month on a ship that was constantly shaking and vibrating. Hmm, maybe not so surprising after all?

Jose and I smoked cigarettes: how were we going to get a replacement screw? John Pengelly came to the rescue, in that he let us take the slow running screw from his own mint condition 2CV. Problem solved. Doctor Doug then turned his attention to the No.2

car. It was a simple matter of adjusting the timing and points and within a few minutes both cars were in perfect working order again.

John Pengelly was about to take a month's break at the family holiday home in British Columbia. He cancelled his afternoon flight in order to take care of us. Now that the cars were ok, he bid us goodbye and rushed off to the airport. We promised to get another slow running screw sent over to him from England. John was laid-back about it, laid-back because his 2CV was driven only very occasionally.

Doug lived with his mother and sister. He offered to put us up for the night. We declined the invitation. This guy had given up his afternoon to fix our cars and we did not feel we could impose on him anymore. Instead, we checked into a hotel and bought Doug dinner that evening in a Greek restaurant in the little Athens part of town. Over lamb and rice, Doug and I got into a long debate about how an alternator works. Jose started crying again.

The next day we toured round Toronto in a three vehicle convoy. Doug drove his Truckette. A Truckette is a 2CV van, as used in days of old by the French post office and by Inspector Clouseau in the Pink Panther movies. Of course, we were posing, just like we had done in Savannah. There are more Citroen 2CVs knocking about in Canada than in America and we didn't turn as many heads as in the southern States. However, there were still plenty of people who stopped and stared and massaged our egos.

Eventually our little attention seeking convoy pulled up right by the front steps of the Ontario Parliament Building. It seemed a good idea to do a photo shoot there. The security guards didn't agree and immediately rushed down the front steps, guns drawn, thinking that we were going to attempt to assassinate the Prime Minister of Ontario. I told them that guns make me nervous and we were from the press, on an important assignment. It worked. The security guards put their pistols away and let us have one minute to do the photo shoot. A tour bus driver joined in for the group shot.

The main purpose of these photo shoots at places of interest was so that we'd have some good pics to go with the Alaska Challenge bulletins. The bulletin from Toronto was the ninth one I'd written since leaving London at the end of June. While on board the *Marie Anne*, composing the bulletins had been a pleasure. Once on the road, though, it became a bit of a chore, particularly since we had enough on our hands nursing two knackered 2CVs up to Canada. Jose grew annoyed at the amount of time I spent on the laptop computer. I often used to fall asleep over that computer in the small hours of the morning, and once a bulletin was done we had to find internet connection in order to e- mail it to Tony Carr, so that he could put it up on the web site. It didn't take long before I came to the conclusion that this idea of 'almost live reportage' had been a bad one. In Toronto I also noticed that Tony still hadn't put the charity sponsorship form up on the web site. I sent him another reminder e-mail.

We spent a total of three days in Toronto, our longest break so far on the journey. When we hit the road again it felt good to be back on the move. The two cars were now working properly as we headed east towards Montreal and Quebec City. East to Alaska? Yes, because Quebec City was the starting point of the Alaska Challenge. I was confident that once Tony put the sponsorship form up on the web site, so that people could download it and send it off to the bank with their sponsorship money, we would raise thousand of pounds for the Samaritans and NACC (National Association for Colitis and Crohn's disease).

The 2CV Alaska Challenge had never been conceived as a charity fund raiser. It came about at the suggestion of my dear mother, who did a lot of fund raising for the NACC. Jose used to work for the Samaritans, so we decided to go for it and to split all the monies we raised equally between the Sams and the NACC.

Sounds easy, doesn't it, but as soon as the Alaska Challenge took on a charity angle things became complicated. We had to set-up a separate bank account for 'The Alaska Appeal', as the fund raising became known ("The Alaska Appeal?", people asked, "has there been an earthquake in Alaska?"). A friend of Jose's who worked for the Samaritans became a trustee of the Fund. I was the other trustee. We needed to get authorisation for this from the two charities. Then we had to show this authorisation to the Charity Commission (a governmental organisation) before they would sanction it. All this organisation and paperwork took months to complete, and once it was all set-up I felt more inclined to raise money for people who were suffering from extreme pain in the rear.

But hey, it was for chaaarity, mate, and now all I had to do was figure out exactly how we would go about raising the money. I had enough on my plate with the complex arrangements involved in putting together The 2CV Alaska Challenge, not to mention the tedious task of earning a living, and didn't really want the further hassle of going out and shaking a bloody collection tin, nor did anyone else. So, I came up with a (seemingly) brilliant idea: I decided to attempt to do all the fund raising via the web site. I made Quebec City the 'official' starting point of The 2CV Alaska Challenge, because it's almost exactly 5000 road miles from there to Prudhoe Bay, on the shores of the Arctic Ocean. Five thousand miles, at one penny per ten miles, would work out at a nice round fiver in charity donation terms, an amount that I figured people would be quite happy to pay, and it could be easily donated via our web site. We were going to be the first people to attempt to drive a Citroen 2CV up to the Arctic Ocean in Alaska, and the charity side of things was also another first: no one had ever before attempted to collect charity donations entirely on the internet. Once the Alaska trip got under way I soon discovered why not.

We headed along the north shore of Lake Ontario on the Queen Elizabeth II Way. The Queen Lizzie Way is a large highway and carries a lot of traffic. Jose and I soon discovered that the drivers in Ontario are very law abiding and on the main highways stick strictly to the 90 kilometre per hour speed limit (about 55mph). With your foot to the floor a Citroen 2CV will do more than 120 kilometres per hour (about 75mph), steep hills permitting. However, because the 2CV is so flimsily built it takes some nerve to drive them at high speed, because as soon as you go above 50mph they start shaking and rattling and swaying about most alarmingly. Of course, being intrepid adventurers, Jose and I drove the Queen Lizzie Way with foot to the floor, weaving through the traffic, overtaking, undertaking, and racing each other - *this is the self preservation society*. Jose, being

71

Dutch, always drove like a maniac and I struggled to keep up with her. Some of the other drivers gave friendly toots and waved at us as we sped past them. Others shook their fist angrily. Being overtaken by a 2CV can be a bit like a red rag to a bull for some drivers. However, they all stuck to the 90kmh speed limit. They obviously knew something we didn't.

We spent the night in Cornwall, on the north bank of the St. Lawrence Seaway. On the south bank of the river lay the USA. The St. Lawrence Seaway is 183 miles (295 km) long and runs from Lake Ontario to Montréal. The St. Lawrence river has many rapids, making it unnavigable, so in the 19th century, Canada very sensibly constructed a series of canals and locks to allow commercial vessels to reach Lake Ontario. The commercial vessels were very grateful and happily paid the tolls. Cornwall is the headquarters of the St. Lawrence Seaway Authority. The town dates back to the 1700s yet nothing of its heritage has been preserved. We discovered a sprawling grid of streets set back a mile or so from the river. It wasn't exactly ugly, but it wasn't exactly pretty either. In the distance a huge bridge could be seen spanning the river. It looked like it was built out of Mechano. This was the Seaway International Bridge, which connects Cornwall with Rooseveltown, N.Y.

That evening the local paper contacted us, asking if they could do a piece about our trip. We obliged and I was reminded of another Cornwall back in England, and a photo shoot we'd done with the *Cornish Times*. Jose and I, of course, were no strangers to publicity.

Using complicated mathematics, which involved the number of people connected to the Internet in the UK in 1999, the entertainment factor of being able to follow the Alaska Challenge almost as it happened, and the movement of the planets at the time of the spring equinox, I figured that we could raise at least £20,000 for the two charities. However, we needed to let the world know about us first, so it all hinged around how much publicity we could get for the 2CV Alaska Challenge. During April, May and June of 1999, we took the No.1 car on publicity tours all over the UK and received coverage from nearly 60 newspapers (not to mention the occasional tv station). We used the regional branches of the Samaritans and the NACC as the 'local angle' so that the local media would cover us. I would ring the Director of a particular branch of the Sams or NACC to get their permission for the publicity. Once I'd got that permission I would fax a press release to the local media, telling them when we'd be at that particular Sams or NACC office. The press release contained our web site address, where curious news editors could find out all they wanted to know about The 2CV Alaska Challenge. A few days before the off I would ring the news editors and pester them further. Most times it worked, and on the few occasions when not one single newspaper bod showed up we took our own photos and sent them to the papers. I didn't really care what the Fourth Estate said about us, as long as they mentioned that donations can be made via the web site and gave the web site address.

Jose accompanied me on approximately half of these publicity tours, my cousin Andre on the other half. My cousin was no longer Alaska bound and instead had become 'Andre the Canadian Mountie', the mascot of the 2CV Alaska Challenge. The Mounties uniform consisted of a wide brim hat, a red jacket with gold braid, dark blue baggy trousers with yellow stripes on the side and a pair of long black boots. However, the costume had been to one too many fancy dress parties and looked a bit worse for wear; not helped by the fact that the costume had been made for someone with a much larger build than Andre. It kinda hung on him.

Andre loved the publicity. Jose hated it. I suppose I was somewhere in-between. One thing we all disliked was the dreaded 'roof shot'. A large number of the press photographers liked to get a picture of the car with its canvas roof rolled back and us standing up through the roof. We hated doing this because: A) it's difficult to clamber in and out of a Citroen 2CV and stand up through the roof, and B) you looked like a right pratt when doing it. In late May I did a photo shoot on my own, at my local branch of the Samaritans. The press photographer asked for the roof shot. I obliged. The woman Director of that branch stood beside the car. The photographer asked me to hold out my arms (the 'Jesus pose'). I threw out my arms and my left hand whacked the woman in the face. Tears came to her eyes and she started sobbing. This was just one of the hazards of the dreaded roof shot.

Cornwall became another half forgotten memory when the next day we left Ontario and drove into Quebec Province. Quebec is nicknamed *La Belle Province* (The Beautiful Province). The main highway to Quebec City runs along the north side of the St.Lawrence River, passing through lots of towns. Jose and I decided to take the smaller road on the other side of the river, which skirts to the south of Montreal and traverses a much less populated area. As with the drive up from the southern states of America, we wanted to avoid the hustle and bustle of big places. We wanted to be alone. Trouble was, we were still stuck with each other.

Quebec City was a delight. It's located on Cap Diamont and the banks of the St. Lawrence River and is Canada's most historic city. Vieux-Québec, surrounded by solid fortifications, is the only walled city in North America, a fact that prompted UNESCO to classify it as a World Heritage Treasure in 1985. Quebec City has a population of half a million, yet it retains a distinctly provincial air. In both parts of the Old City - Haute and Basse - the winding cobbled streets are flanked by seventeenth and eighteenth century stone houses and churches, graceful parks and squares, and countless monuments. Jose and I were able to count at least eight monuments before we had a big row while trying to find a hotel. Jose was tired after a hard days driving and wanted to check into the first place that had a room available. This meant one of the chain hotels: Comfort Inns, Best Westerns, Motel 8's, Days Inns, the sort of places we'd mostly been staying in thus far. These chain hotels provided a good standard of accommodation for the price, yet they were all exactly the same. The layout and decor of the hotels were identical, whether you were in Georgia or Pennsylvania or Ontario or Quebec or Mars. Some mornings we awoke and looked around at our hotel room and for a moment had no idea of where we were. That's ok for 1960s rock stars, but in a wonderful place like Quebec City I wanted something with a bit more atmosphere. That 'something' was a loft apartment in the old part of town. Even Jose was impressed and our argument went from red to amber. It didn't last long, though, because Jose didn't like the Jacques Brel tracks I was playing on our old, beat-up cassette player, nor did she like what I'd got in for dinner, or the way I'd been driving the No.1 car, or the fact that I had to write another Alaska Challenge bulletin. I was only just getting started on what I didn't like about Jose when she grabbed some of her things, screamed that she'd had enough and was going home and stormed out of the apartment, slamming the door behind her. Once again we were actors on an Eisenstein film set.

This particular Eisenstein film set has always been shaped by wars between England and France and their battle over acquisitions in North America. A French explorer by the name of Jacques Cartier first visited the area in 1535 and by 1608, Quebec had become the first permanent French base in Canada. In 1629, Quebec was captured by the British, who held it until 1632, when the Treaty of Saint-Germain-en-Laye restored Quebec to France That is, until the fleet of Sir William Phipps, governor of Massachusetts, attempted to take Quebec in 1690 but was beaten back by the French. In 1711 a second attempt to take the city also failed when a British armada crashed on the reefs of the St. Lawrence before reaching Quebec. The city finally fell to the British in 1759 and was ceded to Great Britain by the Treaty of Paris in 1763. And just for good measure, during the US War of Independence, the Americans failed in an attempt to capture the city.

I went to a nearby bar and was met by the pungent aroma of Gauloises cigarettes, rude waiters and the smell of coffee and croissants. It was like being in Paris and it seemed strange and inappropriate to be paying for things in dollars. No one spoke English. Nevertheless, after America, with its car culture, those endless straight roads with malls, gas stations, burger joints and car dealers, it was a refreshing change to be immersed in European culture again, even if the waiters were rude.

Later that afternoon Jose and I encountered each other again in a launderette near the apartment. Before having our row we'd left a huge load of washing in one of the machines there. We didn't speak to each other as we sorted through our clothes. Afterwards, Jose asked for the key to the apartment. As she left the launderette she slammed the door shut so violently that it made the opening hours notice fall off the window. Well, it didn't seem as though Jose was flying back to Europe just yet, so French Canadian doors would have to stay on their guard.

I needed to e-mail my Quebec City bulletin to Tony Carr. The French Canadians are so civilised, because they have internet bars. The computer terminal was literally on the bar and you could sit there on a stool and smoke and drink while surfing the net. Officially, smoking in public places is banned in Canada. Likewise, alcohol is sold only in strictly regulated outlets (you can't buy alcohol in a supermarket in Canada). In Quebec Province these regulations were interpreted loosely; ie, you could smoke just about anywhere and you could buy booze just about anywhere. This probably had something to do with the fact that the Quebec Minister of Health was a heavy smoker who liked his wine (note the past tense). It was also to do with politics. Due to its history, Quebec has always been a different entity from the rest of Canada. The separatist issue refuses to go away, because the economic activities of the province have always been controlled by the tiny minority of English speakers. This discrimination has made the French Canadians fiercely nationalistic. Some of them get so angry that they even go around slamming doors.

Early on Sunday 8th August, after three nights in Quebec City, Jose and I checked out of the loft apartment. Tony still hadn't put the charity sponsorship form up on the web site. I e-mailed him yet another reminder just before we left the city. The official starting point of The 2CV Alaska Challenge was Place D'armes du Fort, in the old walled town and overlooking the St. Lawrence River. It was pelting down with rain when we arrived. There was no one else around. The two cars had been running perfectly ever since leaving Toronto. Full of confidence, we took some photos and then set off along the empty, rain drenched streets. The previous two weeks had seemed like a preliminary to the main event. As we drove away from Quebec City the curtain raised for the Main Act. From now on we would be heading due west, across the continent of North America, 5000 miles to Alaska.

Chapter 3. The Wild West

On the road out of Quebec City I drove fast. Jose was being cautious in the rain and struggled to keep up with me. I slammed on the brakes as we came to a red light and Jose slammed into the back of me. Speed and wet road conditions are such fun. We got out of the cars to inspect the damage. So far we'd covered less than two miles of the official 2CV Alaska Challenge, not even the first penny of charity sponsorship. Fortunately, the No.2 car was directly behind the No.1 car when the collision occurred. The bumper mounts hit each other and so the impact of the collision was taken entirely by the chassis. That's one advantage of driving identical cars, with identical bumper arrangements. Damage was minimal. However, Jose and I did not miss the opportunity to have another row. The rain ignored us. Jose was about to throw a piece of bumper at me when we noticed a sign by the side of the road. It said: 'Vancouver 5110 km' (which is roundabouts 3175 miles). Who could resist? and so after some parting shots we jumped back in the cars and resumed our journey along the Trans-Can Highway.

Trans-Canada Highway 1 is known as "Canada's Main Street". It goes from St. John's, Newfoundland, to Victoria in British Columbia, a distance of 7821km (4860 miles), passing through ten provinces and five time zones along the way. It's the longest national road in the world and was formally opened in 1962. I figured that you just needed to know this.

We followed the Trans-Can along the north bank of the St.Lawrence River. The countryside here was more hilly than on the south side of the river. There were lots and lots of trees. The rain followed us all the way from Quebec City to Montreal. Just south of Montreal the Ottawa River joins the St. Lawrence. The Trans-Canada Highway follows the Ottawa River upstream for almost 100 miles until reaching the city of Ottawa, capital of Canada.

Ottawa has three major claims to fame: it's the capital of the second biggest country on the planet, it's the western world's coldest capital, and popular opinion holds that it is one of the world's dullest capitals. It's all Queen Victoria's fault. In the 19th century, Ottawa was a boozy, brawling lumber village. Then Queen Victoria saw some rather pretty watercolour paintings of the area and was so inspired that she declared Ottawa the capital, leaving Montreal and Toronto smarting at their rebuff. Converted by royal mandate into a political cockpit, Ottawa immediately started cleaning up its act and government investment was poured in to redevelop the area. The result is a prim, boring place with a small-town atmosphere, a city dubbed 'too perfect for excitement' which cost the long-suffering Canadian tax payer millions and millions of dollars. No one knows where the boozy lumberjacks fled to.

We didn't stop in Ottawa; in fact, an immaculate highway very kindly sped us straight through the centre of the city. It felt strangely satisfying to break the prim 80kmh speed limit as Jose and I once again did a re-run of *The Italian Job*. Our destination was a little town some 20 miles west of Ottawa, where Barbara and Clive lived. Barbara and Clive were more of our internet contacts in North America, Citroen enthusiasts who were following the Alaska Challenge and asked us to drop by if we were passing. The Trans-Can went right by their place, so we dropped in.

We dropped into a pretty little residential street that screamed 'Family Land'. Jose and I shuddered as we were led out into a pretty back garden, where we sat on pretty chairs and Barbara produced pretty sandwiches and squash. Barbara and Clive were nice people. Their fourteen-year-old son kept asking us questions. Jose spoke to him in Dutch. Fortunately the fourteen-year-old son couldn't speak Dutch. I masticated a small piece of my sandwich as Clive told me about the 2CV he was thinking of buying. Jose kept flicking her spent cigarette butts on to the lawn. Barbara produced a paint tin lid (there wasn't a single ashtray in the house). Barbara and Clive were nice people. They offered us a room for the night. We declined the offer, saying that it was still early afternoon and we had to push on with our journey. What struck me most, as we sat there in the garden, was that it was all so *normal*. It was almost a shock. That's the trouble with intrepid adventuring: it's easy to lose touch with reality.

Since leaving Toronto we'd had six days of trouble free motoring. It was too good to be true. Two hours after leaving Barbara and Clive's place the No.2 car decided to go on strike. The bloody thing gave up the ghost in Deep River, Ontario, and refused to start. By now it was late afternoon. I couldn't be bothered with it all, so we pushed the No.2 car to a nearby hotel and checked in for the night.

The little town of Deep River is named after the Deep River which is so named because, well, apparently it is very deep - the locals told us that at one place the river is bottomless, rather like Jose imagined her credit card limit to be. In 1997, Deep River obtained the highest rating possible in the Communities in Bloom competition. I figured you just needed to know that. The town has a reputation for cutting edge technology and is the home of Atomic Energy of Canada Limited (AECL), which is a harder act to sell. On Monday 9th August 1999, Deep River also became home to two intrepid adventurers and two knackered 2CVs.

On the following morning, Jose and I could be found in the hotel car park, gazing forlornly at our own particular piece of not-so-cutting-edge technology. It was an ignition problem, we decided, after a process of elimination that left us both covered in grease and oil (it was always an ignition problem, because it's the only complicated part of a 2CV). We looked at the spare engine, gearbox, suspension arms, etc, in the back of the car: all useless. We needed to fiddle around with the points, which lurked at the back of the fan. However, the bolts holding on the fan mesh cover had been tightened too much and the heads of the bolts wore away as I tried to undo them. Man, we needed this like a hole in the head, but violence prevailed and after much struggle with a monkey wrench the bolts relinquished their grip and turned. Blood and oil mixed as my knuckles were smashed against the raw edges of the fan casing. Well, driving a 2CV to Alaska had seemed like a good idea at the time.

So, the fan cover was bloodily removed and the fan was taken off by means of the two Billys' wrench and a big whack with a hammer. The whack caused a huge cloud of rust to fall from the No.2 car. We tactfully ignored it and put in a new set of points and condenser, and it worked: the engine fired into life at the first attempt. For a moment we were stunned, then, Whoopee! We were on our way once more, for about 100 yards, when the No.2 car's engine died again. The ignition timing needed doing, and we were doing it for another two hours before the car deemed to start. The feeling of getting a knackered Citroen 2CV working again can be compared to childbirth... and so we continued bowling westward, chewing up the miles/kilometres across the spectacular scenery of northern Ontario.

Our last night in Ontario was spent in Terrace Bay. This little town sits at the northernmost point of Lake Superior. Terrace Bay is known as the "gem of the north shore". It's surrounded by rugged beauty which to the north is total wilderness. The tourist office town guide lists "54 things to do in Terrace Bay", amongst which are walking along the beach and visiting the tourist office.

Jose and I did neither of these things. Instead we had a row. Well, it was due, we hadn't had a bust-up since the car collision in Quebec City. The cause of our conflict began as soon as we got up to the hotel bedroom, where I immediately started working with the laptop computer. The Alaska Challenge bulletins were a bit behind schedule and this was an opportunity to bash one out. Jose had been growing increasingly annoyed over the amount of time I was spending on the laptop. I told her to get lost. After all, there were 54 things to do in Terrace Bay, and one of them most definitely did not involve unplugging the mouse from the laptop just as I was reaching the end of my scribblings. This caused our feeble little computer to go into a spin. I lost my work. I had to re-type the bulletin all over again. I was not pleased. In the dining room that evening we sat at separate tables.

The next morning we were up early, This was the big day. We were on schedule to reach Winnipeg that evening. Tony lived in Winnipeg and we would be staying at his house for three days. I felt somewhat apprehensive about it all. I'd been e-mailing with Tony for almost a year now and had spoken to him on the phone only once. Now I was going to meet him in the flesh, the man who was running the Alaska Challenge web site for us, the man who still hadn't put up the charity sponsorship form, and we were already well into the journey from Quebec City to Alaska.

It's a very arduous 970km (600 mile) drive from Terrace Bay to Winnipeg. The No.2 car was running like a constipated pig, which didn't help Jose's mood. We pulled into a lay-by to take a look at the car's engine. Yup, it certainly looked like a car engine. Jose suggested that I have a go at fixing it. I suggested that she get her hands dirty for a change. A nearby information board saved the day by informing us that we were on the Terry Fox Courage Highway, which is a 50 mile stretch of the Trans-Can that leads to Thunder Bay. We'd seen similar Terry Fox signs ever since leaving Quebec City three days previously. This was one of the last memorials that we came across, because Terry Fox never made it beyond Thunder Bay. That made us think.

In 1977, when Terry Fox was only 18 years old, he was diagnosed with bone cancer and forced to have his right leg amputated. Terry's observations of the intense suffering of cancer patients led to the Marathon of Hope, when in 1980, Terry attempted to run across Canada on an artificial leg. His mission was to raise money and awareness for cancer research.

Terry Fox started his journey in St. John's, Newfoundland, running 26 miles each and every day through Canada's Atlantic provinces, Quebec and Ontario. However, after 143 days and 3314 miles, Terry was forced to stop his Run outside of Thunder Bay, Ontario, because the cancer had reappeared in his lungs. He was showered with awards and honors, including the Companion of the Order of Canada. Terry died on June 28, 1981, shortly before his 23rd birthday. The heroic Canadian was gone, but his legacy was just beginning. Every year Terry Fox Marathon's of Hope are run in Canada and all around the world, raising millions of pounds for cancer research.

Despite our early start it was late afternoon by the time our two little Citroens reached the prairies. The prairies suddenly came upon us. One minute we were driving through hilly, wooded country, the next minute the trees stopped and we were out on an endless flat plain. The sky was incredible, so huge that it looked like it was about to swallow up the land. A sea of golden wheat bowed before us in the wind. *Hello Manitoba!*

Manitoba is in south central Canada and the easternmost of Canada's three prairie provinces. It's located at the geographic center of Canada and has been known as the Keystone Province ever since Canada's Governor-General Lord Dufferin described the province in 1877 as "the keystone of that mighty arch of sister provinces which spans the continent from the Atlantic to the Pacific." Perhaps the term 'old duffer' derives from the Governor-General?

Much of the countryside in southern Manitoba is farmland and gives the impression of a vast plain with a perfectly level horizon as far as the eye can see. As you move further north, to the center of the province, the flat farmland gives way to vast areas of forest interspersed with hundreds of lakes. In the extreme north, where only a few hardy souls live, the land is much the same as it was thousands of years ago, with a bleak array of stunted trees, exposed rock, and swamps.

I rang Tony on his mobile and gave him our location: "the start of the prairies". Tony seemed to know where we were, and it wasn't Manitoba. We were still in Ontario. My God, Ontario seemed to have the proportions of the planet Jupiter. Tony said he would drive out and meet us half way, at the border between Ontario and Manitoba. The border? it sounded like something out of the Cold War. Sure enough, after driving for an hour or so we came across a border post. It lacked barbed wire and searchlights, and it was unmanned, yet this was a real border control. We later found out that cigarettes are very much cheaper in Ontario and Quebec than in Manitoba and the other prairie provinces. The border post was an attempt to stop cigarette smuggling.

Dusk was falling as the No.1 car and the No.2 car arrived at the border carrying cartons of cheap cigarettes bought in the southern states of America. Tony stood there with James, his eleven-year-old son. The two of them had been waiting for some time. Tony was a big man with a round face, glasses and short greying hair. He gave Jose and I a bear hug and welcomed us to Manitoba. Tony told us that he'd heard the distinctive *phut phut phut* of the 2CV's engine before he spotted us coming down the road. It was an emotional moment as we discussed compression ratios; well, Jose seemed to be getting all emotional as she began dabbing her eyes. Tony took a look at the two cars in the fading light. His face dropped when he saw the No.2 car, but he made no comment. We followed Tony and James west on the Trans-Can Highway. It was an hour's drive. On the outskirts of Winnipeg we saw an overturned trailer on the hard shoulder. Dead pigs were scattered over the highway.

In early April I e-mailed Tony a photo of a 2CV that was for sale just down the road from me. It was cream coloured with a black and white stripy roof, and it had round headlights, like all of the older 2CVs have. The bodywork was in very good condition. Tony loved the car so I told him I'd buy it. However, those round headlights had deceived me, because in the event the car wasn't quite as old as I thought. The age of both the No.1 and No.2 cars was very, very important, if they were going to have any resale value in North America.

Citroen 2CVs were never sold in North America because they did not meet the strict safety and emission standards. However, if a car is 15 years or older in Canada, or 25 years or older in the US, it's classified as a 'vintage car' and is exempt from the standards. The No.1 car had been registered in 1984, making it 15 years old and a vintage car in Canada. The cream coloured 2CV was 13 yeas old. It was not exempt from the standards and to drive it legally in Canada a fortune would have to be spent modifying it so that it met the standards. I would have to find Tony another car, one that was at least 15 years old. In all the excitement I forgot to tell him this. He still thought we were shipping over the cream coloured car with the stripy roof and round headlights.

In mid April we did finally buy the No.2 car. A young girl called Nicola, who lived near Bedford, was reluctantly selling her much loved 2CV. It was a 1983 2CV6 without too much rust. Both its bodywork and roof were a sort of bluey green colour (the cars paperwork described it as opal). It looked ill, and it had the horrible rectangular shaped headlights that one finds on later built 2CVs. However, the car drove like a bomb. We bought it for £400. On the drive back to London I was behind the wheel of the No.1 car, Jose was behind the wheel of the No.2 car. We encountered heavy traffic on the M1 and drove fast, overtaking and cutting in and out of the other cars. It was our first experience of driving the 2CVs in convoy. It was fun.

Tony lived with his wife Wendy and son James in the south east of Winnipeg. The single storey house was in a leafy residential street. Jose and I were quartered in the large basement. We felt shattered after a long day's driving and went to bed early. The next morning I explained to Tony about the No.2 car. He thought he was getting a cream coloured car with a stripy roof and round headlights. Instead, we arrived with a bluey green 2CV which looked ill and had horrible rectangular shaped headlights. Tony said he didn't mind, really, but I could tell he wasn't happy. Matters weren't helped when we tried to start the No.2 car and it refused to oblige. We went inside the house, where Wendy had prepared breakfast. Wendy was a small woman with long, dark hair and a pleasant disposition. Her and Jose seemed to be getting along ok, and real bread was placed on the table, not the cardboard variety so favoured by Canadians. Things were looking up. Tony joked about the No.2 car and told us that he had taken two days off work to look after us during our stay. We were scheduled for some sightseeing and once breakfast was done and dusted we headed off to see some sights.

Winnipeg is the capital city of Manitoba and with a population of over 600,000 it accounts for more than two-thirds of the province's population. The city lies at the confluence of the Red and Assiniboine rivers, 60 miles (95 km) north of the US border. It was named after Lake Winnipeg, derived from the Cree Indian words *win nipee* ("muddy water"). A settlement was first established there in 1738 by the French voyageur La Vérendrye. In the following century, settlers from Scotland, England, Germany, Poland, the Ukraine, from all over, found a home there.

This mass immigration was engineered by the Canadian government, who in the late 1800s were concerned that if the Canadian west was not quickly populated it would be grabbed by the Americans. They were looking for people who could endure the hardships of homesteading the Canadian west, especially people with strong backs. Among these early settlers were the Mennonites. The Mennonites are devout Protestants who broke away from the more highly organised form of Protestantism to form their own church. Their doctrine stressed simplicity of life and devout belief in God. This, of course, meant that they were heavily persecuted in Europe and were ideal candidates for a new life in the New World. A Canadian envoy in Russia reported that he was impressed by the Mennonites he met there: "They are a hard working, sober, moral and intelligent people". In 1873, the Canadian Department of Agriculture formally invited the Mennonites to settle in southern Manitoba. The government offered the Mennonites an "entire exemption from any military service" and set aside special land reserves for their settlements. These reserves were around the Red River, in what is now Winnipeg city. Between 1874 and 1879, almost 18,000 Mennonites left Russia for the New World. Entire villages moved from the Russian steppes to the virgin soils of southern Manitoba.

The 1999 Pan-American Games were held in Winnipeg and they drew to a close shortly before we arrived there. Posters and banners marking the event could still be seen all around the city. Needless to say, the Americans scooped-up most of the medals. Earlier in the year, Tony had been in touch with the CBC (Canadian Broadcasting Corporation) with regard to the 2CV Alaska Challenge. The CBC were going to send a film crew along with us, from Quebec to Alaska, in order to make a programme about the Alaska Challenge. This would have been rather jolly. However, due to the delays on the Atlantic crossing our road journey coincided with the Pan-American Games: all the available CBC film crews were covering the Games and noone could be spared for our little jaunt to Alaska. I think Jose was relieved that our two ring circus hadn't been turned into a three ring circus.

Tony took us down to the newly developed riverside area. It looked nice. He took us to the Railway Museum. It seemed interesting. He took us to the highest hill in Winnipeg, which rose a towering 50ft above the city and was formed from an old garbage dump. It entertained us... the trouble was, Jose and I were somewhat reluctant tourists. We'd been spending as much as 16 hours a day on the road. That was our tourism. During breaks in the journey we found that we didn't have much inclination to go sightseeing. The idea was to relax, to do nothing, and to occupy ourselves with our favourite passtime: arguing.

On the evening of the second day in Winnipeg, Tony held a barbeque in our honour. Earlier that day, Jose and I had words, each accusing the other of being selfish. We went off on separate long walks. Winnipeg was perhaps the lowest point in our relationship on the road journey. I was fuming. Before changing her mind, Jose had originally intended to fly home from Winnipeg and now I was tempted to drive her to the airport. At the barbeque we tried to act like a team. However, observant barbeque guests would have noticed that Jose and I never actually stood together. We drifted around separately, answering the same old questions about the Alaska Challenge. When we did happen to be in earshot, Jose and I flung polite insults at each other, in Dutch. I think those twenty or so barbeque guests would have been rather startled if they'd known what the dynamic duo were really saying to each other.

After doing some research on the internet, Tony became happier about the No.2 car. Apparently, Citroen had sold only one hundred and two 2CVs with this particular colour scheme (I wonder why?). The only other ill-looking 2CV still on the road was owned by a guy in Australia. The No.2 car was a rarity, a collectors car, which made Tony very happy. He adjusted the wing mirror and it came off in his hands: nothing some duct tape and a big whack with a hammer couldn't fix. I leaned casually across the windscreen, hoping Tony wouldn't notice the rusty hole in the bodywork. Tony didn't notice the rusty hole in the bodywork, and so the No.2 car found a new home in Winnipeg.

We had agreed a price of two thousand Canadian dollars for the No.2 car. This was about $1000 less than the cost price of buying it in the UK and getting the damn thing to Winnipeg. We were doing Tony a favour in the form of a cut price car, because he was running the web site for us. Tony was most grateful and said that he'd hold on to the money in case we needed it later. We didn't argue; we were too exhausted from arguing with each other. I sat Tony down and had a little chat with him, about the 2CV Alaska Challenge, and about how it was also raising money for charity, and how the charity fund raising had all been set-up officially in the UK, and how I could get into deep shit if we didn't actually raise any money. I told Tony that the charity sponsorship form was a matter of urgency. It had to go up on the web site. Tony said he'd make it top priority.

It was an emotional moment bidding farewell to the No.2 car, a duck which had been our faithful, if somewhat temperamental companion on the tortuous 3650 mile (5850km) journey from Savannah to Winnipeg. Au revior little duck. Jose got quite sentimental and gave the No.2 car a last kick for luck (she's funny that way). And so after a somewhat strained three day break in Winnipeg it was just Jose, me and the No.1 car that set off into the sunset, west across the prairies. We'd had a short intermission. Now Part Two of the 2CV Alaska Challenge was getting under way.

The prairie skies continued to be amazing. Huge cloud formations hung overhead. The clouds looked solid and Dali-esque, their hues ever changing in the wind. We passed grain elevators and impossibly long freight trains; went through small towns that were instantly forgotten; tanked-up at tiny gas stations which came from another era. The stalks of wheat stretched to the horizon. Our little duck was crossing a golden sea.

The Trans-Canada Highway takes the shortest route across the prairies, and thereby manages to avoid nearly everything of interest on the 850 miles (1350km) from Winnipeg to Calgary. Many Canadians prefer to do this drive at night, when they say the scenery is better. However, I found the landscape so extreme in its monotony that it held a kind of fascination. We had the roof down on the car and soaked-up the summer sunshine. In the winter the temperature on the prairies can fall to -40°C as the wind rips down from the arctic. It's hard to imagine how the European pioneers managed to survive, huddled together in remote log cabins or even sod huts. Yet survive they did, and between 1895 and 1914 the great swathe of land that makes up the wheat belt was turned into one of the most productive wheat-producing areas in the world. By any standards, it was a remarkable achievement, but the price was high: the nomadic culture of the Plains Indians was almost entirely destroyed and the disease-ravaged, half-starved survivors were dumped in a string of meagre reservations. Similarly, the Métis, descendants of white fur traders and native women, found themselves overwhelmed by the European settlers; and so, under the leadership of Louis Riel, the Métis rebelled against the settlers, culminating in the 1885 battle of Batoche, in which the Métis were soundly beaten. With the natives now out of the way, the European immigrants concentrated on their wheat yields, but they were the victims of a one-crop economy, their prosperity dependent on the market price of grain and the freight charges imposed by the railroad. Throughout the 20th century the prairie farmers have experienced alarming changes in their fortunes as bust has alternated with boom, a situation that continues to dominate the economies of Saskatchewan and eastern Alberta today. Hmm, considering that the European settlers in effect occupied land which wasn't theirs, I'd say it serves them right.

Among those early European settlers were the Doukhobors, who were possibly the world's first hippies. The Doukhobors, like the Mennonites who settled in Manitoba, came originally from Russia, where they were heavily persecuted. The Doukhobors were pacifists and very strict in the observance of their religious beliefs. They refrained from drinking, smoking and eating meat, and practiced a form of communal living in which all property belonged to the group. In 1898, the Canadian Government offered the Doukhobors free land in the west under the Homestead Act. The following year several thousand Doukhobors migrated to Saskatchewan, where they were soon busy farming and driving away injuns. However, they did not want their children to speak English and refused to send them to Canadian schools. When the government built schools, the Doukhobors burned them down, and as a form of protest some of the Doukhobors appeared in public without their clothing. In 1924 their leader, Peter Vasilevich Verigan, was killed in an explosion. Some believe the explosion was set off by his own followers, who had become disenchanted with his leadership style, and also disenchanted about appearing in public in the nude – it gets a bit nippy in Canada. Following Verigan's death, the Doukhobors became more integrated into Canadian society. Many of them settled in Regina.

We broke our journey across the Prairies in Regina, the capital of Saskatchewan. Regina began life as an inconsequential dot on the map called Pile O'Bones, so named after the heaps of bleached buffalo bones left along its creek by generations of native hunters. The settlement served as the administrative headquarters of the Northwest Territories from 1882 until 1905, when it was selected as capital of the newly formed province of Saskatchewan and renamed Regina after Queen Victoria. Louis Riel, leader of the Métis rebels, was tried for high treason and hanged in Regina in 1885. I liked Regina. It has a population of less than 200,000 and feels friendly and manageable. Likewise, Jose was starting to feel more friendly and manageable. Very strange: when we were in separate cars we were at daggers drawn for most of the time, yet once we were both together in the No.1 car we started getting along surprisingly well. Hmm, I wonder what a psychiatrist would make of it? Yin and Yang, or is that a Chinese take-away in downtown Regina?

On Sunday 15th August we crossed into the neighbouring province of Alberta, named after Princess Louise Caroline Alberta, fourth daughter of Queen Victoria. What an ego trip it must have been for Queen Vicky to look at a map of the world and see all those distant, far flung places named after her and her family. But the province of Alberta didn't seem to care. The horizon was largely undisturbed and we were saluted by nodding donkeys on either side of the Trans-Can Highway. Medicine Hat was the first big town we hit in Alberta. It's the site of a huge gas field and the pong of the refineries could be smelt for miles around.

I took the wheel for the last few hundred miles of the highway to Calgary, which were across a flat, featureless landscape. I felt apprehensive. So did the weather. Huge billowing blue/black clouds hung from the sky. We switched on the headlights and drove through heavy rain bursts. The radio reported tornados in the area. The emergency services were on a high state of alert. We stopped for gas at a small place called The Middle Of Nowhere. A sign flapped violently in the wind. On the distant horizon I could see three small twisters developing. They weren't coming in our direction. The huge, bruised clouds were. It grew so dark that I could hardly see the dollar bills I counted out to pay for the petrol. The woman who ran the gas station asked us to come inside for a coffee, until the severe weather had passed. We declined the offer and continued on our way. There was no other traffic on the road.

First, the CNN tower peeped at us from over the stormy horizon. Then the skyscrapers came into view. Then the City of Calgary could be seen laid out in a valley beneath us. I was back, after almost 12 years, and as we drove towards downtown Calgary it felt like I'd never left the city. Everything seemed so familiar; every street corner, every building sparked memories, and the memories weren't as painful as I thought they'd be. Jose and I checked into the Ramada Hotel on 8th Street. There was an irony here: when I left Calgary in February 1988, supposedly for ever, I caught the airport bus from outside the Ramada Hotel.

The Ramada was a bit more expensive than our usual hotels. However, we'd saved on three nights hotel accommodation while staying with Tony in Winnipeg; and besides, after more than two weeks on the road we figured we needed some pampering. Jose loved our plush hotel room. Jose also loved Calgary. I knew she would, most people do. Calgary? I know you're just dying to ask... back in the 1870s the Northwest Mounted Police were sent to south central Alberta to put an end to the illegal whiskey trade. They built a fort at the confluence of the Bow and Elbow rivers. A jock by the name of Colonel James Macleod was in charge of the Mounted Police. He named the settlement Calgary, possibly because this was the name of his ancestral home back in Scotland, or perhaps because 'calgary' means 'clear running water' in Gaelic, or perhaps because Calgary Bay, on the Isle of Mull, was where shiploads of destitute refugees set sail for America in the early 1800s. In otherwords, no one seems to know just how the hell Calgary got its name. Personally, I think the most likely explanation is that in the dialect of the local Indian tribes, Calgary means 'bunch of white dickheads who are stealing our land'. Anyway, with the arrival of the Canadian Pacific Railroad in the 1880s the population of the settlement boomed, and the rest, as they say, is history.

Calgary has a reputation for being a cowtown (it hosts the annual Stampede, one of the biggest rodeos in North America), but the discovery of huge oil reserves in Alberta in the 1960s transformed it into a major metropolis and administrative centre of the oil industry. Forget the cowboys, black gold is what Calgary is really about. You can see it everywhere, from the gleaming downtown skyscrapers of

---

the oil companies, to the nodding donkeys beside the runways of Calgary International Airport. Calgary = oil, billions and billions of dollars worth of oil. The cowboy image is just an echo from its frontier past.

It felt nice the next morning to wake up in a plush hotel room. One of our company sponsors was based in Calgary. They were called Vitacorp and Jose went off to pay them a courtesy visit. Meanwhile, I picked up the phone and rang the news desk of the *Calgary Herald*. Thus far we hadn't done much publicity in North America. There was no need to: all the charity fund raising was coming from the UK. It would be nice to get some publicity for Vitacorp; however, I had other motives.

During the winter of 1987/88, I was 23-years-old and living in Calgary and hopelessly in love with a girl who didn't love me. In the subzero temperatures of a Canadian winter this little drama was set against the much bigger backdrop of the forthcoming XV Winter Olympic Games.

I could have won a medal for persistence back then, my persistence in pursuit of *her*. Our relationship had always been somewhat stormy and it reached a crescendo during that winter in Calgary. But it was time to bury the past, so while Jose was down at Vitacorp I took a drive around Calgary, looking at all my old haunts. For the first time in North America I was highly conscious of being in such a visible car. I didn't want to be noticed on the streets of the city. I wanted to keep a low profile. I did not feel like contacting anyone from the old days, least of all *her*.

My navel gazing was interrupted by the car. For the last two weeks, since Doctor Doug's operation in Toronto, the No.1 car had been running as sweet as a nut. Now, in Calgary, the brakes on the car started playing up. Every time I hit the brake pedal my foot went to the floor. There was no pressure until the pedal was pumped two or three times. Oh, brilliant. I pulled into a parking lot beside a church. A group of worshippers had to quickly step out of the way as I pedal pumped to a halt. The worshippers were Mormons and didn't seem to mind that I'd almost run them over. They politely asked me the usual questions about the Alaska Challenge and I gave the usual answers.

I'd seen lots of Mormons during my previous encounter with Calgary. The ones dressed as cowboys had the most sinister appearance: boots, jeans, shirt and hat, all black, like some kind of Roy Rogers antichrist. Manitoba got the Mennonites, Saskatchewan got the Doukhobors and Alberta got the Mormons (also known as Latter Day Saints - LDS). In this instance, though, the Mormons weren't settlers coming directly from Europe, they were fleeing from persecution in the United States, persecution which largely centered around the Mormon practice of polygamy. It's a bitch being a Mormon, because shortly after the Mormons arrived in southern Alberta the Canadian authorities also banned polygamy. Despite this the Mormons stayed in Alberta because the Canadian Government's policy of populating the west meant that free land was available under the Homestead Act. Actually, I think it must be rather handy to have more than one wife, particularly when it comes to pushing a broken down car.

The Mormons were most helpful and after I'd put some brake fluid in the system we decided that the car could be driven safely, depending on your definition of 'safely'. They had God on their side, whereas I had to rely on luck. That luck got me back to the hotel in one piece, where Jose informed me that the big boss at Vitacorp was taking us out to dinner that evening.

The big boss was a guy called Alan, in his early thirties and wearing a thousand dollar suit. Alan came from eastern Canada and was going prematurely bald. He was a company man through and through and talked business all the time. He didn't appear to grasp the concept behind The 2CV Alaska Challenge: *it's a fun thing, Alan, it's FUN*. Alan seemed a nice enough guy though, particularly when he said he would pick up the tab for the meal. A generous sponsor indeed, who was accompanied by Adina, his Head of Marketing. Adina came from Romanian stock. I didn't know the Romanians had made it this far west, but there again, when the government offered free land in these parts they came from all over the world to get a slice of the action. Adina was small, slim, dark- haired and 28-years-old. I'd already spoken to her on the phone earlier that day, asking if Vitacorp were ok about us doing some publicity. She agreed to it and became the spokeswoman for Vitacorp.

"So, you're from England, Jose's Dutch and you're driving a French car to Alaska: how come a Calgary company are one of your sponsors..?" a *Calgary Herald* reporter had asked me. Hmm, good question, and one I didn't have an answer to, nor did I have an answer when the reporter asked me what sort of business Vitacorp were involved in. I mumbled something about Adina handling that side of things and quickly changed the subject.

Adina was more relaxed than Alan, who seemed unable to click out of business mode. The restaurant was perched on Princes Island, in the Bow River and just across from downtown Calgary. Judging by the clientele, the joint was obviously the latest in-place for wealthy Calgarians. The four of us sat outside at a table. The menu had poncy descriptions of what was just basically meat, potatoes and two veg. Despite the fact we were sitting outside, smoking was banned. Jose lit-up a cigarette and had an argument with the waitress. Jose was wasting her breath. In some states of America, where they still have the death penalty, condemned prisoners are not even allowed to have a last cigarette. Political correctness, don't you just love how wonderfully screwy it is. After we'd finished the meal our argumentative waitress brought over the bill. I looked at it and then looked at Alan, who didn't blink an eyelid as he produced his credit card. I would have been having heart palpitations. Afterwards, Adina came back to the hotel with Jose and I and we all had a drink together in the bar.

The next day, Tuesday 17th August, we made it into the *Calgary Herald*, page 3 of the entertainment section. The headline ran: 'Tin snails bound for Alaska Highway'. The piece carried a photograph, taken from the web site, showing the No.2 car beside a wigwam and a covered wagon. They used this photo of the No.2 car because it carried Vitacorp's banners and the No.1 car did not. Looking at the article in the paper, I was once again dragged back to the past, to a 15th February 1988 copy of the *Calgary Herald*, which became the last thing to go into my suitcasebefore I crept out into the snow and headed for the airport.

Since arriving in Calgary in October 1987, I'd been working illegally without a permit and it had been a constant battle to keep one step ahead of the immigration people. After Christmas I lost my job and from then on I suffered acute poverty. I struggled to pay bills; I struggled to put food on the table; and all the while there was heartache and the hustle and bustle and excitement of the approaching Olympic Games. It really was the best of times and the worst of times, hammered home by my final encounter with *her* on Christmas Eve. We met amidst the tinsel of a downtown bar, where she had the last word on our relationship.

I felt like a cad, a complete and utter cad. My luck had run out and my money had run out. Now I was skulking back to London, leaving behind me a score of unpaid bills, like losing betting slips after a big race. I owed back rent on the apartment. I felt really bad about this. My landladies, two young American girls, were nice people who had taken care of me. But if you ain't got any money you ain't got any money; and so I did a runner from the apartment, using the service alley between the backs of the houses in the hope that no one would notice me. It's not easy being furtive when you have a large suitcase for company. I slipped and stumbled through the snow and came out on 14th Street, which at this point is a busy shopping area. It was midday. I did the dirty at this hour because I knew there was less chance of running into my landladies or any of their friends. But still some chance, so I hid behind a wall while I waited for the downtown bus. I was wearing many layers of clothing to keep out the fierce cold. The temperature was hovering at around 30 below freezing, yet I was still drenched in sweat. It's no pushover being a cad, you know.

After the bus had deposited me downtown, I left my suitcase in the reception of the Ramada Hotel, from where the airport bus departed. My plane wasn't due to leave until six that evening. The subzero temperatures made it impossible to contemplate any outdoor time wasting, and I didn't fancy spending six hours drinking coffee in an airport lounge. The solution was simple: I had put aside fifty dollars, so in the meantime I would get gloriously drunk.

Every bar I visited became yet another farewell to Calgary. I eventually found myself at a hotel bar near the airport, where I got tangled-up with an Aussie businessman who had a wild mane of hair. He offered me a job. I pondered over this offer and bought the Aussie another drink. After paying the barman for the drink I had twelve dollars and fifty cents left. That was it. I had nothing else. My bank accounts were empty. I had nothing valuable I could sell. That twelve dollars and fifty cents *really* was everything I had left in the world.

With a resigned sigh I asked my old pal the barman for another refill. The sands had run their course. I now had seven dollars and fifty cents and I knew there was no going back. No last chances from mad Aussie businessmen. This was goodbye Calgary, for about the eighth time that day.

The bitter sweet irony of it all cracked me up. In fact, I couldn't control my laughter. Most of the bar crowd were in town for the Games. They were in a holiday mood and dollar bills were thrown across the bar with carefree abandon. I got rather caught up in it all and almost missed my flight to London. I only made it because the plane was delayed due to technical reasons. I don't remember the take-off. I staggered on to the plane, did my seat belt up and fell into a deep sleep. I awoke many hours later to find the plane over the Welsh mountains. I was home. The next day, nursing a hangover, I watched the opening ceremony of the 1988 Calgary Winter Olympics on my television set in London.

More than 11 years later, with that article in the *Calgary Herald*, I was trying to have the last word over *her*. Childish, isn't it.

It was Wednesday 18th August 1999 when we resumed our journey west on the Trans-Can Highway. I felt no regrets when we left Calgary. I felt no guilt either. All those debts I left behind in a previous life had been paid off a few months after I got back to London in 1988. All that remained was the emotional tug which Calgary still exerted on me. There wasn't an awful lot I could do about this and so I concentrated on the job in hand: getting an old, beat-up 2CV all the way to the Arctic Ocean in Alaska. As Jose and I drove away from Calgary we were only one and a half weeks from our goal.

In this instance, the old, beat-up 2CV also had dodgy brakes. We discovered, though, that if we kept the brake fluid level topped up,

most times the brakes worked when you hit the pedal. We just had to hope that on those rare occasions when you had to pump the brake pedal we weren't aiming for an emergency stop. Looking back, I suppose we should have got the brakes seen to before we continued with the road journey. I think that Calgary had been a strange experience, not only for me, but also for Jose, and perhaps we weren't thinking straight. This might also explain why we decided to change our route to Alaska. The original plan was to head due north across the prairies from Calgary to Edmonton, and then north west to Dawson Creek, the start of the Alaska Highway. But hey, the No.1 car had iffy brakes, so we thought we'd head straight for the Rocky Mountains, and to stay in the mountains on BC Highway 97 all the way up to Dawson
Creek.

Jose and I weren't the first people to have wonky thinking. Neither were we the first to take a Citroen up into the northwest wilderness. In July 1934 an expedition left Edmonton bound for Telegraph Creek, on the Stikine River. The purpose of the expedition was to explore and map the region and to test out Citroen's new half-track vehicles. It was led by a French millionaire, Charles Eugene Bedaux, who tried to take a little bit of civilisation with him into the wilderness.

Bedaux and his wife and friends had a valet and maid-in-waiting to look after their personal needs, and a vast support company of vehicles, animals and men. The convoy of 2 limousines, 5 Citroen half-tracks, and 130 horses was loaded with cases of champagne, exotic foods such as caviar and truffles, and clothing suitable for society balls. Bedaux also brought along a noted surveyor called Frank Swannell to draw maps of the route. However, Swannell's surveying equipment was among the first items to be discarded when the going got tough as the rough terrain destroyed the vehicles one by one. The logistical difficulties of moving a large entourage through the northern bush were far beyond what any of Bedaux' 'experts' had expected, and in late October, with snow falling heavily, the order was given to abandon the project and flee back to civilization with all possible haste. At a cost of over $250,000 for the expedition, Bedaux had provided a great deal of interesting copy for the newspapers, none of it complimentary to his sanity.

Although not well planned, Charles Bedeaux' little jaunt had, as he remarked once back in Edmonton, made a start on a land route to Alaska. Mount Bedeaux in northern British Columbia now honours his efforts. Legend has it that the wreck of one of the Citroen half-tracks can still be found in a remote mountain valley, along with some empty champagne bottles.

The Rocky Mountains just sort of suddenly hit you. One minute you are driving across prairie land, the next you're surrounded by brutal rock faces and towering peaks. Needless to say, the scenery was spectacular. We followed the Bow River valley as the Trans-Can began its steep climb up to Kicking Horse Pass. On either side of the highway there were high wire mesh fences. These fences are designed to keep the wildlife at bay. Signs were posted at regular intervals, warning about the wildlife, and in particular not to feed the animals. As the No.1 car crossed into British Columbia we saw our first bear. It was small, brown and hid shyly in the trees. Not worth photographing. I had set myself a challenge on the Alaska trip: I was determined to get a shot of a grizzly bear standing beside the No.1 car, and perhaps I could also have Jose standing there with her arm around the bear's shoulders. I was still waiting for a good moment to put this proposition to Jose.

At the top of Kicking Horse Pass we pulled off the road and admired the scenery. The pass was discovered in 1858 by James Hector, and yes, you've guessed it, his horse kicked him while he was crossing the pass, hence its name. Kicking Horse Pass is best known for its railway. In 1881, the Canadian Pacific Railway finally began building the transcontinental railroad. When the line got to the Rocky Mountains they were faced with a seemingly insurmountable obstacle. Various areas were surveyed and it was decided that Kicking Horse Pass was the only viable route across the Great Divide. They achieved it by cutting two, long tunnels into the valley sides to reduce the gradient of the railway. The tunnels were complimented by a series of switchbacks. It was completed in 1911 and at 5,338 feet it's the highest point on the Canadian Pacific Railway. By way of contrast, the Trans-Canada Highway didn't come through the pass until the 1960s, which gives some indication of just how difficult it is to get roads and railways over high mountain ranges.

Jose and I could see one of those impossibly long freight trains on the valley floor below us. We were looking down on a toy train set. The weather was glorious so we lingered awhile at the top of the pass. The toy train entered the first tunnel. Fifteen minutes later it emerged from a tunnel mouth higher up the valley wall. There was a bridge and the front of the train crossed over its rear section, which was still disappearing into the tunnel mouth below. The CP Railway over Kicking Horse Pass is an incredible piece of engineering, and a wonderful example of lateral thinking.

There wasn't much lateral thinking when it came to driving the No.1 car across the mountains. We really should have had the brakes checked in Calgary... three hours into the Rockies, and after a lot of heavy braking as we came down the west side of Kicking Horse Pass, we stopped for fuel at a Husky petrol station in Golden, a little town nestling in a scenic mountain valley. I went to the restaurant to get some coffee and left Jose to park the car. Jose, being Dutch, drives like maniac, which you can sort of get away with if your brakes work, but... Jose zoomed into a parking space, hit the brake pedal and nothing happened. Meanwhile, the car mounted a six inch curb, demolished a rubbish bin, ploughed across a lawn, caused a small poodle to run for its life and came to a halt within inches of a picnic table, where, of course, a family were picnicking. The family carried on as if nothing had happened. I was reminded of my shipmates on the *Marie Anne*.

I ran over to the car. Dust hung in the air. Jose was white-faced. I asked her if she was ok. She nodded, then got out the car and slammed the door before storming off to the restaurant. Ah... I reversed the No.1 car back into the parking place and gave a feeble wave through the windscreen to the picnic family. They waved back, leading me to think we were very, very lucky that no one had been in the way of the careering car. It could have been a pretty nasty incident, but on this particular afternoon the Gods were smiling. I shuddered at the thought of the steep mountain roads and hairpin bends we had negotiated just minutes before.

The No.1 car took a pounding during this incident, mostly because of that six inch curb. The protective steel plate beneath the fuel tank had become a different shape, but the fuel tank was still intact, and miraculously none of the tyres blew out with the impact. It took three cups of coffee to calm Jose down. Amazingly, the accident didn't spark off a row between us. There's never a psychiatrist around when you need one, so we carefully drove the car to a nearby garage, where two taciturn mechanics hoisted it up and bleed the brakes. As green liquid squirted out from the bleeder screws one of the mechanics informed us that someone had put in antifreeze instead of brake fluid. We were still too shaken up to explain the peculiarities of a 2CV's braking system - which uses green fluid, not red fluid. I gave the mechanics twenty bucks for their trouble and we continued on our way.

This little incident in Golden somewhat spoilt our first day in the Rocky Mountains. However, as we continued west on the Trans-Can Highway the scenery was so awesome that it soon took our minds off near misses with Death. We ended the day in Salmon Arm, on Lake Shuswap, high up in the Rockies. There was a huge electrical storm that night, lighting up the mountains and the lake. Electrical storms in the mountains are pretty trippy, because as well as the fireworks happening above your head you also get lightening in the adjacent valleys. The mountain peaks are above the level of the storm clouds so when there's a lightening flash in another valley it looks like the light is coming up from the ground, as though a bomb's gone off. Amid all this natural wonder the little town of Salmon Arm looked like an insignificant speck. A marquee had been erected on the shore of the lake. A rock band were playing a concert. What with the lightening and all, it looked like a scene from that Vietnam war film, *Apocalypse Now*.

We are stardust, we are golden
We're gonna get right back, to the garden...

Jose went down to the lake shore to listen to the music. I stood a little way from the rock concert and attempted to get a photograph of fork lightening. Have you ever tried to do this, to capture on film the precise moment when lightening hits the ground? Not easy. As I stood there fiddling with my camera a woman came up to me. She was around 60 years old. We got talking and she told me her name was Pam. Pam had a strong southern accent and hailed from New Orleans. Thirty years ago she left America by way of protest, to show her disgust at the Vietnam War. Pam kept moving until finally she settled in Salmon Arm, which she said was paradise. Well, Salmon Arm is certainly paradise for the Western Grebe. It's the world's last nesting area of this particular bird specis. By now I was feeling peckish, so I bid farewell to Pam and wandered off in search of a Kentucky Fried Grebe joint. Instead, I found an internet café where I discovered that Tony still hadn't put the charity sponsorship form up on the web site. I sent him an e-mail, reminding him how important it was to get the charity side of things moving.

Lake Shuswap and the surrounding region take their name from the Shuswap natives, the northernmost of the great Salishan family and the largest single tribe in British Columbia. The town of Salmon Arm is so called because at one time salmon were so plentiful in the lake that you could just stand on the shore and spear them. These days, Lake Shuswap still provides an important sanctuary for hatched salmon fry before they make their long journey down the Thompson and Fraser rivers to the sea. The Fraser River system is North America's greatest salmon habitat. In October each year anything up to two million fish brave the run from the Pacific up to their birthplaces in the river system. During the peak week of the salmon run, 250,000 make the journey to the rivers. No, not salmon, but a quarter of a million human spectators. Frightening, huh?

On our travels the next day we were surprised to find ourselves in desert country. The landscape around the town of Kamloops was dominated by strange, bare-earthed brown hills with bits of scrub and failing stands of pines. Rock and clay outcrops looked down upon the bilious waters of the Thompson River. The land looked very sick indeed. Had someone accidentally released Agent Orange? No, the desert-like conditions in this part of the Rockies are apparently caused by a lack of weather fronts; ie, it doesn't rain much. The locals joke that the area is the northernmost point of the Mohave Desert.

Kamloops is located where the South and North Thompson Rivers meet, hence the name "Kahm-o-loops", the Shuswap Indian word for "meeting of the waters". It's the largest town in the Canadian Rockies, with a population of 75,000, and serves as a transport hub. The main north/south highways, the Yellowhead and the Coquihalla, cross the Trans-Canada Highway here. It's also the junction of the Canadian Pacific and Canadian National railways. Yup, it all happens in Kamloops, if you're into transport. Apart from that, the town doesn't have much else going for it, and when the wind blows from the saw mills it smells as if something's been dead for a week. We stopped for gas and a quick cup of coffee and were grateful that we didn't live in Kamloops.

Roads are taken for granted, a method of getting from A to B. They've become an intrinsic part of our lives, yet how often do we wonder what mission the other road users are on? What's brought them to travel on this road in and that direction? A road is a story, a romance, a mystery, an intrigue... for 12 days and 3000 miles we had been heading due west on Trans-Canada Highway 1. Forty five miles out of Kamloops we reached Cache Creek, where we left the Trans-Canada Highway to head north on BC Highway 97. One story ends and another begins.

Cache Creek is a tiny place, yet it was once an important supply stop for prospectors on their way north to the Cariboo Mountains. Highway 97 follows the route of the old Cariboo Wagon Road and as we drove along we saw 'Gold Rush Trail' signs, pointing down dusty tracks to long forgotten ghost towns. The Cariboo gold rush was the second of the three big stampedes for gold in North America (the first was the 1848 California gold rush), stampedes that had a huge impact on the history and development of the wild west.

The Cariboo gold rush started in 1862, when a Cornishman named Billy Barker idly staked a claim in the heart of the Cariboo Mountains, in what is now central British Columbia. After digging down a metre or so through the clay he was about to pack up and head north. However, urged on by his mates, Billy dug another couple of spadefuls and turned up a cluster of nuggets worth $1000, which was an awful lot of money in 1862. Billy then sunk a shaft 52 feet deep to get through the clay and hit the richest pay dirt ever seen in the region.

Gold had been discovered in this part of British Columbia a decade previously, but not at the rate of $1000 per spadeful. As soon as word of Billy Barker's gold strike got out there was a stampede for the Cariboo district. Within a few months the site of the find near Stouts Gulch had become a huge shanty town of more than 20,000 people parked in the middle of the wilderness. It became known as Barkerville, but getting to Barkerville was no easy task. First you had to go to Fort Victoria (now the city of Victoria, on Vancouver Island) in order to purchase a mining licence and supplies. Then you'd travel by paddle-wheeler or canoe across to New Westminster on the mainland, and find a steamer to take you up the Fraser River to Fort Yale, which was as far as the steamers could go. After that, travel was on foot along rough trails, carrying all your extremely heavy supplies for hundreds and hundreds of miles through what was then largely uncharted territory. It was tough going, but they did it, tens of thousands of them from all over the world who were prepared to risk their lives and their sanity in the north west wilderness in pursuit of gold.

Things were made easier with the construction of the Cariboo Wagon Road. The Wagon Road stretched all the way from Fort Yale up to Barkerville, which was now a boom town. As with other gold rushes, entrepreneurs followed the miners. Soon dance halls and saloons sprang up to help the miners forget the hardships they endured. A troupe of Dutch and German dancing girls, the "Hurdy Gurdies", came up to the Cariboo from the dance halls of San Francisco. They were featured as the main attraction in a saloon in Barkerville, where miners were charged one dollar to dance with them. With so few women in the town, an Anglican Minister, Robert C. Brown, initiated the Columbia Emigration Society. Its purpose was to arrange for young women from England to be sent to the Cariboo as potential brides for the miners. A lot of English women took up the offer and went to live in rough conditions in the wilderness with equally rough miners, which just goes to show how silly people become at the mention of that magical word: gold.

Within a decade the Cariboo gold rush was over, most of the claims having either run out or been bought up by big mining companies. As for Billy Barker, he and his wife both loved to party and spent most of their money in saloons in Victoria and Barkerville. They say that when Barker entered a saloon he would dance a jig and sing a ditty:

I'm English Bill, Never worked and never will,
Get away girls, Or I'll tousle your curls!

Barker also loaned his friends lots and lots of money to help them search for gold, but they weren't as lucky as him, or else they had a huge thirst. When Billy Barker inevitably ran out of money he returned to prospecting and made just enough to prevent himself from starving. He died in the Old Men's Home in Victoria and was buried in a pauper's grave. The boom town that was named after him all but disappeared until the Canadian Government created a Provincial Historical Park to protect it. Now it's a tourist trap and no doubt Billy is shifting uncomfortably in his grave. Tourist dollars have always been more valuable than prospector's dollars.

Despite our near miss in the high Rockies, Jose was still driving like a maniac. My co- driver had a penchant for accelerating when she saw brake lights or red traffic lights, before braking hard at the last moment. She also continued pulling into parking spaces at high speed, which caused our mishap in Golden. Likewise, the careful drivers in North America drove her mad and she would tailgate all the time. The slow RV's (Recreational Vehicles) raised her blood pressure the most and I had to keep telling her that we were also driving an RV; a Ridiculous Vehicle: SLOW DOWN!

But there was still a screech of brakes and a cloud of dust when we stopped in at the Pengelly place on Clearwater Lake, near 70 Mile House and approximately 50 miles north of Cache Creek. We'd last seen John Pengelly two weeks previously in Toronto, when he kindly saved the Alaska Challenge by supplying us with a slow running screw for the No.1 car. On that day in Toronto, John was about to head off for a vacation at the family holiday home in British Columbia. Another one of those strange coincidences ensured that we were driving right past the family home a fortnight later, which gave us time to get a new slow running screw sent over from England. John got his screw back, gift wrapped. If only the rest of the trip had been that simple.

If only Jose hadn't attempted to water-ski on Clearwater Lake. It was obvious from the way she kept falling over that Jose had never water-skied before. On her 3rd attempt to stay upright, one leg went one way and the other leg went the other way. Jose felt her left leg click. She limped from the water in considerable pain. Rob's co-driver was now injured and suddenly her Dutch method of driving didn't seem so bad after all.

It appeared to be a hamstring injury and the next day, Friday, we went to the Cariboo Memorial Hospital in Williams Lake. I reassured Jose, and told her about the reciprocal agreement between Canada and the European Union, whereby free medical treatment could be obtained by tourists. The receptionist in the emergency department didn't seem to know about this and Jose was told it would cost $150 to see a doctor. What?! We tried to explain to the receptionist about socialism and a national health service, free at the point of use. It didn't wash, and so we were directed to a nearby clinic, where Jose could see a doctor for $40. I waited outside the clinic and studied road maps. How badly was Jose injured? It was still a long drive to Alaska.

On the way up from Cache Creek are the three tiny settlements of 70 Mile House, 100 Mile House and 150 Mile House. These were the old roadhouses of the men who built the Cariboo Wagon Road. The road builders were paid by the mile, which is doubtless why 100 Mile House is well short of one hundred miles from Cache Creek, which is the start of the road. Williams Lake is just north of 150 Mile House, which means it's about 120 miles up from Cache Creek, Canadian road builders being what they are. Williams Lake is a busy and drab transport centre that huddles in the lee of a vast rocky crag above the lake of the same name. Just to the east of Williams Lake, in the Cariboo Mountains, is the site of Barkerville. However, gold fever never really affected Williams Lake. Settlers who followed the prospectors up the Cariboo Wagon Road in the 1860s were after the rich agricultural land in the area, and thus managed to avoid dying destitute in old people's homes. Today, Williams Lake is best known for its famous rodeo, held on the first weekend in July. Oh, c'mon, don't tell me that you've never heard of the famous Williams Lake rodeo?!

Jose had never heard of the famous Williams Lake rodeo and our suspicions were confirmed: it was a pulled hamstring. The $40 doctor wrote out a prescription and advised rest. This meant that from now on 'moi' was doing all the driving. Jose's injury put us a bit behind schedule, so I hammered the No.1 car up Highway 97, Dutch-style. We drove through Quesnel and left the Gold Country behind in a cloud of dust. There was no time for a look at Prince George, the biggest town in central British Columbia, and north of Prince George we came into Peace River country, driving hell-bent through an unbroken tunnel of conifers. The road twisted and wound through hills, passing small lakes and offering occasional glimpses of the mountains. Soon we were in the mountains again and crossed the Continental Divide at Pine Pass, which is one of the lower altitude road routes over the Rockies and therefore one of the least dramatic. The road then dropped steeply to the small town of Chetwynd, where we spent the night. Jose limped heavily, her hamstrung left leg dragging behind her. Hopalong was now on pain killers and dry white wine and was speaking Dutch more than English. Hadn't her mother warned her about liquor and pills?

We made the short drive to Dawson Creek the next morning. Dawson Creek is a dump. It's only claim to fame is that it is Mile Zero of the Alaska Highway. It's a very small, unpreposing town in the north of British Columbia, only ten miles or so from the border with Alberta. Our itinerary managed to avoid an overnight stop in Dawson Creek, so we thankfully ate breakfast in a grotty diner and contemplated what lay ahead.

Following the Japanese attack on Pearl Harbour in December 1941, American War Department Officials became worried about the vulnerability of Alaska, since at that time there was no road link to the lower 48 states. US Army bases in Alaska had to be supplied by sea, but the supply shipping was now in range of Japanese aircraft carriers. The solution was the Alaska Highway, which runs from Dawson Creek to Fairbanks, in the Alaskan interior. This 1500 mile stretch of road was built in an astonishing eight months and twelve days under the direction of the US Army Corps of Engineers.

The urgency behind the construction of the Alaska Highway was further highlighted in June 1942 when Japan invaded the Alaskan Aleutian Islands. This invasion occurred while the highway was still being built. The Aleutians are a chain of small islands more than 1000 miles long that jut out south west from Alaska across the Pacific Ocean, like a line of washing. They had to divert the International Date line to miss the Aleutians, so keeping them in the western hemisphere. These islands are about as remote as you can get and are constantly swept by freezing winds and often engulfed in dense fog. The Japanese occupied Attu and Kiska islands at the western end of the Aleutians. The Americans succeeded in winning back the islands during the summer of 1942. This campaign in the remote Aleutian Islands is often overlooked yet the battle for Attu Island was one of the most costly assaults in the Pacific war, second only to Iwo Jima in terms of human life.

Against this background, that astonishing eight months and twelve days to build the Alaska Highway was perhaps not so surprising. The highway crosses rivers, swamps and mountains as it winds its way through some of the wildest terrain in North America. To this day, the Alaska Highway remains one of the world's great engineering feats.

In the half century since its construction other roads have been built to take travellers to Alaska, but even using the alternate routes - the Cassiar Highway, the Klondike Highway - you still have to drive part of the Alaska Highway, also known as the Alcan, Alaska-Canada Highway. The Alaska Highway remains as the only complete land route to Alaska. It is one of the world's great roads, and we were going to drive the length of it, in a Citroen 2CV. From Savannah, Georgia, we had driven 5546 miles / 9012Km to reach Dawson Creek and it had taken us 23 days.

Hopalong insisted on taking the wheel for the all important drive out of Dawson Creek, and on Mile 2 of the Alaska Highway she almost put us in a ditch. There were strong cross winds and even our heavily laden 2CV was bouncing around all over the place. The landscape reminded me of England, what with its farm land and rolling hills.

The weather, too, made me homesick: it was overcast and rainy and there was a definite nip in the air. It wasn't a very spectacular start to our drive up the Alaska Highway.

Our first overnight stop on the highway was at Fort Nelson, 285 miles up from Dawson Creek. Fort Nelson is a gritty kind of place, more a frontier supply depot than a town. It's dour buildings stand in a battered sprawl around a windswept grid. Even in the late 1950s, Fort Nelson was a community without power, phones, running water or doctors, not even $40 doctors. Life's always been tough in Fort Nelson and is geared towards survival and exploitation of its huge natural gas deposits. The town does, however, have one extraordinary claim to fame, namely that it's home to the world's largest chopstick factory, which is located south of the town. This has nothing to do with a gargantum demand for Chinese food in Fort Nelson, but more with the region's high- quality aspen, a wood apparently perfectly suited to producing the dream chopstick. The Canadian Chopstick Manufacturing Company produces an incredible 7.5 million pairs of chopsticks a day, or 1.95 billion a year.

Saturday night in Fort Nelson found Jose and I in the hotel restaurant, where I had one of the best steaks I've ever eaten. Afterwards, I dragged Jose to a nearby bar, which was packed with a boisterous crowd. We played darts with some of the macho lumberjack types and got slightly drunk. On the way back to the hotel I noticed that it didn't get dark until very late in the evening and the air was chilled. We were now up in the far north and the arctic wilderness beckoned; or at least, it seemed that way after six glasses of beer.

"The Alaska Highway
winding in and winding out
fills my mind with serious doubt
as to whether "the lout"
who planned this route
was going to hell or coming out!"

(Retired Sergeant Troy Hise)

Work began on the Alaska Highway in Dawson Creek on March 9th 1942, when more than 11,000 American soldiers, 16,000 civilian workmen and 7,000 pieces of equipment were thrown into the herculean task of building a 1500 mile road through a vast untamed wilderness. Conditions were horrific. Mud, mosquito-ridden bogs, icy rivers, landslides, extreme weather, all had to be overcome. There are numerous curves along the route and all sorts of ideas have been put forward to explain them: that they were to stop Japanese planes using the highway as a landing strip; that the road builders simply went where ever the bulldozers could find a route; or that at one point they even followed the trail of a rutting moose. The main reason for the curves, though, is that surveying often amounted to nothing more than a finger pointed at the horizon.

Some of the toughest sections of the highway were given over to black GIs, few of whom were given any credit for their part in its construction. You won't see any black faces amongst the white officers in archive photos of the ribbon cutting ceremonies. The native Indians also suffered during construction of the highway. Scores of them died from epidemics brought in by the workers. Wildlife en route was also devastated by trigger happy GIs taking recreational pot shots while they worked. Several specis were almost brought to extinction by this casual slaughter. Another controversial part of the Alaska Highway was the Canol Pipeline. The pipeline was needed to supply oil for the thousands of pieces of equipment that were used to build the highway. The nearest oil supply was way up in the North West Territories, at Norman Wells, on the Mackenzie River, so a 600-mile-long pipeline was built from Norman Wells to a refinery in Whitehorse. It wasn't an easy undertaking:

June 15 1942
THIS IS NO PICNIC
Working and living conditions on this job are as difficult as those encountered on any construction job ever done in the United States or foreign territory. Men hired for this job will be required to work and live under the most extreme conditions imaginable. Temperature will range from 90 degrees above zero to 70 degrees below zero. Men will have to fight swamps, rivers, ice and cold. Mosquitos, flies and gnats will not only be annoying but will cause bodily harm. If you are not prepared to work under these and similar conditions
Do Not Apply

The Canol Pipeline was a major engineering feat, a forerunner of the trans-Alaska pipeline, and its construction caused huge dumps of poisonous waste, which was added to by the junk from the pipeline crews. Much of this detritus is still up there, rotting away in the arctic wilderness.

Our second day on the Alaska Highway involved a 350 mile drive from Fort Nelson to Watson Lake, in the Yukon. The somewhat tame landscape at the start of the Alaska Highway had been replaced by endless forests and distant towering mountains. We became aware that we were now uninvited guests in the wilderness, but the residents didn't seem to mind our presence and were pretty laid back when we stopped to photograph them. We saw caribou, elk, deer, beavers, eagles and hippies, but we didn't get close to the lead actor in the Rocky Mountain drama: the bear.

We stopped off at Liard Hot Springs, at Mile 475 of the Alaska Highway. The water in the springs comes from a volcanic fissure and is at a temperature of 32 degrees. Tropical plants grow there. Strange fish swim in the waters. This, in a region where winter lasts for six months of the year and the temperatures regularly freeze the balls off brass monkeys. The warmth at the springs attracts a lot of wildlife and it's not unusual to see larger animals like moose, and bears. Wooden walkways have been built to take human visitors to a big pool at the centre of the springs, which is ideal for bathing, even when balls are dropping off brass monkeys. Liard Hot Springs is a rather interesting place. It was also our last chance to rendezvous with a guy called Chris Freeman.

Chris hailed from Seattle. I'd been e-mailing with him for a year. He was a Citroen buff who owned a Truckette (a 2CV van). That summer, Chris and his brother also planned to drive the Alaska Highway, in the Truckette. We thought it would be neat to join up and agreed to meet at Dawson Creek, then head up to Alaska in convoy before continuing on the Dalton Highway. However, due to the delays crossing the Atlantic, Jose and I were running two weeks behind schedule. The reason I hammered the car up from Williams

Lake to Dawson Creek was to try and catch up with Chris and his brother. I'd been keeping Chris informed of our progress all the way from Savannah to the Rockies. Problem was, whereas Jose and I were intrepid adventuring for however long it took, Chris and his brother had work commitments back home. They could only spare a maximum of three weeks for their vacation, and they'd already hung around for the best part of a week waiting for the No.1 car to show up. Chris and bruv were pissed off with it all and the last e-mail I received from them said that they might still be at Liard Hot Springs on 23rd August. We were there on 23rd August; Chris and his brother were not: they'd gone on ahead without us. This put my ego in a bit of a spin, because although Citroen 2CVs had been driven up the Alaska Highway before, no one had ever taken one up the Dalton Highway to the Arctic Ocean. Would Chris and his brother beat us to it?

Jose didn't really care and flicked spent cigarette butts into the hot springs. She called us all anoraks and said that no one would give a toss about who was first to drive a 2CV up to the Arctic Ocean in Alaska. Jose was in a relaxed mood, and remarkably we still hadn't had a row since leaving Winnipeg together in the No.1 car. This might have been a good moment to launch my photo challenge proposition on her, whereby I'd get a shot of Jose and a grizzly bear standing beside the No.1 car. Thing is, there were warning signs everywhere about how dangerous bears are. A few years previously at Laird Hot Springs, two people were killed by a bear. It was a brown bear that was sick, weighing just a few hundred pounds, half its normal body weight. The bear went for a mother and her child. Two people tried to help. The child and one of the rescuers were killed. The others were badly mauled. This was a rare event, but you should never mess with bears.

A bear can outrun a human, but can it outrun a Citroen 2CV? Luckily, we never had to put this to the test and reached Watson Lake without incident. Watson Lake is at Mile 637 of the Alaska Highway and is really just a spit on the map, a weather-beaten junction that straddles the 60th Parallel and marks the entrance to the Yukon Territory. Watson Lake's one claim to fame is its 'Signpost Forest', which came about when a homesick US Army GI working on the construction of the Alaska Highway in 1942 erected the first group of signposts. Travellers from all around the world have added other signposts in the intervening years, and now there's more than 20,000 of the damn things. We didn't bring a signpost along with us, although we did have a spare gearbox, just in case we came across a Gearbox Forest further along the highway.

The Alaska Highway can get rather confusing as far as distances are concerned. In Canada everything is in kilometres. In the US of A everything is in miles, and all along the Alaska Highway, in both Canada and the USA, there are 'Historical Mile Posts'. These are the original distance markers of the Alaska Highway, when they took a meandering route from Dawson Creek to Fairbanks, which made for a longer road mileage. In the intervening years the Alaska Highway has been improved/straightened-out; which means that it is now a shorter road. Hence, if you come across a 'Historical Milepost' of, say, 496 miles, it is probably nearer 450 miles up from Dawson Creek. Not that the moose care.

Most of the Alaska Highway, 1200 miles or so, is in Canada. The final 300 miles is in the state of Alaska. The highway was an American gig and in exchange for right of way across Canadian soil the yanks paid for its construction. Back in 1942, with a little help from the US Army, you could build 1523 miles of road through the wilderness in less than nine months for 140 million US dollars, which included 133 major bridges and more than 8000 culverts. On a cold, bleak day in November 1942, a group of shivering soldiers, civilians and RCMP watched as officials from the United States and Canada cut the ribbon to officially open the road. The ceremony took place at Mile 1061, known as "Soldiers Summit". The first full convoy of trucks to reach Fairbanks crawled along at 15 miles per hour during one of the worst winters in memory. Later in the war, 8000 planes were transported up the Alaska Highway to Fairbanks, where they were picked up by Soviet pilots and flown to the Siberian front.

The United States turned over the Canadian section of the Alaska Highway to the Canadian army in 1946. It was opened to the public in 1948, but within months of its opening there'd been so many accidents that it was closed for a year. The Canadian army retained control of the highway until 1964, when it was turned over to the

Federal Department of Public Works. Since then there's been a continual program of upgrading, widening and straightening. Nowadays, according to officialdom, most of the Alaska Highway is paved. In reality the never ending road improvement schemes mean that you're just as likely to find yourself on rock and dirt than on a finished road surface.

At Mile 917 of the Alaska Highway we found ourselves in Whitehorse, capital city of the Yukon Territory. Jose became very introspective and went into one of her 'moods'. It seemed a good idea to separate for a while, me trying to find internet connection, Jose wandering along the banks of the mighty Yukon River, which gave Whitehorse its name - the rapids and foaming white water look like the flowing manes of white horses.

After trying unsuccessfully to find an internet café, I soon discovered that Whitehorse is also the world's capital for eccentrics. The No.1 car attracted them like bees to honey. Within the space of fifteen minutes I found myself talking to a professor of higher mathematics, who told me he was in the process of patenting a new formula for calculating the surface area of snowflakes, and an elderly man with a long white beard who said that he was related to Adolf Hitler. They both had the dress sense of a rutting moose, but I got the feeling that no one in Whitehorse really cared about such things.

Later, over dinner, Jose told me she felt homesick. This wasn't surprising, here in such a remote and harsh place. The Yukon Territory is vast (bigger than France and Germany put together), yet only 30,000 people live there, and 23,000 of them are residents of Whitehorse. The Yukon's capital is a small, friendly place that constantly reminds you of its location. Splat bang at the end of Main Street there are rocky outcrops and fir trees as the wilderness tries to encroach. It's also a somewhat incongruous place: what's a town of this size doing here, in the middle of nowhere? The answer, of course, is gold.

On August 17th 1896, two Indians and a white man stopped to rest beside a tiny stream called Rabbit Creek, which flowed into the

Yukon River. There on the creek bottom they saw glistening flecks of gold, "caught between rocks like cheese in a sandwich". The men's names were Skookum Jim and Tagish Charlie, members of the Tagish tribe, and George Carmack, a Californian man who had moved to the Yukon and joined the Tagish band, marrying Jim's sister, Kate. Lucky old Kate, because George and his two partners struck it rich that day and quickly re-named the creek Bonanza. They would become immortalized as the co-discoverers of gold which, by today's standards, would be worth over a billion dollars.

Word of The Bonanza Discovery spread fast among northern prospectors, but the Arctic winter was on its way, cutting off the Yukon from the outside world. It wasn't until the following year that news of the gold strike reached beyond the northwest wilderness.

"At 3 o'clock this morning the steamship Portland, from St. Michaels for Seattle, passed up Puget Sound with more than a ton of solid gold on board and 68 passengers."

When this magic sentence appeared in the July 17, 1897, issue of *The Seattle Post-Intelligencer*, it triggered what was probably the last and the greatest gold rush in history. Before noon that day every berth aboard the Portland had been sold for the return trip north and telegraph wires hummed with news of the 68 miners who carried boxes of gold down the gang plank at the Seattle wharf. When it was actually weighed, the gold amounted to more than two tons, but by then it didn't really matter. The stampede to the Klondike in north western Canada was underway.

The site of the Bonanza Discovery, near the confluence of the Klondike and Yukon Rivers, turned into a sea of tents as miners rushed in to stake claims. The new settlement became known as Dawson City. By the summer of 1897, Dawson had become the largest city west of Winnipeg and north of San Francisco, with a population of 40,000. Dawson soon developed the raunchy character of a 19th century frontier town, its ragged streets and rowdy saloons becoming the centre of the Klondike Gold Rush. Fortunes were won and lost as dancehall girls performed high kicks in the Opera House, the Palace Grand and the Monte Carlo, where the biggest poker game ever recorded in the Klondike took place, with a pot of one hundred and fifty thousand dollars.

Prior to the gold rush, Whitehorse had been a tiny Indian settlement. As the gold rush got under way it became a natural resting place for prospectors on their way to the Klondike. Dawson City lay 400 miles to the northwest, along the Yukon River, which meant negotiating the Whitehorse rapids. After the first few boats through the rapids had been reduced to matchwood, the Mounties laid down rules allowing only experienced boatmen to take craft through - writer Jack London, one such boatman, made $3000 in the summer of 1898, when more than seven thousand boats attempted to make the journey to Dawson City. In the late 1800s, Whitehorse became a boom town with a population of more than 10,000. After the gold rush it's population dwindled to about 400 and for the next forty years it slumbered. Whitehorse's second boom arrived with the construction of the Alaska Highway, a kick-start that swelled the town's population to 40,000 almost overnight, and has kept it going ever since.

The next morning we were still trying to find internet connection... ok, it's simple really: if you're driving a weird car with foreign number plates and company banners plastered all over it that adds up to news, so you go to the nearest newspaper office, which in Whitehorse happened to be the *Yukon News*, and these days newspapers always have internet connection. We were able to send our latest Bulletin, and the *Yukon News* got a story, of sorts.

I was a bit depressed to discover that Tony still hadn't put up the charity sponsorship form on the web site, but by that time I was almost beyond caring. Here in Whitehorse it didn't seem to matter so much; and besides, I was still tiptoeing around Jose's mood. She didn't like our hotel room,which was small and a bit tacky. Peak season hotel rooms in the wilderness are expensive. Our company sponsorship money had run out shortly after we left Calgary and we were now surviving on our own funds. We needed to budget sensibly. Jose didn't see it like that. I'd been asking around town to find out how far behind Chris Freeman we were, since 2CVs are such noticeable cars and everyone noticed when Chris and his brother passed through Whitehorse four days previously. Jose thought I was too obsessed with beating Chris to the Arctic Ocean. I took Jose to a nearby bar in the hope of relaxing things between us, but the black cloud followed us. The bar was part of an old gold rush hotel which had been restored. In otherwords, a real tourist trap. We sat tensely at a table. Eisenstein directed. An out of work actor was dressed-up as a Canadian Mountie type clown. It was his job to jolly along the tourists. When the Mountie tried to jolly us along, Jose told him to fuck off, in English. My, she really was in a bad mood. We then had an argument about who was going to pay for the drinks. I tried to look on the bright side: it was out first argument for nearly two weeks, since we'd left Winnipeg together in the No.1 car. I paid for the drinks and wondered why we hadn't been a bit more careful with the company sponsorship money. Both Jose and I had plenty of our own funds. I think it just came as a bit of a shock when we started having to dip into them.

News of the Bonanza Discovery jollied everyone up, because at the time North America was locked in an economic depression that came from the Panic of 1893. The Panic of 1893 was sparked at first by the collapse of an important railroad company, and then the collapse of an industrial corporation that had been paying dividends illegally. On top of this there was also an underlying weakness in the US economy, caused by the reckless spending of the Democrats. The naughty old Democrats had also been intentionally inflating the money supply by overvaluing silver relative to gold. It's no wonder that everyone panicked.

The Panic of 1893 resulted in destroying some 172 State banks, 177 private banks, 47 savings banks, 13 loan and trust companies and 16 mortgage companies. It also placed the United States Treasury in the position of being bankrupt for the first time in its history, as a massive drain on its gold reserves was unleashed when fear spread throughout the public that the government would be unable to honor its debts. Historians say that the global depression produced by the Panic was sharper than the great 1930s Depression.

During this period many people were out of work and finding it difficult to feed themselves. However, those magic words: "a ton of solid gold from the Klondike" changed all that. Business doubled, then tripled, as more than one hundred thousand people from all over the world stampeded to the site of the Bonanza Discovery. The Mayor of Seattle was in San Francisco when he heard news of steamships from the Klondike carrying tons of gold. That was it. He immediately wired his resignation as Mayor and before the month was out he bought an ocean steamer, formed a Yukon trading company, and set sail for the Klondike. Most of these gold seekers didn't have much idea of where the Klondike was; few really cared. They might have cared more if they knew what lay ahead: thousands of miles of wilderness, murderous rapids, mind- numbing cold and frontier gun slinging quite literally stopped many stampeders dead in their tracks.

The Klondike Gold Rush had an immediate and lasting impact on Western Canada and the United States. Seattle became a major staging point for fortune hunters on their way north and the populations of Vancouver and Edmonton doubled and tripled respectively. The Klondike Gold Rush was one of the greatest mass movements of people in history. It was one hell of a party, the like of which will probably never be seen again.

'Yukon' comes from a Dene Indian word meaning "great". The Indians refer to it as the land of little sticks, because the trees are so spindly. The white inhabitants simply call it the Far North. People who live in the Far North call the rest of the world the 'outside'.

I really liked the Yukon. Robert Service, a famous Yukon poet, called it the "cussedest land I know". It's a land where in the winter the temperature can drop to more than 80 degrees below freezing, so cold that petrol turns to slush and water tossed into the air turns to ice before it hits the ground. It's a land where the sun can shine at midnight in July, but vanish entirely during December. It's a land of natural wonders, such as the Virginia Falls, a giant waterfall that is twice the height of Niagara Falls. It's a land which has huge mineral riches, but they are so far from civilisation that transportation costs make them worthless. The Yukon is also a land of legend and mystery, and for a region with such a small population, over the years there's been an extraordinarily large number of UFO sightings. Most common of these sightings are glowing spherical objects, about the size of a basketball, usually red in colour, sometimes green or white.

The Shaman call these objects "Grandfather and Grandmother lights" and say they are the souls of departed ancestors.

Jose and I set out from Whitehorse on Tuesday 24th August. Ahead of us lay 305 miles to the Alaska border. We were now driving along the most remote stretch of the Alaska Highway. It was also the most beautiful. In fact, it was so beautiful, what with the distant mountains and the endless forest, that I just had to get a good shot of it. We pulled over at a suitable spot. I got out the car and gazed around at the awesome scenery. There was no sign of human influence at all; no houses, no pylons or telegraph poles, no other cars, no nothing, just wilderness that seemed to go on for ever. The silence seemed magical. I felt so lucky, so privileged to be able to experience this place. Then I noticed the bear. It was a black bear and it didn't look that big, that is, until it came out of the tree line and started cantering towards us. I leapt in beside Jose and told her to burn rubber. We never did get that shot.

One hour later I was still trying to calm my shaking hands when the scenery dramatically changed. The flora had died a horrible death. The fauna probably met a similar fate. Maybe that's why the bear was so pissed off? The landscape had been devastated by fire and looked like some of those horrific World War One battlefield pictures. The magnificent green carpet of conifers had been reduced to a desert of charred stalks, some of which were still smoking. The destruction went all the way up the slopes of the surrounding mountains. We later found out that the forest fire started the previous summer at a small place called Burwash Landing, just off the Alaska Highway. Someone from the Canadian Forestry Service had tried to burn off a small garbage heap, but things got out of control, causing one of the biggest forest fires in recent Yukon history. Someone from the Canadian Forestry Service was now probably looking for other employment. Really, though, the guilty party was probably the Canadian Forestry Service. Wild fires are a part of nature. It's part of the circle of death and regeneration that keeps things healthy. When man intervenes, with misguided ideals of the natural world, and tries to prevent wild fires it just causes more damage. The forest overgrows and becomes a tinder trap. The recent spate of huge forest fires in the United States is a direct result of man interfering with nature. Forests are meant to burn now and again. By preventing these small, natural fires you end up with one big catastrophic fire.

This one had been catastrophic indeed. We were driving for nearly an hour before we left the last of the burnt trees behind and arrived at the south eastern end of Lake Kluane. The Lake Kluane area has some of Alaska and the Yukon's greatest but most inaccessible scenery. The St Elias Mountains contain Mount Logan (5950m), which is the highest point in Canada, and Alaska's Mount McKinley (6193m), which is the highest point in North America. These mountains are part of the world's second highest coastal range (the Andes are the highest). Below the mountains is a huge base of mile-deep glaciers and ice fields, which form the world's largest non-polar ice field, and it has just one permanent resident, the legendary ice worm.

Ice worms..? Ok, the origin of ice worm lore is probably from Tuchone Indian legends. Glaciers along the St. Elias Mountains were rumoured to be inhabited by giant white worms. The Tuchone Indians smoked anawful lot of strange substances, but in fact there are real ice worms, and they live on the surface of temperate glaciers and eat airborne pollen grains, fern spores and the red algae that grows in snow. Ice Worms are the only known creatures that spend their entire lives covered in, ice. Ice worms are tiny, roughly three quarters of an inch in length. They are similar to common earthworms, except that they need to stay inside a very specific temperature range to survive, ideally 32 degrees Fahrenheit. A few degrees warmer and they disintegrate, a few degrees colder and they freeze, the poor buggers. On cloudy days they are common on the snow surface. They neither bite nor sting nor hurl abusive language at you, but if you pick up an ice worm in your hand your body heat will kill it in seconds. Yup, it's not easy being an ice worm.

However much travelling you've done, however many wondrous sights you've seen, however hardened you are, you cannot fail to be impressed by Kluane Lake. At 400,000 square kilometres it's almost as big as Wales, but without Cardiff and Swansea. The lake is surrounded by scenic splendour, but what really grabs the eye is the water. It has a kind of blue/white translucent colour, like washing machine powder has been dissolved in it. This strange colour is because glacial sedimentation is held suspended in the water. Dip your hand into Kluane Lake and you're literally dipping your hand tens of thousands of years into the past.

The Alaska Highway follows the south shore of Kluane Lake for 30 miles. This area is known for its huge variety of wildlife, yet the only really wild things we saw in great abundance were mountain goats. I'm not sure what they were wild about but they were everywhere and seemed to be suicidal. After negotiating a hairpin bend you'd suddenly find a group of goats in the middle of the road, and when you jammed on the brakes and swerved to avoid them they would run directly into your path. These goats were obviously very depressed about something and wanted to end it all. They had wild, staring eyes and reminded me of the sheep in the Outer Hebrides (the previous March, Jose and I had taken the No.1 car up to the Outer Hebrides for a dress rehearsal). I wondered who had the toughest time, the Kluane mountain goats, which had to survive subzero winters and weeks on end without any sunlight, or the Hebridean sheep, who had to survive howling gales and almost constant rain. It would be fun to put the Kluane mountain goats up against the Hebridean sheep and just let them try to outstare each other.

We spent our final night in the Yukon at Beaver Creek, Canada's westernmost settlement. Beaver Creek has a year round population of 140 which swells enormously to 200 during the summer months. This tiny place sits right on the Alaska border. However, following protests from its inhabitants, Beaver Creek no longer houses the customs post - this has been moved a couple of kilometres up the road because of the flashing lights and sirens that used to erupt whenever a tourist forgot to stop. Beaver Creek is a tiny place, yet it is within a day's drive of Fairbanks and so has cornered the tourist market in this part of the world. Americans come across from Alaska to have a little taste of Canada, and in particular the Yukon.

We stayed at the best hotel in town, the Westmark, which was full of American tourists. Behind the hotel there's a large log pavilion which is home to the Beaver Creek Rendezvous, a rollicking musical show set in the early days of the Yukon. Jose loved the show. I found it a bit too am-dram and was more impressed later that evening by an excellent production of the Aurora Borealis. I stood under the night sky with a glass of beer and watched shimmering, dancing, luminescent curtains of colour. Very trippy. The Aurora Borealis (also known as the 'Northern Lights') is named after the Roman goddess of dawn. Some Inuit tribes believed the lights were the spirits of animals or ancestors; others thought they represented evil forces. Old-time gold prospectors thought they might be vapours given off by ore deposits. The Japanese believed a marriage would be particularly successful if consummated beneath them. The phenomenon is still not fully explained, although it's thought that the Aurora Borealis is caused by solar wind hitting the atmosphere and being attracted to the poles by the earth's magnetic field; although I'd rather go for the Inuit's take on things.

After breakfast the next day we drove the short distance to the Yukon/Alaska border, where US Customs gave Jose a hard time. Hey, what's wrong with a Dutch Passport? Have the gentle, peace loving Dutch ever harmed anyone? What surprised us most, though, on all the border crossings, was that the Customs officers never checked the contents of the car. We could have had a case of Kalishnikov rifles, 8 kilos of heroin and ten illegal immigrants hidden in the back of that car, and no one ever checked to see; but there again we were driving an RV (Ridiculous Vehicle) and I suppose no one took us seriously.

Delta Junction is the official end of the Alaska Highway, and we rolled into this small Alaskan town on the afternoon of Wednesday 25th August, having clocked-up 1437 miles (2335Km) from Dawson Creek. At the Visitor Centre we learnt that Chris Freeman and his brother had passed through the previous weekend. We were also surprised to discover that Rob Godfrey was some kind of celebrity. Both staff and visitors took pictures of probably the most famous Citroen 2CV in the world.

All this hoo hah was because we knew someone in Delta Junction: Barbara, who worked at the Town Hall and was one of our internet contacts in North America. Barbara lived in a big log cabin about fifteen minutes drive from the Visitor Centre. She invited some friends over and held an afternoon barbeque for us. We had our first taste of bear and moose steaks. It was a nice welcome to Alaska. We were also given some good advice about driving the Dalton Highway, and in particular how to deal with the many bears up north. Stan, one of Barbara 's friends, said that he had a pepper spray we could have, for warding off any stroppy bears we might encounter. But surely, if you spray pepper into the face of a marauding bear wouldn't that make it even angrier? Apparently not. Jose, though, started becoming angry with me when Barbara invited us to stay over at her place and I replied that we had to reach Fairbanks before nightfall. Barbara was also driving to Fairbanks later that day, to catch a flight down to Seattle, where she was visiting some friends. We could stay at Barbara's place while she was away. Jose liked the idea. The log cabin was very plush, and even had its own family of bears living at the bottom of the garden. Well, by this time I'd had enough of bloody bears. However, my main reason for wanting to push on to Fairbanks was because I figured Chris and bruv would rest there for a number of days before heading up the Dalton Highway: there was just a chance that we might be able to catch up with them, at last.

Jose mouthed the word 'anoraks' as she took her place beside me in the No.1 car. We then followed Stan and Barbara the short distance to Stan's log cabin, where he gave us the pepper spray. We also got our first taste of the Alaskan's obsession with firearms. Stan's gun collection, which he proudly showed us, was more of a small arsenal than a collection. I asked him what on earth he needed twelve handguns, nine rifles, five semi- automatic rifles and a machine gun for? He offered me the largest handgun, a 45, as if by holding it I would instantly understand why he needed twelve handguns, nine rifles, five semi automatic rifles and a machine gun. A machine gun?! Stan said that it was fun to go into the bush with the machine gun and just let rip with it. He gave us some bullets to take away as souvenirs.

The No.1 car moved in the shadow of Barbara's huge 4WD as we drove the 98 miles (158 km) along the Richardson Highway to Fairbanks, which we reached at dusk. After our thanks and farewells, Barbara drove on to the airport and Jose and I took a room at the Comfort Inn next to Alaskaland, on the banks of the Chena River. Alaskaland is a very touristy adventure park themed mostly around the pioneering days. I was somewhat relieved when Jose went into one of her moods, thus relieving us of the task of visiting Alaskaland.

In some respects, Fairbanks is similar to Whitehorse, in that it's located splat bang in the middle of nowhere. The difference between the two is that Whitehorse is really just a town, whereas Fairbanks is quite a large city with a population of more than 70,000. Most cities have other population centres near them. Not Fairbanks. As soon as you leave the city limits you are in the wilderness. The only other city in Alaska, Anchorage, is nearly 400 miles away on the south coast. There are settlements within 100 miles of Fairbanks, but they contain a sprinkling of people and are more or less just frontier outposts.

It makes you wonder why Fairbanks, in the frozen north, in the middle of nowhere, has grown into a large metropolis. Well, that can be largely blamed on war: the Second World War, when several huge military bases were built to thwart possible Japanese attacks, and the Cold War. Geographically, Alaska is a stones throw from Siberia, which is just 22 miles away across the Bering Strait. In the bad old days, when the Soviets and Americans were waving thermo-nuclear weapons at each other, Alaska became a place of strategic importance. The state still has a large military presence, particularly in Fairbanks, and is the site of early warning radar posts. In the bad old days the Alaskans would have given their countrymen in the lower forty eight states the three minute warning. Whether or not those decrepit Soviet missiles would have actually managed their trans-continental flight was never put to the test, thankfully.

History is littered with ironies: Alaska used to be Russian territory. Russian fur traders first arrived there back in the 1700s and established a settlement on Kodiak Island, on the south coast. The Spanish and the English also made an appearance and tried to claim Alaska as theirs, but they didn't like the cold weather and so the Ruskies maintained ownership. However, by the mid 1800s the fur trade was in decline and the Russians wanted to get Alaska off their hands. They managed to bamboozle the Americans into buying it in 1867, just a few years after the American Civil War. The price was $7.2 million, or about 2 cents an acre. Sounds like a bargain? Well, what did the Americans get for that 2 cents an acre: mostly arctic wilderness where it was impossible to grow anything in the hard permafrost. The place may be scenic in parts but it is also largely barren. This is the main reason why for many years Alaska remained just a territory of the USA and didn't became the 49th state of the Union until 1959, when the Soviets were lurking just across the

Bering Strait.

Kurt Benz had supplied me with a list of contacts in Fairbanks, people he'd met on his numerous visits to the city. I figured I should look up at least some of them and dragged Jose along for the ride. We managed to get lost and ended up in a downtown car park. I saw a woman putting shopping into the back of her car and went over to ask directions. The woman jumped as I approached her. My, folks were certainly nervy in these parts. However, the woman calmed down and became friendly when she heard my English accent and saw the No.1 car. She introduced herself as Lynn and I was somewhat surprised to find myself talking to a fellow Londoner. At that moment her husband, Guy, appeared on the scene; also English and very curious about the No.1 car and the 2CV Alaska Challenge. We agreed to meet Guy and Lynn later that afternoon for a drink in the Dog Sled Salon, a popular hangout in Fairbanks.

When we got back to our hotel, Jose said she had something to tell me. She'd been making mysterious phone calls all day and I kinda knew what was coming... Jose had decided to go home. Homesick and hamstrung she had booked herself on the Friday night flight down to Seattle, and thence on to London. I was left somewhat surprised by Jose's decision to bow out, because ever since leaving Winnipeg in the No.1 car we'd got along together just fine. Now, in Fairbanks, we were just two days away from the Arctic Ocean, providing the No.1 car made it up the Dalton Highway. As far as the 2CV Alaska Challenge went, we were almost at journey's end.

But Jose wanted to be somewhere else, Europe, London, home, wherever that was; no doubt somewhere that didn't have Rob Godfrey as part of the scenery. Jose and I had our ups and downs. There were times when we could have quite easily strangled each other, but in the end we always stayed together. I suppose we were a bit like an old, married couple, the marriage being a road journey across North America. Now it was not so much a divorce, but more an amicable separation. I felt hurt by Jose's decision to leave the 2CV Alaska Challenge. I also felt sorry for her, because she wouldn't get to see a part of the world that few people have the chance to visit: the Arctic; let alone visiting it in a Citroen 2CV.

The Dog Sled Salon is on the ground floor of the Captain Barlett Inn, on Airport Way. It's what's known as a 'Yukon bar': sawdust on the floor, overflowing ash trays, heavy drinking and lots of colourful characters. The sign outside the salon said: "All firearms must be left with the cloakroom attendant before entering". In Alaska you can legally carry a firearm without needing a permit, as long as your firearm is clearly visible (to carry a concealed weapon you do need a permit). However, firearms are not permitted in bars, where only slow death is allowed.

It was a sunny afternoon so the four of us sat out on the terrace. Guy and Lynn were ex-pats who had been living in Fairbanks for eight years. Lynn used to work in a jewellery store in downtown Fairbanks. It got held up by an armed man. Six months later the jewellery store got held up again, by the same armed man. Lynn resigned from her job and was now on trancs for her nerves. Previously, she'd always been afraid of guns, now she kept a forty five magnum in the house, a shot gun in her car and a 22 in her handbag (when I approached Lynn in that downtown car park I was lucky I didn't get shot). Guy sold real estate. He was well known in Fairbanks and was one of the people involved in the redevelopment of the downtown area. Guy and Lynn were nice people. We chatted for an hour, then they had to go on to a wedding reception.

That evening, Jose and I had dinner at the Captain Bartlett Inn. Afterwards we went back to the Dog Sled Salon for a drink. It was then that I hit upon the idea of taking a sex doll up to the Arctic with me. It seemed a good way to end the Alaska Challenge, which had been a wacky venture right from the start. More than anything, though, I find all those 'adventure journeys' that one sees rather tedious. It's all the same sort of macho rollocks; 'endurance', 'hard going', 'gee aren't we tough guys'. I was both the producer and the director of the 2CV Alaska Challenge, and now that the leading actress was no longer sticking to the script it was time for a bit of improvisation.

The following morning we checked out of the Comfort Inn and I took a room at the Captain Bartlett. This was Jose's last day in Alaska.

The plane for Seattle left at midnight. But first, we had to buy a sex doll. This didn't prove easy, because despite the large military presence there's no red light district in Fairbanks. In fact, there didn't seem to be any sex shops at all. We pulled into a gas station. A young chap lounged behind the counter. Jose asked him where we could buy a sex doll. The young chap's mouth dropped open and for a few seconds he was speechless. It was an interesting meeting between American prudishness and Dutch liberalism. The young chap recovered his composure and became bashful. It turned out that in the whole of northern Alaska, a place the size of western Europe, there is just one sex shop. Luckily, though, it was situated only twenty miles from Fairbanks, out in the wilderness. We headed off down the highway.

We'd never have found the sex shop if it wasn't for the fact that the chap told us it lurked near a small lumber yard. The sex shop was set back from the highway, down a small dirt track that led into thick forest. We pulled up outside a long, wood cabin without any windows. It looked abandoned. There were two cars parked outside. A ha.... we cautiously pushed open the battered metal door and found ourselves inside a large emporium of the flesh, no different from any you'd find in Europe. A bored, fat guy sat at the counter. He was watching a ball game on a small portable tv. His eyes met ours for a fraction of a second. The only other customers in the sex shop were a GI and his girlfriend. They were holding up and admiring various sized dildos. Their eyes met ours for a fraction of a second.

We wandered around the shop. There were videos titled 'Sex the Greek way', 'Cowboy Brothel' and 'Masturbation Danish style'. There was the 'Orgasmo electric vagina', the 'Clitofing', 'Chinese Erekto Cream', and the 'Giant Strap-on Cocky'. There was also a large selection of sex dolls. Linda Lovelips, 'fully equipped with three holes for pleasure'. Doll Mate, 'you can vary the grip of her soft, inviting vagina during intercourse'. The Sexy Doreen Doll, 'with lifelike pubic hair'. Naw, I didn't like the look of any of them. I plumped for Jamie the Love Doll, because at forty bucks she was the cheapest. I handed over my cash at the counter. The fat guy's eyes met mine for a fraction of a second.

Now that I'd acquired my new co-star I just had to get some good shots of her, to put up on the web site. So, the three of us drove to the airport. Fairbanks International Airport is not a huge place, yet because of its location it used to be a major stop over for trans-Pacific and trans-Arctic flights. Those glory days are gone now, but the airport still handles a lot of traffic from Canada and the lower forty eight states. The alternative to flying is a five day drive along the Alaska Highway, as we knew all too well.

A little way down from the modern terminal building there were some old Dakotas parked by the perimeter fence. We parked the 2CV just in front of them. An old car with some old planes in the background. I took shots of Jose waving her hand and walking away from the No.1 car towards the Dakotas. Then Jose took shots from the same angle of me and Jamie standing by the car. Our photo shoot attracted a small crowd. The pictures went up on the web site two hours later, along with a bulletin announcing that Jose was going home. As I e-mailed the bulletin and pics I noticed that Tony still hadn't put the charity donation form up on the web site.

Looking back on it, I should have considered how the sex doll thang would have appeared to the large audience that was following the Alaska Challenge, and particularly the two charities we were supposed to be raising money for. All I can say is what I believe I've already stated in this book: when you're intrepid adventuring it's very easy to lose touch with reality!

Back at the Captain Bartlett Inn, we thoroughly cleaned the No.1 car and got it shipshape for the trip up to the Arctic. It reminded me of that film, *The African Queen*, where Humphrey Bogart and Katherine Hepburn get their little boat ready for the attack against a German warship. In our film, though, Hepburn would not be joining Bogart for the big finale.

All that remained was for Jose and I to have a last meal and drink in the Dog Sled Salon. Then, at just after 11pm, I took her back to the airport. It became another one of those strange farewells, late at night at an airport on the other side of the world. Jose and I had done some hard travelling together: Savannah to Fairbanks in 31 days and 7000 miles in an old, beat-up Citroen 2CV. It had been a slice (of life).

Neither of us liked lingering farewells, so I didn't wait with her in the departure lounge. I told Jose that if she changed her mind at the last minute – something that women have been known to do - I would be leaving for the Arctic at 8.00am the following morning, Saturday 28th August. Jose and I embraced, and then me and the No.1 car drove off into the Alaskan night.

I drove back to the Dog Sled Salon, where I got rather drunk in the company of some dentists from Seattle. I wasn't overly upset that Jose had gone, just disappointed. More than anything, I think my return to Calgary after all those years had finally caught up with me, on an emotional level. The wounds were still deep. Jose's departure had rubbed salt into those wounds. To me, it seemed like I was always being abandoned by women when I was in far flung places; but at least I knew that Jamie the Love Doll would not let me down; unless she had a puncture.

Chapter 4.   The Arctic

Do I know where hell is? Hell is in hello.
Heaven is in goodbye for ever, it's time for me to go.
I was born under a wandrin' star, a wandrin' wandrin' star.
Mud can make you prisoner, and the plains can bake you dry.
Snow can burn your eyes, but only people make you cry.
Home is made for comin' from, for dreams of goin' to,
which with any luck will never come true.
I was born under a wandrin' star,
I was born under a wandrin' star.

Wandrin' Star, music by Frederick Loewe, lyrics by Alan Jay Lerner

For some reason I knew the date, Saturday 28th August, yet I couldn't remember where I was. Staying in a different hotel almost every night for a month can leave you a touch disorientated, to put it mildly. The large amount of beer I'd consumed the night before didn't help. I looked around for Jose. She wasn't there. Had I left her somewhere..? Then it all came back to me: I was in Alaska; Jose had flown back to London the night before. I opened the window and felt fingers of cold air on my face. This revived me somewhat, but the energy expended to stay in a vertical position was too much, so I laid down on the bed again and let out a loud groan. I glanced across the room and saw the grinning face of Jamie the Love Doll. How the hell could a guy screw one of those things? I remembered just what Jamie was doing here in this hotel room in Alaska. Oh shit. I remembered that I was an intrepid adventurer, that today I was driving up into the lonely, desolate wastes of the Arctic, in an old, beat-up Citroen 2CV. I began to pull the bed covers back over me.

But onwards and upwards; after all, I was an intrepid adventurer. I scrabbled around for my travel alarm clock. It showed just after half past nine. Right, time to get moving. I felt fired up, a reaction against the fear that was starting to grip me. I got dressed and then managed to force down some breakfast in the hotel restaurant. Without Jose around it all felt fresh and new. The parameters had changed. The landscape was different.

It was gone eleven by the time I carried my rucksack and Jamie the Love Doll out to the hotel car park. The No.1 car gleamed in the sunlight. It felt like an old friend. This old friend, though, might very soon die on rock and gravel roads that ran 500 miles due north from Fairbanks up to the Arctic Ocean. I could hardly bear to start the engine. It fired into life at the first attempt. Once again I found myself amazed at the stamina and durability of this car. How could I risk killing it in the Arctic?

The Arctic... it seemed sensible to stock up with some essential supplies for the trip, so I drove to a nearby supermarket. Supermarkets always give me anxiety attacks, and this one, crowded with weekend shoppers, was no exception. I shot round and picked up the essential supplies, which consisted of two packets of crisps, one bar of chocolate, a carton of cigarettes and four crates of beer. All set, and at twelve minutes past midday I drove out of Fairbanks and headed north on Highway 70. On the seat beside me was Jamie the Love Doll, who was strangely silent.

Highway 70 is paved, that is, until you leave Fairbanks City limits and it becomes a rutted dirt road. I didn't know at the time that the pounding the No.1 car was now receiving would be nothing compared to what lay just a short distance ahead, on the Dalton Highway. It's a 73 mile drive north from Fairbanks to the start of the Dalton Highway. The dirt road wound through gently rolling hills and thick forest. The No.1 car bounced, lurched and shuddered. Spruce, birch and aspen stretched in all directions. A lumberphiliac's paradise. The weather was glorious, the sky so blue that it seemed as if you could reach up and scrape bits of it off with your hand. A strange day indeed to be a polar explorer. A sled and thermal clothing? a deckchair and suntan lotion would have been more appropriate; and I should have brought along *The Observers Book Of Pipelines*, because since leaving Fairbanks the road had been shadowed by a weaving, silver worm, glimpsed every so often through the trees. According to *The Observers Book Of Pipelines*, the Trans-Alaska Pipeline is one of the seven wonders of the modern world.

In some respects, the construction of the Trans-Alaska Pipeline had echoes of the construction of the Alaska Highway, in that it was an emergency project. Arab-Israeli wars were putting Middle East oil supplies in jeopardy. The announcement in 1968 of a large discovery at Prudhoe Bay by the Atlantic Richfield Company (ARCO) confirmed what many people had suspected all along: beneath the frozen landscape of Arctic Alaska there lay no less than 10 billion barrels of oil, the largest ever find in North America and as much as the combined reserves of Louisiana, Oklahoma, Kansas and half of Texas. Against the prevailing political climate it wasn't a question of if the oil could be recovered, but how soon it could be recovered.

The biggest problem lay in transporting the oil back to civilisation. It was estimated that to transport it by road would require a fleet of 60,000 tanker vehicles operating around the clock, seven days a week, 365 days a year. Likewise, to move the oil by rail would involve building two sets of tracks, one for the loaded wagons going out and the other for their return. A 100-wagon train would have to leave the oilfields every 23 minutes of the day and night. I'm sure the polar bears would have complained about the noise, and so the oil companies came up with the idea of building an 800-mile pipeline from Prudhoe Bay on the shores of the Arctic Ocean, through some of the most desolate country in the world, much of it perpetually frozen hard, to the ice-free port of Valdez on the southern coast of Alaska.

In 1969 a Japanese company started delivering sections of the new steel pipeline to Valdez. However, the project took a while to get going because of law suits filed by various environmental groups, and because of Native land claims. Congress passed the National Environmental Protection Act to keep the environmentalists happy, giving them a supposedly eco-friendly pipeline, and the Natives were bunged one billion dollars and 40 million acres of land by way of the Alaska Native Land Claims Settlement Act, which was signed into law in December 1971 by President Nixon. The final impetus for the pipeline occurred on 6th October 1973, when Egypt and Syria invaded Israel. Arab members of OPEC stopped exporting oil to the United States in retaliation for US aid to Israel. This put the US in a state of emergency and the Trans-Alaska Pipeline Authorization Act was passed by the House and the Senate on 16th November 1973. This Act was a carte blanche to get the pipeline built as soon as possible, and nothing would be allowed to stand in its way. Construction of the Trans Alaska Pipeline System (TAPS) began on 29th April 1974. It was run like a war-time project. Money was no object; time was of the essence as 28,000 men and women across Alaska worked furiously around the clock and in all types of weather conditions to get the job done. Three years and eight billion dollars later, the 800-mile long Trans-Alaska Pipeline was opened for business on 20th June 1977. Thirty one people died during its construction.

It took more than two hours to cover the 73 miles to Livengood. I found myself amazed that the No.1 car had made the distance, such was the pounding it received on the journey up from Fairbanks. We passed a sign which said: 'Livengood City Limits'. Someone obviously had a sense of humour, since the 'city' consisted of a scattering of log cabins set back from the road. Livengood is so named ('living good') because it was the site of a rich gold strike in 1914. Apart from that, it's only other claim to fame is that the Dalton Highway begins there. Highway 70 crossed a small bridge over a gully and then climbed up a steep bank, away from the huge metropolis of Livengood. At the top of the bank, Highway 70 curved round to the left and went on its way to Manly Hot Springs. Leading straight off the bend was another dirt road: the Dalton Highway.

I'm not quite sure what I expected at the start of this infamous highway. Cheer leaders, a marching band, perhaps flashing neon signs? No, it was just another innocuous dirt road making a tiny dent into the wilderness. But this road went all the way to the Arctic Ocean. There were cheery road signs at the start of the Dalton Highway: 'ALL VEHICLES DRIVE WITH LIGHTS ON FOR NEXT 425 MILES'. 'NO SERVICES FOR NEXT 100 MILES'. 'YOU ARE LEAVING 911 AREA'. 'CAUTION: HEAVY INDUSTRIAL VEHICLES USE THIS HIGHWAY'. I felt fear again. I got out the car and took some pictures. The sky still looked a scrapable blue. It was a lovely August day. There wasn't a soul around. All I could hear were birds singing in the trees. Ah, to hell with it. The Dalton Highway is what put the 'challenge' in the 2CV

Alaska Challenge. It needed to be seen through to the end. I had to make that drive up to the Arctic Ocean... as long as Chris and his brother hadn't got there first. I asked around in Fairbanks: no sightings of Chris, but there again, it's a big place. I was almost certain that after staying in Fairbanks, Chris would have gone on to tackle the Dalton Highway. He was as obsessed about it as me. The 64,000 dollar question being, how far up the Dalton would Chris take his 2CV van?

The thing about the Dalton Highway is, it's a road that goes to the ends of the earth. If you make the 500 mile drive all the way up to Prudhoe Bay there's nowhere else to go. You have to drive those 500 miles all the way back down to Fairbanks. That's a four day round trip, if the Gods are smiling and the weather's good and your vehicle survives the pounding... I drove past the warning signs, north towards the Arctic. I now needed every ounce of my concentration to keep the car moving along the highway. I was on rock, gravel and mud. There were deep potholes that pummelled the underside of the car like artillery fire, mean ridges that violently shook the car, big rocks that suddenly bounced us up in the air. Jamie slid down off her seat and settled on the floor. On three occasions I burnt my nose while trying to light a cigarette. I kept the car moving and passed abandoned vehicles on the side of the highway, rugged four-wheel drives that couldn't take the pace. How the hell was a Citroen 2CV going to survive if these big beasts couldn't?

But survive she did and after an hour and a half we reached the Yukon River crossing. Suddenly, all became smooth and quiet as we drove on to the wooden decking of the bridge. I managed to light a cigarette without burning my nose. A short distance away the Trans-Alaska Pipeline crossed the river on suspension wires. The Yukon River road bridge is the largest and most expensive bridge ever built in Alaska. It spans 2,295 feet and swallowed up 4,838 tons of structural steel and 170,000 bolts. I pulled up half way along the bridge to count the bolts and gaze at the muddy Yukon River below. Patches of mist hung above the water. I'd last encountered the Yukon River in Whitehorse and knew that it's the fifth largest river in North America, 2000 miles long, and empties 2 million gallons of water into the Bering Sea every second, although I'm never quite sure how they measure these things.

The Yukon River bridge goes down at a sharp angle from the cliffs on the south bank to the flat north bank. Here, a little bit of civilisation can be found, a settlement known simply as 'Yukon River Crossing', which consists of a large barn workshop and garage and near the river bank a hotel. The hotel was my first taste of arctic architecture. It was made of prefabricated box-like structures bolted together to form a rambling sort of building. There were about half a dozen big 4WDs parked by the riverbank. These were the first serviceable vehicles I encountered on the Dalton Highway.

We had covered 130 miles since leaving Fairbanks. An inspection of the car showed that it was still in one piece. The Yukon River crossing is one of only two gas stations along the Dalton Highway. You tank-up at every opportunity. I also carried 30 litres of petrol in jerry cans. The gas station attendant grinned back at Jamie and told me that another weird looking vehicle had come through earlier in the week. So, Chris and his brother had made it this far. I also learned that this was the first weekend of the hunting season. The Yukon River crossing is a popular base for hunting trips. The hunters use flat bottom boats propelled by small aero engines. The engines are quiet. The boats can navigate very shallow water. This enabled the hunters to go deep into the bush using the river. They were after moose, and any of these unfortunate creatures who went down to the river bank for a drink would receive a lead sandwich instead.

In the wilderness you can hear things miles away. It's the lack of other noise, you see. There's no roar of traffic, or aeroplanes, or other kinds of machinery. There's no sound of people. There's no movement at all, except by the wildlife, and they keep as quiet as possible. It's kinda like the silence in a church. *Sqwump, sqwump, sqwump*, a big station wagon came down the bridge from the south side. It was pulling a boat on a trailer. The guy at the gas station knew all the signs and started getting his tyre equipment ready. We watched as the station wagon carefully negotiated the rutted ground in the parking area. It came to a slow halt on the other side of the gas pumps. One of the trailer tyres had punctured and ripped. The garage carried in stock all the popular makes of tyres. The guys in the station wagon were out of luck. The trailer had a rare make of small tyre. It might take anything up to a week before a spare could be found and sent up to the garage. I carried six spare tyres in my 2CV. I felt reassured.

The highway wound away from the Yukon River crossing, up into gently rounded hills. I stopped at the top of the rise and looked back. You could no longer see the small settlement. The course of the Yukon River was marked by low rolling mist as it wound through the wilderness. The Dalton Highway was completely deserted. Just me, Jamie the Love Doll and the No.1 car bounced, shook and rattled on our way. By now I had become more adept at handling the car in the rough conditions and was able to drive a bit faster than the crawl at the start of the highway.

The endless forest began thinning out. The trees were noticeably smaller. Soon we were driving across what looked like moor land. I saw a cloud of dust coming towards us. The huge 18-wheeler truck did not slow down. I pulled over to the side of the highway. The ground began to shake. A rain of gravel and dust fell on the No.1 car as the truck thundered past. The driver gave a friendly toot on his horn. In five hours he would be back in Fairbanks and civilisation. This was the first of many 18-wheelers I encountered on the Dalton Highway. They take supplies up to the Prudhoe Bay oilfields, which is why the Dalton is also known as the Haul Road. I took the same action each time I encountered one of these trucks: get out of the way!

The silver, snake-like pipeline was our only companion in the increasingly bleak landscape. Back in 1974 they built the 440 mile long Dalton Highway in just five months. As well as a supply route to the Prudhoe Bay oilfields it's also a service road for the Trans-Alaska Pipeline. You're never far from the pipeline when you're driving on the Dalton Highway. You are a very long way from civilisation, though, and I was amazed to come across a solitary house set back from the road. It wasn't your usual Alaska-style log cabin, but a stone cottage. I could see a hand painted 'Hotel' sign on the gate. Who the hell lived here? or more to the point, who the hell would stay in this godforsaken place? I didn't stop to find out but got an answer to the riddle a little further up the road. Another sign pointed to a lay-by. It said 'Arctic Circle'. There was an observation platform and picnic area in the lay-by, also the official Sign telling you this is the Arctic

Circle, 188 miles north of Fairbanks, where at 5.30pm on Saturday 29th August I reached latitude 66° 32' north, and in so doing became the first man ever to cross the Arctic Circle with a fully inflated sex doll.

I didn't linger in the lay-by. My destination for the day was more than sixty miles further north and it was getting late. This stretch of the highway was in appalling condition and it took us more than two hours to cover those sixty miles. The No.1 car took a terrible pounding. Rock and gravel flew around all over the place. One of the headlamps was smashed. The exhaust pipe broke. The windscreen got cracked. Jamie once again slid off her seat and on to the floor, where she stayed until we arrived in Coldfoot.

Located in the foothills of the Brooks Mountain Range, Coldfoot is 250 miles north of Fairbanks and is the half way point of the drive to Prudhoe Bay. Originally named Slate Creek, the settlement began in 1898 when thousands of stampeders flooded to the area in search of gold. The town's name was changed when a group of prospectors got "cold feet" about wintering in the district and headed south. At its height, Coldfoot had one gambling hall, two roadhouses, seven saloons and ten working girls (many of the local creeks are named for these friendly women). The town also had its own post office. Mail was delivered once a month from Fort Yukon, in the winter arriving by dogsled.

By 1912 the gold stampede was over and Coldfoot become an Arctic ghost town, with only the wolves for company. It came alive again during the 1970s, when it was used as a construction camp for the Trans-Alaska Pipeline. Once the pipeline had been built, Coldfoot once more became a forgotten place; that is, until Alaskan dog musher, Dick Mackey, set up an old school bus on the site and began selling hamburgers to the truck drivers. Coldfoot is a convenient place for a rest stop during the long drive to and from Prudhoe Bay. All that was left from the gold prospecting days were a couple of tumble down cabins and a graveyard. The truck drivers wanted to make Coldfoot a bit more comfortable, so they helped build a restaurant with old packing crates that had been used to haul supplies up to Prudhoe Bay. The names of these truck drivers are engraved on the centre pole inside the restaurant, which is now used as a communications centre with messages hung for the truckers, miners and other folk in the area.

Coldfoot experiences long, cold winters, with 24-hour darkness. Summers, by contrast, bring 24 hours of daylight with temperatures that approach 100F. It's a place of extremes. On January 26th 1989, Coldfoot recorded the lowest ever temperature in this part of North America: 82 degrees below freezing. Mind you, 1989 was a particularly bad winter and for seventeen consecutive days the temperature in Coldfoot remained at more than 60 below freezing. Coldfoot bills itself as 'the northernmost truckstop in the world'. Here, in the midst of the Arctic wilderness, as well as the original restaurant built by the truckers you'll now also find a gas station, hotel, post office, general store and first aid post, specialising, no doubt, in the treatment of frostbite.

As soon as I arrived in Coldfoot I asked after Chris Freeman. I received some cheery news: mine was the first weird little car to have recently come through these parts. This told me all I needed to know. Chris and bruv had got as far as the Arctic Circle and then turned back. Most people who drive the Dalton favour this option, because it's an easy drive from Fairbanks and you can say you've been to that famous imaginary line. Calculating the driving distances, Chris and I must have missed each other in Fairbanks by just a day or so, him southbound, me northbound; northbound for the Arctic Ocean: I was going to be the first man to drive a Citroen 2CV this far north in Alaska. The record was mine.

My elation was somewhat tempered when I discovered the price of a hotel room in Coldfoot: $120 a night. I was also dismayed to find a young, smartly dressed English couple staying at the hotel. They were from Epsom and had flown to Fairbanks for 'something different', which involved hiring one of those huge 4WDs and doing the Dalton. Epsom?! The Arctic is supposed to be a place for teeth-gnashing intrepid adventurers who wrestle grizzly bears and bite the heads off bald eagles, not sedate couples from bloody Epsom. And worse, they didn't take to Jamie the Love Doll at all. I explained my mission in the Arctic and told them that when they got back home they could tell everyone that they had met Rob Godfrey. This didn't get much reaction. The young couple took a quick picture of me and the car then hurried into the hotel.

That 120 bucks a night bought me only a small room in the Slate Creek Hotel, a haphazard array of prefabricated box-like structures that smelt strongly of sweat and hot radiators. On the road journey, Jose and I were paying between $60 and $80 per night for hotel rooms. The thing about the Arctic is, all provisions and supplies have to be shipped in from down south, hundreds and hundreds of miles away. This bumped up the price of everything, including hotel accommodation. Petrol is also horrendously expensive in arctic Alaska, which seemed rather ironic, since we were near the biggest oil field in North America. However, that oil is in crude form. It has to go south via the Trans-Alaska Pipeline to refineries. Then it's shipped back up to the Arctic as petrol, with a suitable price tag attached.

The Trans-Alaska Pipeline has a diameter of 48 inches. It zigzags along its 800 mile route. This is to allow for expansion and contraction caused by temperature extremes, and to allow the pipeline to move in the event of an earthquake. There are a total of eleven pump stations located along the pipeline which move the oil at a velocity of 6 miles per hour. It takes five-and-a-half days for the oil to make the journey from Prudhoe Bay to Valdez, where it is loaded into waiting tankers - about 70 every month. These tankers are escorted to and from the port by specially equipped Escort Response Vessels, to ensure safe passage to the sea. Well, that's the theory... in 1989 the tanker Exxon Valdez ran aground in Prince William Sound, spilling 12 million gallons of oil into the sea. It was an environmental catastrophe and some of the oil still remains on the beaches to this day. Exxon paid for the oil clean-up but didn't pay a cent in compensation to people whose livelihoods were affected by the spill. There's still a legal battle going on with regard to the $5.3 billion in compensation that it's claimed Exxon owes the victims of the oil spill.

I ate some rubber chicken and chips in the truck stop then wandered back over to the Slate Creek Hotel. The bar by the entrance lobby was dry. Welcome to the arctic, a place of big corporations making money and governments making war, and lots of strict control; which means that you can't sit in a deckchair or on a bar stool and just relax and get pissed. The ethos in the Arctic these days is puritan hard work. People mostly come to this harsh land to make a buck, lots and lots of bucks. It's all dreadfully serious and macho. That's why the buildings are strictly utilitarian; ugly assemblies of what are basically shipping containers and portacabins. One day someone will build a beautiful structure in the Arctic. It's just begging to happen, much like the world peace that Miss World contestants blather on about.

I sat up at the counter and drank a coffee. The bar was deserted. I thought about tomorrow, when, if my luck and the car held out, I would reach the Arctic Ocean and the record books. I wondered if they sold anoraks in Prudhoe Bay. My thoughts were interrupted when a group of men began assembling in the bar. They were all big, rugged types, and one looked bigger, older and more rugged than the others. He went by the name of Joe and he was the leader. They were a road gang, about 15 in all, who came from Arizona. Joe settled on a bar stool beside mine. He told me that every summer for the last four years he and his men had taken the shilling from the Alaska government, to come up here to this remote spot and repair the Dalton Highway. The Alaskans wouldn't break their backs here, in this godforsaken place. The Alaskans are spoilt. The oil is to blame.

BP, ARCO and the rest of the oil companies pay the State of Alaska land taxes, for both the Prudhoe Bay oilfields and the Trans-Alaska Pipeline route. These levies go into what's called the 'Permanent Fund'. We'd all like to have a bank account like the Permanent Fund, because there's billions of dollars slopping around in it and it pays out huge amounts of interest. In fact, it pays out an annual check of $1000 to each and every Alaskan. More than 600,000 people live in the state of Alaska, and unlike the rest of the folks in America, the Alaskans don't have to pay a state income tax. Oil revenues pay for most of Alaska's state spending. It's a similar set-up in some of the Middle East oil countries, like Saudi Arabia, where the citizens pay no income tax and get a pay out every year from the oil revenues. A nice gig if you can get it.

Arizona Joe and his gang did four months work during the summer and earned a very large sum of money. Repairing the Dalton

Highway basically meant filling in the pot holes and trying to level it out. This was a never ending task. The condition of the Dalton varied from year to year, depending on how harsh the winter had been and how much rain fell during the summer months. I met people who told me that the Dalton Highway had been in much worse shape the year before. The Dalton is a rough drive whenever you attempt it. From what I could make out, in the summer of 1999 it was in average condition.

The road repair season was over. Arizona Joe and his chaps were throwing an end of term celebration. Joe's overweight wife had come up to claim him and in the morning they were all flying south, back to the real world. The party was somewhat marred by the fact that there was no booze sold in Coldfoot. Everyone contributed whatever they could, which amounted to a mostly empty bottle of whisky, some rusty cans of Budweiser and two bottles of revolting red wine. Meanwhile, someone called Rusty had been sent to get the road gang's secret stash of beer. We all waited impatiently for Rusty to return. It was a private party, but in arctic climes no one is a stranger and everyone is a guest. Guests, however, are expected to make a contribution. I put a five dollar bill into the hat that was passed around and supped on a rusty can of Budweiser.

Rusty arrived on the scene and soon I was drinking cans of Budweiser that weren't rusty. As the beer flowed the different personalities in the road gang began to emerge. They were a nice, if somewhat rowdy bunch of chaps. A beautiful young Indian girl appeared and began strumming a guitar and singing folk songs. From the looks given by the men it was obvious that some of them had been making whoopee with her. Well, it gets lonely up in the Arctic, particularly if your testosterone is flying around… I could see it coming, and sure enough an argument broke out between some of the men and they started fighting. Arizona Joe's wife managed to restore order. The blood was mopped up and after cheers for an encore the beautiful Indian girl gave another rendition of *Blowing in the Wind*. At this point I left them all to it and walked along the dingy corridor, back to my box-like hotel room. It didn't seem possible that just the night before I'd seen Jose off at Fairbanks Airport. Jose would now be back home in London, back in normality, whatever that is. I missed her. I didn't miss the normality.

Hotel rooms in the Arctic are small but everything else about Alaska is big. It's the largest state in the union, more than twice the size of Texas (much to the chagrin of the Texans) and stretches 2400 miles from its farthest point east to its farthest west, that's greater than the distance from New York to San Francisco. More than half of Alaska's land area is seismically active. Ten percent of the earth's earthquakes occur in Alaska, but because very few people live there no one really notices them. It has the highest mountain in North America, Mt. McKinley at 20,320 feet, and the deepest ocean depth, the Aleutian Trench, 25,000 feet below sea level. More than half the world's glaciers are in Alaska. The Malaspina Glacier, Alaska's largest, is bigger than the state of Rhode Island. Alaska also has the biggest 4-wheel-drives in the world and some of the largest egos to be found anywhere on the planet.

After breakfast, Rob Godfrey had his photo taken again. A man came up to me as I struggled to repair the No.1 car's broken exhaust pipe. He introduced himself as Tom and looked to be about the same age as me, but with longer hair. Tom came from Switzerland and worked as a photojournalist, spending most of his time on assignment in the arctic. His editor in Zurich would request photos of a particular animal and Tom went out and got them. Tom told me that at the moment he was after the Arctic Fox *(Alopex lagopus)*, which is found on the tundra north of the Brooks Mountains. The Arctic Fox is an elusive creature and Tom had already spent two weeks trying to find one. Every week or so he came into Coldfoot or Prudhoe Bay to stock up with supplies. Most of his time was spent out in the wilderness, on his own with just the inevitable howling wolves for company. Unlike most people you meet in these parts, Tom wasn't there for the money. In fact, he had to scrimp and save every penny to be able to go on these assignments, because the payment he received for his wildlife photos barely covered the cost of coming to far flung places like arctic Alaska. The simple fact was, he loved the wilderness, and was lucky to have an understanding wife back in Switzerland.

Tom also knew about hotel prices in the Arctic. He slept in the back of his transit van. He informed me that you don't see much wildlife along the first 250 miles of the Dalton Highway. It's only once you get way up into the Arctic that you start seeing grizzlies, moose, caribou, wolves, and the like, the much famed Alaska Serengeti. He also told me that the last half of the Dalton from Coldfoot up to Prudhoe Bay was a lot smoother than the first half from Fairbanks. This cheered me up considerably. Tom took photos of me and Jamie and the car. He was the first person I met in Alaska who really took to Jamie the Love Doll. Maybe it was her wicked grin.

The sign said: NEXT SERVICES 244 MILES. A beautiful sunny Sunday morning found me and Jamie on the road again. The space and lack of sound in the wilderness give it a spiritual dimension, an 'otherness'. It's the silence more than anything that makes the wilderness special. Of course, I was travelling through it during the height of summer. Jack London found his niche writing about the northern wilderness winter, when the silence is even more apparent. He called it the White Silence:

> *Nature has many tricks wherewith she convinces man of his finity - the ceaseless flow of the tides, the fury of the storm, the shock of the earthquake, the long roll of heaven's artillery - but the most tremendous, the most stupefying of all, is the passive phase of the White Silence. All movement ceases, the sky clears, the heavens are as brass; the slightest whisper seems sacrilege, and man becomes timid, affrighted at the sound of his own voice. Sole speck of life journeying across the ghostly wastes of a dead world, he trembles at his audacity, realizes that his is a maggot's life, nothing more.*

Twelve miles north of Coldfoot we passed a small track that led to the town of Wiseman. In 1911 the prospectors began to abandon Coldfoot as rich finds were found on the Nolan and Wiseman Creeks to the north. A boomtown soon developed. In 1910, the author, Robert Marshall, described Wiseman as "200 miles beyond the edge of the twentieth century". They still pan for gold here. In 1994 a gold nugget was found on Nolan Creek. It weighed 42 troy ounces and was one of the largest nuggets ever mined in Alaska. Wiseman has a year round population of 30 people, which swells considerably each summer as people come looking for more big nuggets. These modern gold seekers are nearly always disappointed. Ironically, just yards from the small community of Wiseman there is a 48 inch diameter pipeline through which flows black gold of almost unimaginable wealth.

We had followed the golden vein all the way up from Cache Creek and the Cariboo Mountains, through the Yukon to Alaska, which both figuratively and literally was the end of the line. It seems incredible now that people risked their lives and their sanity by coming to such a harsh and remote land in search of gold, but come they did. Of the more than 100,000 people who stampeded to the Yukon, only 30,000 actually made it to Dawson City, the site of the Bonanza Discovery, and out of these only a handful made big money from gold prospecting. You'd think that this would deter people; but oh no: by 1899 the Yukon Gold Rush was over. The survivors, the dreamers, the insane, streamed out of Dawson City without a glance back. They were off to the beaches of Nome, Alaska, one thousand uncharted miles to the west, near the Bering Strait, where it was rumored the sand was speckled with flakes of gold.

The Alaskan gold rush started in 1898, with an exploration team prospecting the Seward Peninsular. Bad weather drove their ship into the mouth of the Snake River, about 13 miles west of Cape Nome. While waiting for the winds to subside the explorers passed the time by prospecting the surrounding creeks, where they found gold along Anvil Creek. When news of the strike reached the outside world a flood of prospectors arrived at the site and set about staking claims along Anvil and several other tributaries of the Snake River.

The Anvil Creek strike was good, but it did not outshine the Klondike gold fields, except that it led to an amazing discovery. Many of the stampeders who arrived too late to stake claims along the mouth of the Snake River set up tents on the beach, where they found the sands glittered with gold. In fact, there was gold for 40 miles along the water line in either direction from Nome. A few years earlier those magic words: "a ton of solid gold from the Klondike" had caused the biggest gold rush in history. Now, in 1899, "the golden sands of Nome" produced another big stampede.

Those who managed to survive the journey to Nome must have thought they'd died and gone to heaven. The beach strike became a prospector's paradise where digging the gold was said to be easier than stealing it. The work required only a shovel, a bucket and a crude, easily built rocker. The shallow diggings on the beach were open to everyone, since beach land could not be staked by any individual. If you left your diggings another prospector could move in. Poet Sam Dunham wrote in 1900, "For many miles along the beach, double ranks of men were rocking, almost shoulder to shoulder, while their partners stripped the pay streak and supplied the rockers with water and pay dirt." At the height of the summer mining season, nearly 2000 men, women and children were rocking on the beach. Here, in this remote spot at the end of the world, it is estimated that the "beachcombers" mined as much as $2 million in gold from the sand.

'Nome' probably sounds like a Native Indian word. In fact, it's a spelling mistake by the British Admiralty. Back in the 1850s a British ship was surveying the coast of Alaska. An officer noted on a manuscript map that a nearby headland had not been identified. He wrote "? Name" next to the headland. When the map was recopied at the Admiralty, a draughtsman thought that the '?' was a 'C' and that the 'a' in "Name" was an 'o', and thus the headland became known as Cape Nome. Nome, Fairbanks, Livengood, Coldfoot, Wiseman, it was gold which brought most of the white settlers to Alaska in the early 20th century. I wonder what the Native Indians made of it all? No one knows, because no one asked them.

I left Wiseman behind in a cloud of dust and the bone jarring began again. The rugged and majestic Brooks Range now filled the horizon. The Brooks Mountains are the northernmost arm of the Rockies. I glanced at the pipeline and wondered how on earth it managed to get across the mountains. 'Alyeska' is the name of the consortium of oil companies which built and now manage the Trans-Alaska Pipeline. Alyeska boasted in 1977 that "no spill is likely to flow unnoticed for more than a few minutes". Two years later a pipeline leak occurred here on the south side of the Brooks Mountains. The spill continued unnoticed for nearly four days without triggering any of the automatic alarms. It's estimated that up to 5,000 barrels of oil spilled out into the pristine arctic wilderness. Considering that 1.4 million barrels (that's 44 million gallons) of oil pass through the pipeline every single day, there have been very few leaks during the more than 20 years of the pipeline's operation. However, due to the massive volume handled by the pipeline the potential for an environmental disaster is ever present and leak detection has always been a controversial subject.

I pulled up beside a bedraggled, sickly looking tree. It wasn't a case of oil pollution. A sign by the tree said: *This is the farthest north spruce tree along the Alaska Pipeline. Do Not Cut.* I couldn't imagine who would use this sickly looking thing as a Christmas tree. It told me, though, that we were now really in the arctic, where trees can't grow in the permafrost. In fact, there was hardly any vegetation at all, apart from low shrubby bushes and mean blades of grass. The Dalton began a sharp climb upwards. All around were the bleak, bare mountains. A huge cloud of dust came hurtling down the road towards us. I pulled over to let another eighteen wheeler hurtle by. This one didn't give the usual friendly toot. The sense of isolation was increased by the size of the bare mountains, which now loomed on all sides. Even to this day, most of the Brooks Range remains unexplored. Some of the UFO buffs claim there is an alien base hidden in the mountains. Yeah, and Elvis still holds concerts there.

The UFO stuff stems partly from what became known as the 'Alaskan Roswell Incident'. In late 1954 a bush pilot for Wien Alaska Airlines spotted a dull white object on the ground near the Scheenjek River, north of Fairbanks. He flew down for a look, but because of the rough terrain he couldn't see the object clearly. Word of the sighting soon got round and in the UFO hysteria of the time the object was immediately identified as an alien spaceship. It made newspaper headlines and would have caused a War of the Worlds type panic, if it were not for the fact that very few people lived in Alaska and they didn't really have anywhere to run to.

The 7th Cavalry arrived in the shape of The 7th Air Rescue Squadron and an H-5 helicopter. Lieutenant Harold Hale was assigned the task of saying 'hi' to the aliens. "After coming upon the wreckage, I didn't actually know what I saw", Hale reported. "At first I thought it was a parachute. But after discovering that the 'chute' was made of a kind of rice paper and the gondola contained some bamboo parts, I knew that whatever the object might be, we could be

---

reasonably sure that it was of Japanese origin." The strange find was loaded aboard the helicopter and transported back to Ladd Air Force Base, where personnel of the 5004th Air Intelligence detachment made a thorough study of it. The official report of this study said that the strange object was a Japanese incendiary balloon, from the Second World War. During the latter part of war the Japs launched many of these balloons, which were carried by the prevailing winds to the United States. US pilots based on the Aleutian Islands reported shooting down as many as ten of them a day. The balloons were cleverly designed to drop a 5 kilogram thermite incendiary bomb after travelling thousands of miles across the Pacific Ocean. The incendiary balloons were found as far east as Iowa and as far south as Mexico. None had ever before been discovered as far north as the Arctic Circle. Two people in the US were killed by the bombs. At the time the US Government kept all knowledge of the incendiary balloons from the public, afraid that it would start a panic. This only contributed to the hysteria that ten years later surrounded the Alaskan Roswell incident, because of course no one trusts the military and to this day there are many people who swear that it was all one big cover up.

The Brooks Mountains looked like some kind of alien landscape. However, as we drove up Chandalar Shelf I didn't have much time to keep a look out for ET and Co. We were making our way up a sharp incline leading high into the mountains. This was the climb up to the infamous Atigun Pass, which at just under 5000 feet is the highest mountain pass in Alaska. In some places the Dalton Highway went through a 1 in 3 climb as it crawled up the side of the mountains. Eighteen wheelers and Citroen 2CVs have to go into first gear to get up this steep gradient, not helped by the fact that the rocks and gravel slide away from under your wheels. The approaches up to the Atigun Pass are the only parts of the Dalton that have crash barriers. The dents and smashes on the barriers proved how much they were needed. The skeleton of a truck laying on the valley floor below showed that the barriers didn't always do their job properly.

It took 30 minutes to cover the two miles or so to the top of the pass. The smell of burning oil and an overheated engine filled the No.1 car, but we made it. At the summit there is a short stretch of level road before it plunges down over the other side of the mountains. We paused for breath, here at the top of the world, where the air is so clean and clear that you can see for 50 miles in every direction.

The Atigun Pass had always been the biggest hurdle to overcome on the journey to Prudhoe Bay, and that incredible little car got us up there. Jamie and I danced around on the rocks and gravel. Light snow fell from the sky. The wind moaned. It was just us and the aliens and a horizon that seemed to stretch to infinity. *Hello the Arctic!*

The Arctic officially begins at latitude 66° 32', the imaginary Arctic Circle. However, local geography determines where the Arctic really begins. In some parts of Siberia you get arctic conditions way below the official line. Likewise, around Hudson Bay in northern Canada, where in Churchill, hundreds of miles south of the Arctic Circle, polar bears congregate in large numbers. In north east Alaska the real arctic begins once you reach the snow capped Brooks Mountains, seventy or so miles above latitude 66° 32'. There are no trees; very little vegetation; no people, no houses, no nothing. It's as bleak as a Munch painting, and just as exciting.

At the other end of the world, Antarctica is a huge continent surrounded by oceans, whereas the Arctic is an ocean surrounded by continents. Most of the Arctic Ocean is an ice sheet, up to 10,000 feet thick in places. At the North Pole the ice is thin enough to enable submarines to break through. Maps of the world tend to distort the perspective of the Arctic. If you were up in space, directly above the North Pole, you'd see it is encircled by the northern extremities of Russia, Finland, Sweden, Norway, Iceland, Greenland, Canada and America. Thus, the shortest distance between Fairbanks and Moscow is not along the line of 60 degrees latitude, but in a direct line passing over the North Pole.

It's also the shortest distance for intercontinental ballistic missiles and during the latter part of the 20th century the Arctic became a tripwire for Armageddon. Conversely, the Cold War was at its hottest here, where nuclear submarines used to play games of cat and mouse beneath the ice and air defenses were forever being probed and tested.

The indigenous peoples of the Arctic have lived in the region for thousands of years and never had much time for listening posts and missile silos. Their main concern was day to day survival in an incredibly hostile environment. In the Eurasian part of the Arctic can be found the Sami (or Lapps), the Komi, the Khanty, the Nenets, and the Yakuty. In the North American part of the Arctic, from Greenland all the way west to Russia's Chukchi peninsula, there are only the Inuit - also called Eskimos, a name many of them don't like. The Inuit have always been very isolated from the rest of the world, yet the Cold War did impact on them. In the Bering Strait, Little Diomede Island, Alaska, and Big Diomede, Siberia, are only two and a half miles apart. The International Dateline divides the islands, making Little Diomede yesterday and Big Diomede tomorrow. For nearly forty years the islands were also divided by an 'ice curtain'. It was only in 1988 that the Inuit were able to renew ties and travel without visas across the narrow expanse of water that divides them.

The snow was beginning to settle on Jamie. It didn't seem advisable to hang around for too long at the top of the pass, where in the bat of an eyelid the weather can deteriorate dramatically. Some years previously another intrepid Englishman had attempted to cycle from Prudhoe Bay to Peru and got caught in a blizzard at the top of the Atigun Pass. The chap nearly got buried alive in the snow. I didn't want to repeat his mistake and the No.1 car kicked gravel as it accelerated away towards the north side of the pass. When I came to the gradient I immediately had to jam the brakes on. The car carried so much weight that it slid for fifteen feet down the gravel road before coming to rest inches from a crash barrier. Phew! this road was steep and demanded caution. We crawled down the north side of the pass in much the same way we had crawled up the south side.

Since leaving Calgary ten days previously, and weaving our way up through the Rocky Mountains, this was our fourth crossing of the continental divide. The difference this time was that nothing lay on the other side of the divide. I found myself in a narrow, desolate valley between sheer walls of barren rock. It looked like the dark side of the moon. This was reinforced by the silver pipeline, which had rejoined the road. The Trans- Alaska Pipeline didn't go over the high mountains, it went through them.

The road began a slow descent into a wide valley. The terrain was now covered with lichen and mosses and clumps of stunted grass. At this lower altitude the snow had turned to gently falling rain. Water fell from the surrounding cliff faces. Small streams joined bigger streams that became swiftly flowing rivers. Huge clouds rolled across the sky, their tops lit by sunlight, while beneath them were ever changing pockets of light and shade. The chilled air smelt of wet grass and with each breath filled the blood.

The Dalton Highway crossed the myriad of streams and rivers on small wooden bridges. Some of the bridges were in a bad state of repair, the wooden boards having rotted away. Beneath them the waters were brimming with arctic grayling. I saw what looked like a fox on the distant valley slope (Tom's Arctic Fox?), or maybe it was a wolf. Most fun of all, though, were the lemmings. These small rodents were everywhere. They would stand up on their hind legs and survey their surroundings. Sometimes you'd see three of them standing side by side like sentries. Unfortunately, the highway gave them a good vantage point. It was unfortunate because the lemmings didn't have very good road sense. I often had to brake or swerve to avoid them and despite the fact that there were swarms of the little blighters I didn't kill one single lemming. The 18-wheelers didn't have such qualms. There were splattered lemmings all along this part of the Dalton Highway.

Once out of the valley, and away from the bleak, bare mountains, the landscape became less harsh. We were now on the arctic tundra. This area, which stretches for more than a hundred miles north to the Arctic Ocean, is known as the North Slope. The subsoil beneath the tundra is permanently frozen. During the brief arctic summer the tundra becomes ablaze with brightly coloured wild flowers. It's also home to the Porcupine River caribou herd, which numbers 155,000 caribou. Sometimes on this part of the Dalton Highway you can be forced to wait for up to an hour as some of the herd meander across the road. On the North Slope you'll also find polar bears, muskoxen, wolves, foxes, moose and the occasional Citroen 2CV.

I didn't get to see many of the larger animals; after all, this *was* the first weekend of the hunting season and the wildlife has a kind of sixth sense when it comes to eating lead. Perversely, this meant that here on this most remote stretch of the Dalton there was more human activity than on the more travelled sections south of the mountains. The big macho men were out in their big macho four-wheel drives. Some of the hunters were dressed in combat fatigues and had gunk smeared on their faces. You'd see them stalking across the tundra, looking for something warm and furry to blow away. This hunting is strictly regulated by the U.S. Fish and Wildlife Service. The herds on the North Slope do need to be culled every year. However, it just didn't seem like cricket to me, after all, the animals weren't doing any harm. Almost everyone I met in Alaska was surprised that I did not take a gun with me into the wilderness. My attitude was that if you didn't bother the wildlife the wildlife wouldn't bother you.

It was time to refuel the car. A Citroen 2CV will do 200 miles on a full tank of fuel. It's 244 miles from Coldfoot to the Arctic Ocean, and there are no gas stations along the way - in fact, there's no nothing along the way. From among the junk in the back of the car I pulled out the 25 litre jerry can. While refueling I kept the car's engine running. In the Arctic I never, ever switched off the engine, except when I reached my destination for the day. I didn't want to risk the nightmare scenario of being unable to start the car again.

Not far away I could see one of the pipeline pump stations. It consisted of a large 3 storey structure that housed the workers and an adjoining pumphouse. What went on inside the pumphouse was kept hidden from the world. The pump station was ringed by a chain link fence and barbed wire. If you run into trouble on the Dalton Highway don't expect the people at the pump stations to help you. They have orders to radio for help, but not to lend any direct assistance. Almost 20% of America's oil comes from the Prudhoe Bay oilfields and all of it goes down the pipeline to Valdez. That pipeline is vital to America's economy and is patrolled by armed guards. It is rumoured that these guards have the authority to shoot to kill.

On that Sunday afternoon there were enough bullets flying around the North Slope as it was, so I steered well clear of the pump station. The Trans-Alaska Pipeline looked really ugly as it snaked across the bare tundra; a blot on the landscape. The National Environmental Protection Act is to blame, along with the environmentalists who lobbied for it while the pipeline was being designed. If the pipeline had been buried out of sight beneath the tundra it would have melted the permafrost (the oil is at a temperature of 140 degrees), causing irrecoverable damage to the ecosystem. Instead, it's mounted on insulated stilts to prevent the heat of the flowing oil from reaching the ground. However, on the North Slope some short sections of the pipeline do run underground (these underground sections are refrigerated in order to protect the permafrost). The reason for this is to allow the herds of migrating caribou to pass. But it turned out the that the caribou like scratching themselves on the support posts and enjoy ducking under the pipeline, the heat of the oil no doubt attracting them.

It wasn't just the caribou who were taken into consideration when the Trans-Alaska Pipeline was designed. Before construction began, studies were made as to where fish laid eggs and migrated among the 834 rivers and streams the pipeline would cross. Plans were adjusted so that construction works would not affect the rivers during the egg laying and migrations. One unavoidable aspect of the pipeline was that hundreds of miles of tundra would have to be destroyed, so immediately after construction they planted fast- growing seeds and plants from other parts of the Arctic to protect the land until the tundra grew back. Doesn't it all just make you want to put your arms around the planet earth and give it a hug?

The Dalton Highway gave a smooth ride across the tundra. I no longer needed every ounce of concentration to keep the car on the road and so I relaxed a bit. We were very close to our goal. You could smell sea salt in the freezing air. By way of an early celebration I cracked open a bottle of beer and drove with one hand on the wheel. By the time I was on my second bottle of beer the Arctic no longer looked so lonely and desolate. Even Jamie the Love Doll seemed relaxed. Or maybe it was a slow puncture.

I suddenly noticed something on the horizon. From a distance it looked like a moose or caribou. It came down the road directly towards me. I eased off on the gas pedal and peered through the windscreen. Hmm, it didn't move like a moose or caribou. A bear? Oh dear. I scrambled for the pepper spray on the parcel shelf. As the thing got nearer I was somewhat relieved when I could distinguish human features.

The 'thing' turned out to be a Japanese man. He seemed to be in his late teens and as he walked along he wore a determined look on his face. On his back he carried one of the biggest rucksacks I've ever seen. The top of the rucksack protruded at least 14 inches above the top of his head. The Japanese guy bowed under the weight of it. This is what made him look like some kind of animal from a distance.

We converged on each other and I stopped the car. The Japanese guy couldn't speak much English, but there again, I couldn't speak much Japanese. He told me his name was Kuji. I offered him a beer. He declined. I offered him a cigarette. He declined. In broken English, Kuji explained that he was on vacation and had flown up to the Arctic. He wanted to walk back to Fairbanks from Prudhoe Bay. What! or more to the point, why? I tried to explain to Kuji that Fairbanks was a long, long way away, but he didn't seem too worried about this. He had two weeks vacation and he could walk 500 kilometres in that time and 'get to see the wilderness'. No, Fairbanks was 500 *miles* from Prudhoe Bay, not 500 kilometres, and to leave the Arctic you had to cross over a desolate mountain range. Kuji didn't appear to understand the difference between miles and kilometres and had a laid-back attitude when it came to desolate mountain ranges. He produced a camera and asked me to take a picture of him standing beside the No.1 car. For the second or two while I took the picture, Kuji's face broke into a radiant smile, then it returned to a look of painful determination.

It felt very cold standing there on the side of the road. A brisk wind was blowing in off the Arctic Ocean and across the tundra. We were at least forty miles from Prudhoe Bay, so Kuji must have been walking for two days already. I wished him luck and told him to look out for the hunters further south. I had visions of him ending up as a display trophy on the wall of an Alaskan log cabin. Kuji and I shook hands, then I climbed back into the warm car and watched him disappear in the rear view mirror.

Low clouds hung on the grey horizon. Light snow sprinkled from the sky. The chill breeze got into the car and cut through my summer clothing. Hey, hadn't anyone told the weather we were in August? I zipped up my anorak and began supping on my third bottle of beer. Something that looked like a sprawling junk yard came into view. A sign on the side of the road said 'Deadhorse'. This was it, journey's end. We had driven almost 8000 miles from Savannah to reach this lonely place at the top of the world.

Deadhorse is the support town for the Prudhoe Bay oilfields. It's a white man's settlement, where the buildings are an ugly assembly of portacabins, prefabricated warehouses, workshop units and trailers plonked down on the flat tundra. Amidst the buildings there were storage tanks, cranes, containers, oil drums. The detritus of heavy industry lay everywhere. There are no streets or sidewalks, just a crisscross of dirt roads. The distant Arctic Ocean lay hidden by cloud. It was the sort of place where you could build a holiday camp for manic depressives, and make a profit. As far as The 2CV Alaska Challenge went, Deadhorse and Prudhoe Bay were purely symbolic: the 'challenge' had been successfully completed.

It would be nice to say that Deadhorse got its name after a gold prospector's horse dropped dead there, but that's not the case. The town is named after one of the companies who were involved in establishing the oilfields back in the 1970s, a shipping company that advertised its services with the slogan "we'd even ship a dead horse". Twenty-five people actually live in Deadhorse. Perhaps it's some kind of a dare. The rest of the population – which varies between 2000 and 5000 – work an average of two weeks on and two weeks off. That's about all non-native people can handle in this godforsaken place. The sun sets over Deadhorse on November 24th and does not rise again until January 18th. That's 54 days of subzero arctic darkness, or 1,300 hours to think about it all, with the screaming wind coming in straight off the ice caps.

Surprisingly, perhaps, Deadhorse and Prudhoe Bay are now firmly established on the Alaska tourist trail. Thing is, the planet Earth's extremes always attract people, however ugly those extremes are. A lot of these tourists also go to the southern tip of Chile. It's a kind of pole to pole thing. There's nothing much at the southern tip of Chile either, but you can say you've been there, you've done it. As far as

Prudhoe Bay goes, just about all of the tourists fly up from Fairbanks. A popular option is to then be driven back down the Dalton Highway in a tour coach. It's an expensive holiday and it's fun to watch these tourists arriving at the Prudhoe Bay airport. I'm not quite sure what they were expecting to find here on the shores of the Arctic Ocean, but one look at the surroundings nearly always makes their faces drop.

My arrival in Prudhoe Bay had a kind of symmetry to it. The 2CV Alaska Challenge began 2 months previously in Rotterdam, when the cars were loaded on to the *Marie Anne*. The *Marie Anne* is a working ship, heavy industry on the waves, and making a profit dictated her life. She is strictly functional, no frills, and is staffed by a crew of lonely men working in a harsh environment, the ocean. Here, at the end of the 2CV Alaska Challenge, Prudhoe Bay also existed only for profit, is strictly functional and is staffed by lonely men in a harsh environment, the Arctic.

There are two hotels in Deadhorse, The Arctic Caribou Inn and the Prudhoe Bay Hotel. Both establishments are subsidised by the oil companies and help to house the transient workforce of Prudhoe Bay. Tourists and independent travellers can also use the hotels. I pulled up in front of The Arctic Caribou Inn. The caribou-shaped sign hanging outside was the only pretty thing about the hotel. Other than that it was indistinguishable from the warehouse that stood beside it.

A coach had also just pulled up and a herd of tourists were making their way into the hotel. It was going to take ages for this mob to check in, so I walked across to the nearby post office. The Prudhoe Bay Post Office and General Store is about the only thing of interest in Deadhorse. They sell everything from two-foot-long beef jerky sticks to tiny inflatable sex dolls for the lonely oil workers. For ten bucks they'll also give you a signed certificate saying that you've driven the Dalton Highway to Prudhoe Bay. I didn't ask for a certificate. Parked outside was my mud splattered, beat-up car with British licence plates. That was all the proof I needed. The young guy behind the counter produced a piece of string and asked me to pull on it. I hesitated, but he urged me on and so I yanked the string. Suddenly a sign on a flap came down from the ceiling: PLEASE DO NOT PULL ON THIS STRING AGAIN. How we laughed. Well, there's not much else to make you laugh in Deadhorse.

The herd of tourists were still checking into the hotel, so I decided to head across town. Deadhorse is a small place; you can drive from one end of it to the other in a few minutes. The Prudhoe Bay Hotel is across from the airport terminal. It looked more like a network of old shipping containers than a hostelry. But beggars can't be choosers. I parked up and carried Jamie and my rucksack into the hotel lobby, where I was told a room would cost me 130 dollars. For a moment I considered sleeping in the car, but soon dismissed the idea. The only thing that could sooth the grimness of Deadhorse was a warm bed and a bottle of whiskey.

I got the warm bed but had to forgo the whiskey. Deadhorse is dry, like Coldfoot, like most arctic communities. Firearms are also banned. Deadhorse must be the only place in Alaska where you cannot carry a gun. You are, though, allowed to eat steaks that are the size of bathmats. The hotel restaurant stayed open 24 hours a day and was arranged canteen style, help-yourself. Meals were included in the price of the hotel room. The food was excellent, courtesy of oil company subsidies, and you could eat your fill. There's no cash register or staff keeping an eye on the place. Anyone unlucky enough to find themselves slumming it in Deadhorse could quite easily wander into one of the hotel restaurants and eat like a king, free of charge; but of course, I wouldn't sanction such dishonesty.

The diners in the restaurant were a curious mix of white and black collar workers. There were big roughneck guys who worked on the oil wells. Their testosterone bounced off the walls as they ripped into steaks. There were scientists, hunched over laptop computers, their fingers tapping away as they picked at their food. There were oil company men, who were more used to plush restaurants in Anchorage or Dallas; and then there were the tourists, who on that evening numbered just one: me.

After dinner I went back to my room on the first floor of the hotel. It was quite spacious by arctic standards. I drank the beer I'd bought in Fairbanks and wrote postcards and felt very, very lonely. I turned in early and as I drifted off to sleep I could hear a wolf howling out on the tundra. The howls were drowned out by the sound of a helicopter landing at the nearby airport. Soon I was having industrial dreams.

Deadhorse is actually ten miles from the Arctic Ocean and the Prudhoe Bay oilfields. The oil fields are strictly off limits to the general public, supposedly for reasons of security and visitor safety. There's a barrier across the road preventing access. If you want to drive your vehicle to the shore of the Arctic Ocean you have to get permission from the oil companies. The previous summer a group of people had driven a Rolls Royce Silver Shadow up to Prudhoe Bay. They were well taken care of by British Petroleum, who allowed them through to the ocean beach for that 'must get' photograph. For more than a year I had been trying to get permission to take the No.1 car through to the Arctic Ocean. My requests were met with a wall of silence. If only one of those North Slope oil companies had been French owned.

If you have the urge, tourists are allowed to visit the ocean beach, but you have to do it on an official tour of the oilfields. These tours cost 60 bucks and leave daily from the two hotels in Deadhorse. The tour guide will tell you that Prudhoe Bay encompasses 350 square miles, has nine main drilling pads with 36 to 42 rigs per pad, and is being worked by 11 companies, etc, etc... I gave the tour a miss.

The woman behind the reception desk spoke with a Texan drawl and sported a blue rinse. She wasn't surprised that I was checking out of the hotel after just one night. No one stayed in Deadhorse for long if they could help it. In fact, such was the grim reality of drilling for oil in the Arctic that many tourists only spend an hour or two in Deadhorse before going back down the Dalton Highway or heading for the airport. Blue rinse told me that she had a home down in Fairbanks and during her stints working in Deadhorse she never left the hotel complex. She came to Alaska with her husband during the job boon created in the 1970s by the construction of the Trans-Alaska Pipeline. Back then there were so many people heading for Alaska in the hope of earning big bucks that the state government put ads in the newspapers telling folks not to come.

On the wall of the hotel reception there was a display. It showed photos of various polar bears that had wandered into Deadhorse. One bear was shown in the hotel's parking lot; another going through the garbage bins. The purpose of this display was to warn hotel guests about polar bears. They are not like grizzly or black bears. You can't get near them, and you most definitely must not try to hand feed them. Polar bears are tough muthers who live in a tough environment. They are probably the most solitary creatures on the planet, spending months on their own out on the pack ice hunting for seals. Polar bears can run a two-minute mile - ie, they can easily outrun a human being. They can swim 60 miles without pausing. They are strong enough to hoist from the water a beluga whale several times their own weight... you don't mess with polar bears, which are the world's largest land carnivore.

During October and November many female polar bears come to Alaska's North Slope to build dens and give birth to their young. Many others congregate along the coast of the North Slope. The brief arctic summer, with its rich abundance of wildlife, also attracts the bears as a food source. During this period the pack ice melts for 60 miles off shore and seal hunting becomes difficult. The few scattered outposts of human civilisation invariably attract polar bears. Garbage bins are an easy food source. Throughout most of the year, though, you'll find the polar bears out on the pack ice. Their tracks and droppings have even been found a few miles from the North Pole itself. When you're in the Arctic you are in the kingdom of the polar bear. The place even takes his name - arktos is Greek for bear.

I felt a wonderful sense of freedom as I said adios to Deadhorse (I resolved that the next time one of my enemies had a birthday coming up I would buy them a two week package tour to Deadhorse). For the last few months I'd been incredibly focused on the 2CV Alaska Challenge. Now it was done and dusted. Now I no longer had a duty to perform and felt like a free man. I'd written two bulletins covering the journey up the Dalton Highway, which I would send once I got back down to Fairbanks. However, I still didn't have that 'must get' photograph of the No.1 car on the shore of the Arctic Ocean. The oil companies wouldn't allow me to reach the shoreline, so the ocean would have to come to me instead. Deadhorse is located beside a number of creeks that are like fingers of the Arctic Ocean poking inland. I choose the widest of the creeks and parked the car on its bank. It looked just like the ocean shoreline and captured the desolation of the Arctic perfectly.

Standing there with my camera on the side of that creek I had my first encounter with the natives (who really don't like being called Eskimos). There were two of them, on one of those three-wheeled rough terrain motorbikes. The pillion rider had a rifle slung over his shoulder. The Inuit chaps stopped a little distance from me, curious at what I was doing. I gave a wave which they returned with nods. I would have loved to get a photograph of them standing beside the No.1 car, they didn't want to oblige, though. The natives were friendly enough, but an invisible barrier lay between us. I was a white man. The Inuit have mixed feelings about white men.

Prior to the discovery of oil on the North Slope, the Inuit lived a subsistence lifestyle and were among the poorest people in America. In 1664 the Dutch bought Manhattan Island from the Indians for $24 worth of beads and trinkets. That little stunt wasn't repeated in 20th century Alaska, where the Alaska Native Land Claims Settlement Act was passed. This Act gave the Inuit (who in this part of Alaska number not much more than six thousand souls) one billion dollars and lots of other easy money. In the blink of an eye the Inuit were transported from the stone age to the space age and found their pockets stuffed with cash. This has completely changed their lifestyle and has had a disastrous effect on the fabric of their society. The downward spiral of the Inuit has been further exacerbated by their penchant for booze. It's often said that half of them are practising alcoholics, the other half are potential alcoholics. A lot of Inuit communities vote themselves dry and thus bootleggers make a killing - a pint of whiskey which costs $10 in Fairbanks can be sold for $150 in a dry village. Alcoholism of course brings violence, sexual abuse, family break up and depression. The suicide rate among native Indians - particularly young men - is 125 times the national average.

It sure felt good to be driving south back across the tundra. Just a day or so previously, the journey up from Fairbanks had been a case of confronting fear of the unknown. The return journey was a less tense and much more enjoyable affair. The tundra now seemed much more familiar and friendly. This arctic wilderness is part of the North Slope

Borough, the largest local government region in the United States. It stretches from the Bering Sea in the west all the way across the top of Alaska to the Canadian border in the east. That's 90,000 square miles of wilderness, about the same size as the United Kingdom, yet there are only 6,600 people knocking about in this vast space, almost all of them Inuit Indians, and the only road which goes anywhere is the Dalton Highway.

However, this seems set to change: the tundra I was driving across contains more than just flora and fauna. Texas tea lays beneath the frozen ground. Many geologists believe that the reserves beneath the North Slope are even bigger than those found at Prudhoe Bay. Drilling for oil on the North Slope will mean hundreds of miles of new roads and pipelines, a lot of airports and production facilities, living quarters for thousands of workers, etc, etc... in otherwords it will mean a whole lot of damage to the pristine arctic wilderness. Oil exploration on the North Slope continues to be a very contentious issue, and it's one the environmentalists seem likely to lose because of America's insatiable thirst for oil.

The United States has consumed more energy per capita than any other society in human history, and it remains the world's leading energy consumer (and has to import almost half of its oil to meet demand). In 1990, a North American was using twice as much energy as a European and ten times as much as the average Latin American. A North American family of four consumed as much as an African village of 107 people. The United Nations Environmental Programme estimates that by 2015 these inequalities will worsen to the point where the average American family will demand as much energy as 127 Africans or 42 Latin Americans. But don't worry, folks, a recent prominent study estimated that there are still 6 trillion barrels of recoverable oil on the planet earth, which at present rates of consumption will last for another 230 years (note: estimates of world oil reserves vary widely. Worse case studies say that we'll be out of oil by 2050). We'll let the Americans worry about what's going to happen once those 6 trillion barrels of oil have run out; after all, they're the ones who are gulping up most of it.

The Brooks Mountain Range continued to look extremely foreboding. It would be a perfect setting for a wicked witch's castle, flying monkeys and all. I thought of Kuji with his huge rucksack. We should have passed him somewhere out on the tundra, but he was nowhere to be seen. I assumed that he'd hitched a lift with some of the hunters, or else the wicked witch had got him. The climb up the north side of the Atigun Pass had much kinder gradients than the climb up the south side. Nevertheless, as we reached the summit the smell of burning oil and an overheated engine filled the car. Jamie and I decided not to go dancing again because this time round it was snowing more heavily. Instead we sat in the car for a while, at the top of the world, gazing out at the pristine wilderness, which in reality is not quite as pristine as it looks.

The Brooks Mountains not only mark the start of the real arctic, they also help shield the rest of Alaska from pollution. The Russians are largely to blame. In Norilsk in central Siberia there is a huge complex of smelters which pump more than two million tons of sulphur and other muck into the air each year. Norilsk is probably the largest single source of air pollution in the world, and North America is downwind of it. Antarctica has its hole in the ozone layer; the Arctic has a huge pollution haze which hangs over it for most of the winter and spring.

The Arctic's neighbours from hell also have a penchant for dumping radioactive waste. Effluent from the Chelyabinsk nuclear-weapons factory was chucked into the River Techa, from where it ended up in the Arctic Ocean. Nuclear testing at Novaya Zemlya during the 1950s also contributed to radiation levels in the Arctic. Between 1964 and 1986, some 7,000 tons of solid radioactive waste and 1,600 cubic meters of liquid waste were dumped into the Kara and Barents Seas from the naval base in Murmansk, which serviced the Soviet fleet. Likewise, nuclear reactors from at least 18 nuclear submarines and icebreakers were dumped in the Barents sea, and an entire nuclear sub was deliberately sunk after an accident in May 1968. Another nuclear submarine, the Komsomolets, sank 300 miles off Norway with the loss of 42 sailors. It went down with two nuclear warheads. Jeez, it's a wonder the arctic seals don't glow in the dark. In fact, in 1992 the seals in the White and Barents Sea were found to be dying from blood cancer; and earlier, in 1990, six million starfish, shellfish, seals, and porpoises washed up dead on the shores of the White Sea, while the area's natural fish population migrated away, presumably to purchase some geiger counters.

It's a mistake to think of the Arctic as a clean, crisp, happy kind of place, because it's not. Yet despite the problems the Indians have, and the pollution, and the exploitation of its natural resources, the Arctic is a very special place, it makes one feel humble, and as I drove down the south side of the Atigun Pass I felt sad to be leaving it. Jamie, of course, was very silent.

Back in Coldfoot again, my funds were starting to run low. One hundred and twenty bucks for a room at the Slate Creek Inn now seemed rather expensive. I decided to sleep in the car and found a quiet spot round the back of the hotel where I parked-up for the night. I walked across to the truckstop for a bite to eat. A coach-load of tourists were also eating there. Some entertainment was laid on for them in the form of a guy telling jokes and an Indian girl with a guitar singing songs. It was the same Indian girl who'd played at Arizona Joe's party.

After some rubber chicken I returned to the car and drank a bottle of beer. I contemplated unloading the car, so that I could stretch out in the back and sleep. It would take the best part of an hour to unload all the junk from the back of the car, and it would all have to be reloaded in the morning. I dismissed the idea and instead was faced with the prospect of sleeping on the front seats of a Citroen 2CV, a space some four and a half feet by two and a half feet, with the steering wheel jutting into it. I remained fully dressed and kept my coat on. The blanket I wrapped around myself to help keep out the cold made things difficult as I twisted and turned, trying to find a more comfortable position. Finally I discovered that sitting half slumped in the passenger seat afforded the most comfort. Deep sleep was still impossible in that position. I dozed as the night air caressed my face and tried to suck the warmth from my body.

At just after 4am I gave up the idea of a good night's sleep. I drove round to the truckstop and sat in blissful warmth and drank hot coffee. I didn't linger long. Dawn would be arriving on the scene soon and I wanted to be on the road before then. It would be fun to drive the Dalton Highway in the dark. So, with the headlights at full beam, and the fog lamps blazing, I pulled away from Coldfoot and headed south.

I soon discovered that the array of powerful lights on the front of the car made driving difficult. It produced a glare from the surrounding rocks and trees. With the fog lamps switched off, and the headlights at half beam, it was much easier to see the lie of the land. The darkness also softened the Dalton Highway. Two days previously I had cautiously crawled along this stretch of the Dalton. Now, such was my confidence that I really motored along, riding the bumps and potholes and slinging the car around sharp bends into pitch darkness. I'd got lighting cigarettes down to a fine art. Jamie was strapped in with the seat belt and no longer slumped down off the passenger seat. Every so often I saw red eyes by the side of the highway. I briefly switched on the fog lamps to scare away the wildlife before the careering car got to them.

With a screech of brakes and a cloud of dust I pulled into the lay-by at the Arctic Circle. Dawn was just breaking. There's a big sign in the lay-by that says 'Arctic Circle', giving the latitude and an aerial view of the earth from above the North Pole. I wanted to get my picture taken next to this sign, more to prove to myself that I had actually done it, that these last days hadn't been a dream and I'd really driven a Citroen 2CV up the Dalton to the Arctic Ocean.

There were some camper vans parked in the lay-by. Latitude 66° 32' is a popular place. If you built a hotel here you could make a killing. No doubt someday somebody will. My noisy arrival disturbed some of the sleepers. A light came on in one of the camper vans. I went over and knocked loudly on the door. The door opened and a dazed man stood there. His hair was ruffled. He rubbed sleep from his eyes. He agreed to take my picture and disappeared into the camper van to find his boots. The guy still seemed half asleep when I handed him my camera. There was enough light now to get a shot without using the flash. Jamie and I stood in front of the sign. I had a blanket wrapped around me to keep out the cold. Our picture was taken for posterity. The guy staggered back to his camper van without saying a word.

It was the final day of August. The last vestiges of night were swept away and when we reached the Yukon river crossing the sky was a brilliant blue with the promise of a beautiful summer's day to come. I tanked-up with gas and then went over to the hotel for some breakfast. A big husky dog lounged on the porch of the hotel. It barked furiously as I approached. I said the usual things that one says to aggressive dogs. The beast stood defiantly on the porch and blocked my path. It's teeth looked sharp enough to cut steel. Hair bristled on the back of its neck. It's huge paws stamped the ground. Its half erect penis dripped fluid. Brilliant, after actually making it up the Dalton and back I was now going to get mauled by a randy husky dog.

The door creaked and an elderly woman came out of the hotel: "down Timmy, don't go bothering the Englishman'. I followed her into the hotel. The restaurant stank of the adjoining washrooms. I was the only person in the place. The elderly woman cooked a fry-up for me. She also placed a plate of gruel on the floor beside my table. The Husky dog ate with me and finished its food only marginally quicker than I finished mine. Afterwards it licked its balls.

On the sixty mile drive down to Livengood I had to take things at an easier pace. Now that daylight had come there was traffic out on the Dalton Highway: eighteen-wheelers, tour coaches and hunters. There was also a guy on a motorbike. We pulled-up nose to nose, a battered Citroen 2CV and a beautiful gleaming Harley Davidson. We'd seen quite a few Harleys on the drive across North America. The legend of the *Wild Ones* lives on. We soon discovered, though, that these Harleys were all driven by respectable middle- aged people. They were the only ones who could afford a Harley Davidson motorcycle.

This particular Harley rider was quite young, though. He looked to be in his early thirties and wore black leathers and a German soldier helmet. The cool image was somewhat offset by the fact that he was quite podgy; well, he was an American. The motorcyclist's name was Sam. He came from Austin, Texas. Sam told me that he woke up one morning and just felt the urge to travel. He wanted to hit the open road and go as far as you can, which in North America is Prudhoe

Bay. He'd been on the road for a week now and planned to reach Prudhoe Bay that evening. I gave Sam as much useful information as I could about the drive north, then asked him what he was going to do when he reached the end of the road. It was an obvious question, the same one that people had been asking me for weeks. Sam came up with much the same answer as I: he didn't really know what he was going to do when he got to Prudhoe Bay. By taking off on a whim he would have lost his job in Austin. Getting to Alaska had blown most of his money, and he didn't know anyone in the state. However, if worse came to worse he was sitting astride a motorcycle that was worth twenty thousand dollars. I looked across at the No.1 car. Hmm...

Sam and I went our separate ways. The Harley north, the Citroen south. I envied him. He was about to discover the Arctic for the first time, although I was not quite sure what Sam would make of Deadhorse.

I got to Livengood at lunchtime and stopped at the bend in the road where the Dalton Highway left Highway 70. I'd done it, or more precisely, that incredible little car had done it, all the way up the Dalton and back. I felt a tremendous sense of achievement. There was no one else around to share my jubilation so Jamie and I danced around in the middle of the dusty road. I glanced over at the signs: 'ALL VEHICLES DRIVE WITH LIGHTS ON FOR NEXT 425 MILES'. 'NO SERVICES FOR NEXT 100 MILES'. 'YOU ARE LEAVING 911 AREA'. 'CAUTION: HEAVY INDUSTRIAL VEHICLES USE THIS HIGHWAY'. Huh, been there, seen it, done it. At that point there was a blast on a horn. A huge 18-wheeler came thundering down the road. Jamie and I had to quickly step out of the way. Gravel rained down. We choked on a cloud of dust. The truck did not pause at the junction and continued on down Highway 70 to Fairbanks. It must have left Coldfoot shortly after me and been on my tail ever since.

I dusted myself down and climbed back into the car. When I switched on the car radio someone tried to sell me life insurance. Stunned at this reminder that I was almost back in civilisation, I followed the 18-wheeler down Highway 70 and began singing *Wanderin' Star*. It seemed like an appropriate thing to do. The caribou and the bears seemed to be humming along.

One hour later the bumps, pot holes and ridges gave way to smooth tarmac. After four days of spine-jarring driving the sensation was incredible. The car no longer shook and rattled violently. It went in the direction you steered. Signs appeared. Roads led off in other directions. Log cabins began to dot the landscape. A gas station whizzed by. There were advertising hoardings. A set of traffic lights. A shopping mall. I was back in Fairbanks.

Chapter 5 - Wilderness Blues

When a man's tired of Fairbanks he's tired of life. Well, I had no problem with either Fairbanks or life, but I was dog tired. I checked into the Days Inn on Airport Way. It was early afternoon. I had a quick shower and then went to bed. The bed seemed incredibly large, incredibly soft and incredibly comfortable. Within minutes I was asleep. My dreams were confused, weary and arctic white.

The Arctic had been an interesting experience. Alaska is one of the few places in the world where you can actually drive up to such a high latitude: Prudhoe Bay, 300 miles north of the Arctic Circle and almost 500 miles north of Fairbanks. Ok, Prudhoe Bay's a dump, but that drive up to the Arctic Ocean is not so much about a place but more a concept. You can say: "I've done it!"

My finances were starting to run low so I only stayed one night in the hotel. The next day, which was Wednesday 1st September, I rang Guy Douglas. Guy congratulated me on the successful trip up to the Arctic and said sure, I could stay at his place for a while. Guy and his wife Lynn lived in a cabin on the outskirts of Fairbanks. It was a hard place to find so Guy told me to meet him downtown.

I had made no firm plans about what to do after the 2CV Alaska Challenge, because I had no idea if a Citroen 2CV would survive an 8,000 mile road journey, the final part of which was on dirt and gravel roads. The car might have developed serious mechanical problems along the way, which would have cost big bucks to get fixed and swallowed-up my budget. Or it might have got completely wrecked in the arctic wilderness, ending the 2CV Alaska Challenge completely. Or it might have been abducted by aliens. When Jose and I left Savannah, in the southern States, at the end of July these things were imponderables. All I knew was that I wanted to stay on in North America for the winter and write a book about the trip; and if the opportunity arose, I planned to do this in Alaska. Well, that opportunity had now arrived. The car was still in one piece, in fact it drove better than ever, and I still had a little bit of money in my pocket.

I met Guy in the car park of the *Fairbanks Daily Miner*. Guy walked slowly around the No.1 car and whistled. I suppose it did look a bit of a state. The car had so much mud plastered across it that you could no longer read the company sponsorship banners. One of the headlights was smashed. The windshield was cracked. The exhaust pipe was hanging off. Despite the mess it was still an incredible little car, though.

Guy dragged me into the newspaper office, where he appeared to be on first name terms with everyone, including the Features Editor. I was asked the usual questions then we all went back out to the car park, where I had my picture taken standing beside the No.1 car. For once, my still-unfixed teeth seemed to fit in well with the battered car and the story of the trip up to the Arctic. Next stop was the radio station, where Guy used to work. A crowd of people came out to look at me and the car. I was beginning to feel like a zoo specimen and felt somewhat relieved when we finally headed out to Guy's place.

In 1999 you could rent or buy log cabins in Fairbanks really cheaply. It might sound like a nice concept, but most of these cabins on the outskirts of Fairbanks have no electricity or mains drainage. It's real pioneer living. Guy's cabin was spacious, with two storeys and a large basement. It had both plumbing and electricity. It also had five cats, who immediately attached themselves to me. Guy's wife, Lynn, made us a cup of tea. It was all very British. Ex-pat land.

They call Fairbanks the Sump. This is because it has a history of attracting weird and wonderful characters, square pegs who don't fit in anywhere else. This stems from the gold rush days, when the city was founded. In 1999, Fairbanks was still young and growing. The decrepit downtown area was being redeveloped and for such a small city there was a large amount of building work going on. It's a place where you can do very well and make lots of money if you're prepared to work. But that kinda sums up Alaska as a whole, America's last frontier, a land where you can still go and make your mark in a world that is becoming increasingly bland; and I had it all handed to me on a plate: Guy knew a chap who owned a cabin nearby. I could have the cabin for the winter, rent free. Guy knew a builder who was looking for casual labour, and would employ me cash in hand. Guy had given me his friendship, and that of the people he knew. It was all there for the taking. I could spend the winter in Fairbanks, earn some money and write a book about the 2CV Alaska Challenge.

But, but... well, after travelling nonstop for the previous two months I found it difficult to stay still. The momentum of a big journey is hard to dispel. You feel the urge to keep moving all the time; you can't seem to stop yourself. The 2CV Alaska Challenge was over, yet I saw no reason why it should be over for me as well. Using Guy's computer I sent off the Alaska Challenge arctic bulletins. I noticed that Tony still hadn't put up the charity sponsorship form on the web site. It was done and dusted now, but I still e-mailed him a reminder, just for the sake of it. I spent three nights on Guy and Lynn's sofa, with the cats jumping on me all night, then I made the decision to move on. I would head down to Vancouver Island and write the book there. In retrospect this was a big mistake.

On the morning of Friday 3rd September, Guy and Lynn took me for breakfast at a downtown Denny's Restaurant. Afterwards we shook hands and I bid the two of them farewell. As always, it felt great to be back on the road again. The No.1 car was still a mess as far as its appearance went, however, the engine ate-up the miles as we bowled south east on the Richardson Highway. By lunchtime I was back in Delta Junction, where I called in at the town hall and said 'hi' to Barbara. The girls in the office congratulated me on the successful trip up to the arctic. I was beginning to feel like a bit of a plum; after all, it wasn't as though I'd been to the North Pole or anything like that. But there again, I took a look at that little French car parked outside the town hall.

The Alaska Highway seemed like an old friend. That evening found me in Beaver Creek. It felt good to be back on Canadian soil again (yeah I know, I'm a sentimental fool). The girl at the Westmark Hotel reception desk remembered me from before. She asked where Jose was. Just for fun I told her that Jose had run off with a dog musher in Fairbanks. The girl acted as though this was a normal occurrence in these parts. She wasn't too sympathetic when I tried to wangle a discount and I ended up with a tiny box that cost $80 per night. It was the cheapest room they had.

Things were winding down at the Westmark. The Yukon Review gave its final performance that evening, the Westmark's last night of operation before it closed down for the winter. The tourist season is short in these parts. I had a steak in the hotel bar, surrounded by members of the Yukon Review cast. It was all goodbyes and summer memories and promises to keep in touch. Most of the cast came from metropolitan areas in eastern Canada and it had been their first time in the wilderness. Many of them were young kids. They'd just had an adventure summer entertaining American tourists in the middle of nowhere. They'd just had the time of their lives and were now getting emotional. I didn't belong here.

The next morning I tanked up at Beaver-Creek's one-and-only gas station. As I drove back on to the Alaska Highway someone tooted me from behind. In the rear view mirror I could see bull bars on the front of a 4WD. I pulled over and got out the car. Parked behind me was a Toyota Landcruiser. The Landcruiser was plastered with the banners of company sponsors. Well, well: it was the only other vehicle I came across in the wilderness which also had company sponsorship. I just had to meet whoever was behind the wheel.

The driver turned out to be a guy called Greg, from Boston. 28 years old, tall, slim and dark haired. Greg seemed like a nice fellow. We both spoke at once in attempt to find out what the other was doing. We were both on an adventure, we both had an insatiable curiosity about what lay over the next hill, and we both had other people's money to burn. Greg's little jaunt was called 'East to Alaska'. I couldn't figure that one out, since surely you have to go west to get to Alaska? Greg started explaining the concept behind this label and I soon came to the conclusion that he was madder than me. My Alaska Challenge thing had been successfully completed. Greg, however, had suffered some misfortune on his trip.

Like me, Greg had a web site for his adventure journey, which he promoted as "a 10,000-mile, one man, one dog expedition from Boston to the Bearing Sea." His web site says: "East to Alaska will share with the public a new vision of a distant place, and seed thoughts of distant adventure." Greg also did documentary radio pieces to help spread his message: *"the mystery of Alaska is one that is shared by all Americans, a mystery so large that even today has yet to be cracked. The radio will allow the time to begin the slow access to learning about the large giant, and instill a respect in the listener which the state demands."* Well, I must admit I still found myself a bit stumped by it all. We stood on the roadside in Beaver Creek and Greg told me his story.

Greg and his dog Norman, a 2 ½ year old labrador, began their trip on 4th July in Hingham, Massachusetts (by strange coincidence it was also on 4th July when the *Marie Anne* set sail from Rotterdam). It took them one week to drive up to Alaska, where they spent a further three weeks driving around the state. Their ultimate destination was Prudhoe Bay. However, they only got as far as Livengood, just 80 miles north of Fairbanks, where tragedy struck. Greg came across a pick-up truck with a flat tire and stopped to lend a hand. Norman the dog got loose. At that moment an 18-wheeler came hurtling round the corner and hit the dog. The 18-wheeler didn't stop. Norman was still alive and ran off into the woods. Greg spent 11 hours searching for him, without success. He spent that night camped on the side of the road. The weather began to deteriorate. Greg saw a pair of grey wolves and grizzly tracks. He figured that Norman the dog was doomed. Brokenhearted, Greg abandoned his drive up to Prudhoe Bay and headed back home.

And that's when I met him, a few days later in Beaver Creek. The guy was still beside himself over the loss of his dog. It was obvious that he and Norman had been soul mates. However, I later discovered that this story had a happy ending. Six weeks after the incident at Livengood an emancipated dog was found on the Dalton Highway. Yup, you've guessed it, Norman the labrador. Norman was in pretty bad shape, with a nasty leg wound and a fractured toe. Norman was taken down to the animal shelter in Fairbanks, where they were surprised to see a Massachusetts telephone number on his dog collar. Here's how the *Fairbanks Daily Miner* reported the story:

The number on Norman's tag led to a voice-mail box. The shelter worker dictated a message with no certainty she'd ever receive a response. The shelter heard back from Gregory J. Hren within minutes of opening Tuesday. Gregory was astonished and overjoyed to hear of Norman's survival, six weeks after the dog was injured and lost in the wild. "It's an amazing story," Hren said Wednesday, in a telephone interview from his home in Boston.

For 200 miles Greg and I headed along the Yukon stretch of the Alaska Highway. We kind of shadowed each other. Greg's landcruiser was much faster than my overloaded 2CV, but Greg stopped often to take photographs, giving me the chance to overtake him. The No.1 car bowled along the highway. Despite the incredible journey she'd done from Savannah, and despite the battering sustained up in the Arctic, this car was still raring to go. She loved these wilderness roads and was queen of the Yukon. I resolved that when it was all over, and the time came to finally return home, I would somehow, by hook or by crook, take the *Yukon Queen* with me back to the United Kingdom.

At Haines Junction I gave Greg a final toot and a wave. The brokenhearted Bostonian was heading all the way back down the Alaska Highway to Dawson Creek. I had no desire to cover old ground. It was still a four day drive to Dawson Creek. Fortunately, there's an alternative way to get back down south: the Alaska Marine Highway.

The Alaska Marine Highway is a state run ferry system. It provides services both in the Gulf of Alaska and the Inside Passage. The Inside Passage services are the most popular route, as this connects Alaska with the lower 48 states. Skagway and Haines are at the northern end of the system. From here it's a 1000 mile voyage south through the Inside Passage, a wonderland of pristine waters, towering glaciers and untouched forests, to Bellingham on the US/Canada border. Seattle and Vancouver are a short drive from Bellingham.
It takes three days to make the voyage from Haines down to Bellingham. The cost for myself and the car would be well over $500. It was worth it, though. Driving down south would take almost a week, and then there would also be the cost of fuel, food and accommodation. Besides, the Alaska Marine Highway route through the Inside Passage had always been on my list of things to do.

The Haines Highway runs from its junction with the Alaska Highway for 152 miles to the town of Haines on the coast. Haines is in Alaska, Haines Junction is in the Yukon and the Haines Highway runs through British Columbia as it joins the two. Confusing, isn't it. This part of the world makes you wonder what the map makers were on when they drew up the borders. The south east part of Alaska occupies a narrow strip of the coast and its islands. It runs down from the main part of the state for nearly six hundred miles, biting into half of British Columbia's coastline. South east Alaska is known as the panhandle, because on a map it looks like the handle of a pan, the pan being the main bulk of Alaska. Only Haines and Skagway in the north of the panhandle, and Hyder in the south, can be reached by road. The impenetrable Coast Mountains block off the other panhandle communities from the rest of the world. These communities can only be reached by boat and plane, including Juneau, which is the state capital of Alaska and the only state capital in the US that cannot be reached by road. I figured you just needed to know that.

The panhandle caused one of the most serious disputes ever between Canada and the US, and a lot of it was the fault of the sneaky Russians. The borders of Alaska were agreed between Russia and Britain in 1825. This gave most of the west coast of what is now British Columbia to the British, as common sense would dictate. However, when America purchased Alaska in 1867 the Russian territorial maps showed most of the west coast as belonging to Alaska, thereby just about excluding Canada from the Pacific Ocean. That same year the British granted Canada nationhood. The Canadians, naturally enough, wanted their coastline back, and so a commission of three Americans, two Canadians and one Brit was set-up to decide on the matter. After three weeks of discussion and pouring over every document that was relevant to the dispute, the tribunal voted in favor of the US by four to two. The modern day south east Alaska border was established on paper, swallowing up half the Canadian coastline. The deciding vote came from Baron Alverstone, the British member of the tribunal, leaving the Canadians mightily pissed-off over what they viewed as a betrayal by the British.

You can overdose on spectacular scenery in these parts, yet the

Haines Highway still won't disappoint. Boreal forests, high mountain peaks, glaciers, rivers, lakes, you name it and you'll see it along the Haines Highway. To the west of the highway is a vast expanse of mountain wilderness, home of the "glacier bear," a rare form of black bear that has smoky-blue fur. Well, I suppose the glacier bear has got to live somewhere, and condos are so expensive.

After nearly three hours driving through this wonderland we reached the summit of Three Guardsmen Pass. On the other side of Three Guardsmen Pass the Haines Highway descended steadily into a lush coastal forest. Halfway down the grade were the Canadian and US Customs posts. I was back in Alaska again, but only because of cheating Russian map makers and traitorous Brits.

On the Alaskan side of the border there were road works. The Haines Highway was undergoing major repairs and every few miles or so a flagman controlled the traffic. It was rough going and after clearing the last of the stretches of road works we were following the flats of the Chilkat river; and that's when I got a puncture. It was the first flat tyre on the trip. The rear on the driver's side was the casualty. I glanced at the mileometer and did a quick calculation. The *Yukon Queen* had travelled more than 10,000 miles from Savannah, over some of the roughest roads in North America, until here, in this beautiful spot, she finally needed use of one of the six spare wheels we'd brought along with us.

Certainly a beautiful spot, but it was also probably the worst place to have to change a wheel. Most of the valley floor was taken up by the broad flats of the Chilkat river. On either side were very steep hills that in the west rose to the Takhinsha Mountains. The road clung to the side of the valley. It was narrow. There was nowhere to pull off the road.

I switched on the hazard warning lights. They didn't work; the pounding up in the Arctic had seen to that. The Haines Highway is one of the main routes from the ferries to the Alaskan interior. There was quite a lot of traffic about. To safely jack up the car I would have to remove its contents, but there wasn't anywhere to put a gearbox, suspension arms, six spare tyres, etc, etc. On one side of the road lay the fast flowing Chilkat river, on the other side a rock wall.

I lit-up a cigarette and watched an eagle hovering high above the valley. The Chilkat river is fed by underwater springs that keep it at a constant 40 degrees fahrenheit. The warm water keeps sections of the river ice-free during the early winter and supports a late run of chum salmon. Eagles migrate here from all over the north west to feast on the salmon. Nowhere else in the world do eagles gather in such numbers. Of course, I was back in Alaska, the land of superlatives.

There seemed no choice. To unload all the spare parts from the car and lay them out in the road would present too much danger to other traffic. Due to the peculiar suspension on a 2CV they are extremely difficult to jack up when fully loaded. The car is so near to the ground that you have to lift it twice as much as you would with an unloaded 2CV. I found two flat rocks and put them under the car. I then placed the hydraulic jack on the rocks, hoping they'd give me the extra lift required. I began pumping on the jack and wished I hadn't just had a cigarette. After five minutes the drivers side of the car sat so high off the ground it looked like the car was going to topple over, but the rear punctured tyre was just above the road surface. I grabbed the tyre spanner. At that moment I heard an almighty crack and the car dropped back a short distance. The head of the jack had gone through the underside of the car, but the thicker part of the jack arm beneath the head still held the car up. I decided to risk continuing and began pumping again. This time there were no further relapses and as quickly as possible I put the spare wheel on. Now, the moment of crisis: - as I released air from the jack, and the car began lowering to the ground, would the damaged chassis give way when the full weight of the car rested on the ground..? No, it settled down quite comfortably without any ominous creaks or cracks. I could get moving again. Haines lay just short distance down the road and it was early evening as I rolled into town.

Haines sits on a narrow peninsula between Lynn Canal and Chilkat Inlet at a spot known to the Tlingits as Dei shu or "the end of the trail". Two principle bands of Tlingits inhabited this area, the Chilkat (translated as "basket of many fish") who inhabited the valley to the north, and the Chilkoot ("basket of large fish") who lived to the east along Lynn Canal. The Tlingits had quite an advanced culture, based on fishing for salmon and trading seashells and eulachon oil inland for furs, hides, and meat. They lived in large dwellings made of cedar planks and were renowned for their artistic abilities, which included totem poles, intricately patterned baskets and the distinctive Chilkat blankets.

Explorer George Vancouver was one of the first Europeans to visit this area. He named the deep fjord east of town Lynn Canal, after his home port of King's Lynn in England. In 1879 the Chilkats invited naturalist John Muir and Presbyterian minister S. Hall Young to establish a mission and school at the current site of Haines. The settlement soon grew, with clapboard Victorian houses and tidy, fenced yards. Nowadays it's the venue for the Southeast Alaska State Fair and Music Festival, which is held each August. You can sometimes see humpback and killer whales in the deep waters of Lynn Canal.

Yup, Haines looked a real dandy place, yet I drove straight on through to the ferry terminal, which was a few miles further up the Lynn Canal. I then received the bad news: an extremely pleasant young lady behind a sheet of glass told me that all the southbound ferries were booked solid. Well, how solid is solid, I asked? She tapped away at her computer terminal and frowned. The next available space for a car going south was in eight days time. By way of an apology she told me that next week the tourist season was almost over and there'd be more space on the ferries.

Beautiful as Haines is, I couldn't afford to spend eight days there. Hmm... maybe I could spend the winter in Haines, and get my masterpiece written? I pondered on this idea, but not for long. Haines is a very small town and with the tourist season over it seemed an unlikely place to find work for a down-on-his-luck Englishman without a work permit. If I was going to stay on in North America for the winter I needed to earn some money. I'd left the golden opportunity for this behind in Fairbanks. Therefore I needed to head down south, back to civilisation and a job market.

I'd spent the best part of the day driving down the Haines Highway, and spectacular as the scenery was, I had no desire to spend most of tomorrow driving back up it. I consulted a big area map on the wall of the ferry terminal. Skagway seemed to be the answer, just ten miles further up at the end of the Lynn Canal. From Skagway I could drive back to the Alaska Highway, thereby saving hundreds of road miles.

The pleasant young girl said there'd be no problem taking the ferry to Skagway. That was northbound. At this time of the year everyone was heading southbound at the end of their Alaska vacations. The northbound ferries were largely empty. The next one left at 5am the following morning. I booked myself and the car on the ferry and asked if a sex doll could be taken on board at child rates.

Back in Haines I found Saturday night in full swing. There are only three bars in the town. I avoided the rowdiest one and the quietest one and went for the mid option, a joint called the Blue Lobster. I had a steak there and watched the Saturday night rituals taking place around me. You know that feeling you have, when you just eaten a big and satisfying meal, and are sipping beer, or whatever? That's how I felt, an outsider in this small community in the middle of nowhere. It was the night of the full moon. A huge golden globe hung over the fjord, throwing twilight across the surrounding mountains and forests. The juke box had been playing all night, and then someone put on Neil Young's *Harvest Moon*...

Come a little bit closer
Hear what I have to say
Just like children sleepin'
We could dream this night away

But there's a full moon risin'
Let's go dancing in the light
We know the music's playin'
Let's go out and feel the night

I lingered awhile, listening to the mellow music, before heading out on to the street. A crowd of youths were gathered around the *Yukon Queen*: "Hey man, what's this little buggy?", "where are you headin?", "what yu doing?". They were all drunk, but were not threatening. If this had been on a street in Vancouver, or Seattle, or New York, or Toronto it would have been threatening. It's strange how much the environment influences people's behaviour. Here in the Alaskan panhandle there were still fights and mindless violence, people abused drugs and alcohol, but it had a different complexion. Out here the scale of human development was much smaller. Everyone knew everyone else, while all around the natural world was huge and mysterious and dangerous. It gave a perspective that is lost in the big cities. I could have got my head kicked-in in Haines, but hell, with that huge moon lighting up the surrounding mountains and forests and fjords, kicking someone's head in just didn't seem the right thing to do.

With my money running ever lower, and not many hours to go until the morning ferry, I decided that my still intact head could live without a hotel bed. Near the ferry terminal I found a lay-by and parked up. Once again I was faced with the prospect of sleeping on the front seats of a Citroen 2CV. In preparation for this I'd drunk a lot booze in the bar. It worked. The night was a lot warmer than when I'd slept in the car in Coldfoot. Within five minutes I fell asleep.

It didn't last long. Cars began arriving for the southbound 2am ferry. Their headlight beams swept across the lay-by. Engines roared. Doors slammed. Then, I nearly jumped six feet into the air: the ferry docked and let out an enormous toot on its horn. I don't know what the whales and eagles made of it all. The commotion lasted for an hour or so, then, with another enormous toot on the ferry's horn, I was left in peace and was able to get some sleep.

The northbound ferry arrived right on schedule after its three day journey up from Bellingham. Most of the passengers got off at Haines, the shortest route to interior Alaska. Those who remained on the ferry were bound for Skagway, the shortest route to the Yukon. Dawn began to break as the ferry slipped her moorings and headed up the Lynn Canal. The Canal is about half a mile wide. It has steep sloping walls of black rock. At the top of the walls are forests leading up the slopes of the surrounding mountains. The waters of the Canal were crystal clear. The silence magical.

At the head of the Lynn Canal lay Skagway, nestling at the foot of a steep glaciated valley. A few miles further up the inlet lay the smaller settlement of Dyea, which is now a ghost town. Skagway is derived from a Tlingit Indian name, "Skagua", which means "the place where the north wind blows".

Wisps of mist rose from the Canal waters. On the right I could see the mouth of the Skagway river, where there was a small dock and oil storage tanks. Directly ahead lay the small ferry terminal, and on the left a black sand beach. The chill morning air resonated with history. A hundred years ago stampeders poured from the steamships. They would have dragged their belongings up that black sand beach and found themselves in a place that was often described as "hell on earth". Back in 1897, Skagway grew from one cabin to a town of twenty thousand in the space of three months. It boasted over seventy bars and hundreds of prostitutes, and was controlled by organized criminals.

That single cabin belonged to William Moore, a former steamboat captain who arrived in Skagway ten years before the gold rush. Moore was a smart chap. He believed that gold lay in the Klondike because it had been found in similar mountain ranges in South America, Mexico and California. Skagway lay on the most direct route to the Klondike. Moore and his son built a log cabin, a wharf and a saw mill in anticipation of future gold prospectors passing through on their way to the Klondike. They were going to mine the miners.

And come they did, a decade later, at first just a trickle making their way up the Chilkoot Pass and White Pass, then in the summer of 1897 a torrent of prospectors as news of the Klondike discovery spread across the world. William Moore was overwhelmed and suddenly found himself in the middle of a boom town, where self-appointed officials forced Moore and his family on to a five acre tract of land and turned his log cabin into a hotel; which goes to show that sometimes you can be just a bit too smart.

It was just after 6am on a Sunday morning. Skagway slumbered. Only a lone intrepid adventurer in a 2CV roamed the streets. Skagway has retained much of the Victorian buildings from the old days. I drove past William Moore's log cabin, which is now a tourist trap. Skagway is a small town that lives on its past. As I drove along the deserted streets the ghosts of the gold rush seemed to hang in the air. This place had once been the archetypal wild west. Bandits and bad men ruled supreme, including of course the notorious Jefferson "Soapy" Smith, who was the first successful gangster in the west.

Years before Al Capone had made a name for himself in Chicago, Soapy was running Denver with gambling dens, sly scams and corrupt officials. The gold rush brought Soapy to Skagway, which he ruled with an iron hand. He ran crooked gambling halls, freight companies that hauled nothing, telegraph offices that had no telegraph link, even an "army enlistment" tent where the victim's clothes and possessions were stolen while a "doctor" gave an examination. Eventually the citizens of Skagway bandied together and put an end to Soapy's rule. He was shot dead in a gunfight in July 1898 at the age of 37.

The lawlessness and gun slinging didn't last long, though. In 1898 the 14th Infantry arrived in Skagway to maintain order. They remained in Alaska for 15 months. In May of 1899, they were relieved by Company L of the 24th Infantry, one of the US Army's four black units. Aside from peacekeeping, Company L's principal duty in Skagway was to "show the flag," to maintain a government presence near a border that was still in dispute. The black soldiers spent three years in the area and made a favorable impression on all with whom they came in contact.

Skagway may have become a safer place when the soldiers arrived, but this town was just a staging post for the stampeders. Ahead of them lay a 500 mile ordeal to reach the Klondike gold fields. There were two routes from Skagway and Dyea across the mountains to the interior: the Chilkoot Pass in the west and the White Pass in the east. The twenty-six mile trail over Chilkoot Pass was steep and hazardous. Most stampeders who gave up did so attempting to cross these mountains. In the winter they struggled through blizzards and snow and had to contend with avalanches. The trail rose steeply in the final half mile, where stampeders used a guide rope for support and climbed the "golden staircase", 1,500 steps cut in the snow and ice.

To compound the misery the North West Mounted Police set up a border crossing into Canada at the summit of the Chilkoot Pass. They ordered every stampeder to carry a year's worth of supplies, which amounted to a ton of goods. No stampeder was allowed to pass into Canada without the requisite amount of supplies. The Mounted Police were trying to control a situation that was growing increasingly chaotic. Many of the stampeders came from cities and were completely naive about the wilderness. They expected to be able to purchase food and supplies along the trail. The Mounties hoped that the 'years worth of supplies' would deter people from attempting to reach the Klondike gold fields. Amazingly it didn't.

It was sheer bloody hell. To move their ton of supplies over the pass they had to make up to forty round trips, which involved hiking hundreds of miles back and forth along the cruel trail. One stampeder wrote home about the ardours of the Chilkoot Pass. It took him two long weeks to haul his gear up the pass: "Imagine pulling a sled loaded with three to six hundred pounds over a stretch of ice up a steep grade, strewn with boulders and logs, then crossing over a river bed on a couple of trees laid side by side and you get a picture of our labors. My feet are sore, my heels are blistered, my legs sore and lame, my hands, neck, shoulders, sore and chafed from rope. But boys, don't think I'm discouraged...there is a golden glimmer in the distance".

There is an incredible photograph, taken in 1898. It shows a chain of men, women and children making their way up the Chilkoot Pass. It is winter and heavy snow covers the bare mountainside. The line of figures struggling up the steep incline are bent over. You can almost feel the weight of their packs and the biting wind. This photograph captures perfectly what is meant by the term 'gold fever'.

In April 1898 a major avalanche occurred in the Chilkoot Pass. Hundreds of stampeders were buried alive under tons of wet snow. Volunteers dug for days to rescue the living and retrieve the dead. Things were little better on the adjacent White Pass route, where that same winter three thousand horses perished on the trail. Jack London, who was a witness, renamed it the "Dead Horse Trail". Stampeders had little concern for their pack animals. Exhausted horses starved, were hurt on rough ground and fell over cliffs. The stench of rotting horse flesh filled the canyons during the winter of 1898.

Things weren't much better in the summer. Without a covering of snow and ice the trails to the summit led across giant boulders, over which people literally crawled. Entrepreneurs saw an opportunity here. Three aerial tramways and several surface hoists were built to take those who could afford it over the Chilkoot Pass. These tramways and hoists made the Chilkoot Pass the most popular route to the interior. But not for long, as other entrepreneurs got in on the act as well: in May of 1898 work began on the White Pass and Yukon Route Railway, which ran from Skagway to Whitehorse. The construction employed 2000 workers and took 26 months to complete. From sea level at Skagway, the railway climbs 2,885 feet to White Pass summit in only 20 miles of track, one of the steepest railways in the world. As soon as the railway was opened the Chillkoot Trail and its aerial tramways became obsolete. Now, thousands of prospectors were carried towards the Klondike gold fields in relative comfort, although by the time the railway had been completed the great stampede was already over.

I pulled up by the railway station in Skagway. The coaching stock of the gold rush days has been restored and now the trains carry tourists up the White Pass Trail, following the route of the gushing Skagway River upstream, past waterfalls and ice-packed gorges and over a 1000ft high wooden trestle bridge to the Canadian border. The railway station was closed so I drove across to the small airstrip, trying to discover if there was a petrol station open this early on a Sunday morning. A group were waiting for their pilot, who was going to take them on a tour of a glacier. I was told that a nearby gas station always left one of its pumps switched on. You could get petrol by inserting a credit card.

I'd kept a careful record of all my spending on the plastic. My credit card was nearing its limit but the account contained more than enough for a tank of fuel. I headed out of Skagway on the Klondike Highway, which follows the railway line up the old White Pass Trail. A few miles north of Skagway I passed the Gold Rush Cemetery, which is the final resting place of many stampeders. Among them are Soapy Smith and Frank Reid, the man who shot Soapy dead, who, according to his gravestone "gave his life for the honor of Skagway"; a local prostitute, on the other hand, is remembered for "giving her honor for the life of Skagway".

The White Pass route across the mountains is rather spectacular and now has a modern road. I gazed at the steep gorges and plunging river and sheer rock faces. How on earth did they haul one ton of supplies up here?! Fourteen miles up from Skagway, and still not quite at the summit of the pass, I came upon the border post. Light snow was falling and at this altitude it felt bitterly cold. The customs lady remained in the comfort of her glass booth and waved me through. There was no one else around. I hadn't seen a single other vehicle on the highway. This had to be one of the loneliest customs posts in the world, with only the whistling wind and gold rush ghosts for company.

We were now back in Canada again, or to be more precise, the extreme north western tip of British Columbia. A very steep incline led up to the summit of the pass. Second gear was called for to make the climb. The Klondike Highway is well maintained and paved throughout. There is only one place along the Highway where you'll find services. This is the small village of Carcross, sixty miles from Skagway, which sits within a system of lakes high up in the Coast Mountains. These lakes form the headwaters of the Yukon River. From here it is almost 450 miles down the river to Dawson City. One hundred years ago, when there weren't any roads, the Yukon River was the main transportation artery. In late May of 1898, the North West Mounted Police counted more than eighteen hundred boats under construction on the lakes. It was further estimated that another twelve hundred boats were built in the early part of June. That journey down the Yukon River to Dawson City was no picnic. Ahead of the prospectors lay murderous rapids, starvation and disease.

It was just after 9am when I rolled into Carcross. The Klondike Highway follows the shore of Nares lake and the town is set back from the road. The single track railway line runs straight through the centre of town. There was an Anglican church beside a Baptist church. A general store. A hotel. A jailhouse. Cliché wild west stuff. Carcross has been preserved exactly how it was during the big stampede. Buried in the Carcross cemetery are Skookum Jim and Tagish Charlie, who along with George Carmack were the discoverers of the Bonanza Creek claim which led to the Yukon gold rush. The town's museum relates all this history, and as always history tends to get romanticised. Those who reached the lakes in the mountains were the lucky ones. It is estimated only 1 in 5 prospectors made it up the Chilkoot Pass, and only 1 in 10 made it up the White Pass. The rest either died on the trail or turned back to Dyea and

Skagway, ill and exhausted.

Carcross was the first settlement I came across that had an equal mix of whites and Indians. The Tagish tribe who live in this area were an integral part of the Yukon gold rush (Skookum Jim and Tagish Charlie were members of the tribe) The Tagish Indians didn't miss a trick and milked the gold rush for all it was worth. Chiefs were known to demand one dollar per head for every white man passing through their territory. The Indians also provided packing services to prospectors at prices that ranged from about $5 to $15 per hundred pounds. Other tribes fared less well from the huge influx of greedy white men, who brought illness, alcoholism and the breakdown of the Indian's traditional lifestyle.

From Carcross the Klondike Highway runs for 55 miles to Whitehorse, passing through the world's smallest desert on the way. I didn't really want to see the world's smallest desert, and besides, Whitehorse was due north, I was heading south, so I took the Tagish Road which runs east from Carcross to its junction with the Alaska Highway at Jakes Corner. This route would save me a considerable amount of driving time.

The small community of Tagish lays half way along the road. The lake at Tagish is part of the Yukon River route. The North West Mounted Police built a post here in 1897 and it became the southern police headquarters during the gold rush. Every person passing through the Tagish post was required to register with the police - more than 28,000 prospectors according to some estimates – and their boats were given registration numbers and a safety inspection. The Mounties also collected duties and checked to see that each person carried enough supplies. All this to ensure the best possible chance of survival on the nightmare journey down the Yukon River to Dawson City; which proves that even back in the wild days of the Yukon gold rush the old adage still ran true: the only certainties in life are death and taxes.

The Mounted Police post in Tagish is long gone. There was a lot of activity around the bridge over the river. Colourful boats dotted the waters. It looked like some sort of regatta. They were in fact Sunday fishermen. The waters in these parts are brimming with trout. My rough repair on the broken exhaust pipe had come loose and I went noisily across the bridge. One of the fishermen shook his fist at me. As if the trout cared about broken exhaust pipes.

Thirty minutes later I reached Jake's Corner, on the Alaska Highway. I've no idea who Jake was, but his corner was a quiet spot with only a hotel and gas station for company. All around the hotel and gas station there were old pieces of farm machinery and ancient cars. It looked like a cross between a museum and a junk yard. I tanked-up with gas and then went into the hotel for a coffee. The hotel was built Swiss-style. Its restaurant was on the first floor, amid an Aladdin's cave of old tv sets, ancient typewriters, primitive washing machines and other items of yesteryear. Whoever owned this place had a serious collecting problem. For once, the *Yukon Queen* did not look out of place in the car park.

I was back on the Alaska Highway again, but only for 230 miles down to Watson Lake and the junction with the Cassier Highway. The Cassier Highway would take me down to Prince Rupert, where I was going to try to board a ferry again. If you look at a map of the north west coast, Haines/Skagway are at the top, Vancouver/Seattle are at the bottom. Prince Rupert is half way down the coast. Both the Alaska Marine Highway and British Columbia Ferries served Prince Rupert: there was a better chance of obtaining a passage south. Well, it seemed a good idea at the time.

I reached Watson Lake by early evening. The Signpost Forest was exactly how Jose and I had left it two weeks previously, which for some reason surprised me. The nearby Watson Lake Hotel was closed for the winter. The rest of town looked pretty dead as well. Ah, what the hell: I decided to spend another night sleeping in the car. Steak and chips in a run-down restaurant was followed by the obligatory six bottles of beer. Then I found a quiet spot round the back of the Signpost Forest. The previous night in Haines I didn't manage to get a full night's rest. Now, curled up in the foetal position, the steering wheel jutting into my legs, I fell into an exhausted sleep. I dreamt of crisp, clean sheets, a soft mattress and nuggets of gold.

The next morning frost glittered in the sunlight. I staggered out of the car and stretched my legs, only to find myself being photographed. My hair was all over the place. My face was red and indented where it had been jammed up against the door all night. Smears of dribble ran down my chin. The man with the camera came over to me and started asking questions. He'd seen the piece in the *Yukon News*. Damn. I was rapidly coming to the conclusion that it wasn't much fun being big in the Yukon.

I answered the same old questions and wondered how they managed to get a six feet by ten feet sign from the German autobahn to Watson Lake? The guy left me alone after I'd thrust some of our leaflets into his hand and given him my autograph. I then drove around Watson lake for a while until I found a washroom. One of the worst things about sleeping in the car was finding somewhere the next morning to freshen up. I resolved that tonight I would definitely stay in a hotel, funds running low or not. With gleaming rotten teeth I hit the road. The junction with the Cassier Highway lay just west of Watson Lake. This was goodbye to the Alaska Highway. We wouldn't be seeing each other again.

Old friends and new: from Watson Lake the Cassier Highway runs due south into British Columbia for 450 miles to the Skeena Valley, east of Prince Rupert. The Cassier is a real wilderness road, comparable to how the Alaska Highway was 50 years ago. You get the usual warnings before setting out on the Cassier Highway: don't contemplate the journey unless your vehicle's in top condition, take at least two spare tyres and spare fuel containers, blah, blah, blah After doing the Dalton Highway such warnings were old hat. I wasn't the least bit worried about tackling the Cassier Highway.

The Cassier ran through wild and beautiful country. This drive is probably the most spectacular in British Columbia. It's also probably the roughest. Officially, the Cassier is a paved highway for almost all its length. Unofficially, there's still hundreds of miles that are dirt and gravel, compounded by the fact that when I drove it large stretches were undergoing road works, which meant more dirt and gravel. The Cassier wasn't as bumpy as the Dalton Highway, yet in parts it still felt like driving in a rally event.

The first part of the Cassier from Watson Lake runs through endless, silent birch trees; an enchanted forest. It then climbs up into hills that are the tug of war between the Cassier and Skeena Mountains. There's nothing along this northern stretch except an occasional remote Indian village. There was no other traffic on the road. I drove for a solitary 150 miles before I saw the first gas station. I tanked-up and went to the small store to pay for the fuel. The blinds were pulled down and the door was locked. I knocked loudly. Still no sign of life. I was about to walk back to the car and drive off with a free tank of fuel when I saw one of the blinds twitch. I could hear the sound of bolts being drawn back on the door. The door hinged opened. I cautiously went into the store. A gas stove was going full blast and it felt stiflingly hot. Sitting round a table were eight Indians, men, women and children. They were all hard at work, rubbing away at scratch cards. These cards were a promotion by the gas company. If you bought a certain amount of gas you got a scratch card. You could win anything between one dollar and fifty dollars on the scratch cards. There was a huge pile of them on the table. Losing cards went straight in the bin. The winning cards were stacked in a neat pile beside the oldest Indian. I paid for my fuel. The Indians didn't seem too concerned about taking my money.

It began raining. The road wound through increasingly mountainous country. There were steep gorges and plunging rivers. Streams ran down across the road. There was water everywhere. I passed the tiny Indian settlement of Cassier. A few miles from here there's an open-pit mine that used to supply most of the world's high grade asbestos. The mine closed down in 1992 and Cassier became a ghost town. There's still poisonous asbestos scattered for miles around. The area is off limits to the public until the clean-up is complete. No one seems too worried about the Indians who once worked in the mine.

I ended my first day on the Cassier Highway at Dease Lake. This is the mid way point. Dease lake is known as "The Jade Capital of the World", because of the jade mines there. Sounds rather grand, doesn't it. The reality is a small, ramshackle community of 700 people, strung out between the Cassier Highway and Dease Lake. This is the largest population centre along the Cassier Highway and the only non-native community. It has just one hotel, the Northway Motor Inn, where you can find clean sheets, a comfortable mattress and inviting pillows. Before getting a decent night's sleep I had a meal in the hotel restaurant. The restaurant had large plate glass windows. Parked out front there was a pick-up truck that belonged to some hunters who were eating in the restaurant. On the back of the pick-up there were three caribou. Their glassy eyes stared back at me while I ate. Drops of blood fell from the bed of the pick-up to the gravel below.

Two hundred years ago there were no white settlers in this part of Canada. This was due largely to Chief Shakes, the then leader of the Tlingit Indians. Chief Shakes had a hard and fast rule: *'If any white man comes over the mountains from the east, kill him. He is evil'*. This edict was to protect the Tlingits rich trade in furs and dried salmon with the Tahltan Indians. However, the Hudson Bay Company had other ideas. In the early 1800s they sent Robert Campbell, a sturdy Scotsman, to Dease Lake to establish a trading post. However, that same spring the Hudson Bay Company did a deal with the Russians (who then owned Alaska) and gained trading rights in the panhandle. The idea of a trading post at Dease Lake was abandoned. Robert Campbell went on to undertake further explorations for the Hudson Bay Company and become the 'Discoverer of the Yukon'. Don't you just love those sort of titles!

Many years later, in the latter part of the 1800s, gold was discovered in the Stikine River, just south of Dease Lake. This produced a small gold rush into the area, further enhanced by huge numbers of people who began passing through on their way to the Klondike gold fields. This new influx of gold prospectors was to prove negative to the Tahltan way of life. The white settlers assumed they were superior to the Indians and had a patronising attitude towards them. They also brought alcohol and diseases such as measles. This resulted in lots of very drunk and spotty Indians. The traditional trading patterns between the Tlingit and the Tahltan were destroyed. Once they had been hunter gatherers, leading an uncomplicated life. After the white men came they huddled in their villages and drank too much booze and died a slow death.

The north west Indians were themselves by no means perfect. Slavery existed in every Indian tribe, with the exception of the arctic Inuit (who really don't like being called Eskimos). In some tribes one third of the population were slaves. Some of these slaves were captured during wars, others were born into bondage. Some tribes treated their slaves kindly, others did not. When a Tlingit Chief built a new home for himself it was customary to bury a slave beneath the four corner posts as a sign of luck (not for the slaves!).

There were also wars over trade. These wars, small by the standards of white men, were viciously fought. Wholesale slaughter of opponents was the order of the day. It is a mistake to think of the Indians as being noble and moral, somehow superior. They weren't. Indian society contained as much evil as white society. The Indians, though, had their own unique way of life. This way of life was destroyed when the white men invaded their lands.

Jack London, no stranger to these parts, summed it up 100 years ago...

...the white men come as the breath of death; all their ways lead to death, their nostrils are filled with it; and yet they do not die. Theirs, the whiskey and tobacco and short-haired dogs; theirs the many sicknesses, the smallpox and measles, the coughing and mouth-bleeding; theirs the white skin, and softness to the frost and storm. ...And yet they grow fat on their many ills, and prosper, and lay a heavy hand over all the world and tread mightily upon its peoples.

The second part of my drive down the Cassier Highway was under intermittent, heavy bursts of rain. The road wound through green forests beside towering mountains. On the drive I saw places called Bear Glacier, Bear River, Bear Paw Ranch and the Rabid Grizzly Rest Area. I soon discovered why there were so many references to bears. I'd only been driving for a short time when I saw my first one. I was trying to get the car through another stretch of road works. The rain had turned the road surface into a mud bath. I struggled to keep the car moving. I glanced over to my left. There was a pile of earth beside the road. On top of the pile was a big brown bear. It sat on its backside and gazed curiously at its surroundings. The car was doing only 5 miles an hour and was slipping and sliding through the mud, just yards from the bear. I hoped it wouldn't come over to investigate. I was acutely aware that all I had over my head was a canvas roof, and all I had under the bonnet was a 600cc engine which struggled to keep the car moving in these conditions. The pepper spray was close to hand. Fortunately I didn't need to use it. The bear remained up there on top of the earth pile. It seemed to enjoy being king of the castle.

I saw my next bear shortly afterwards. It was another brown bear, smaller, foraging in the undergrowth beside the road. I was through the road works now and was making good speed. I put my foot down. The bear glanced round at me as I whizzed by. There were others, glimpsed in the forest, on the distant hillsides. Why so many? Did bears like rain? By now I was becoming used to the critters. Throughout the 2CV Alaska Challenge I had unsuccessfully tried to get a photograph of a bear beside the No.1 car. Now I had my chance. I saw a small bear messing about in a stream on the hillside. It looked harmless. This was my chance. I pulled up and carefully positioned the car to get a good shot. Then I walked a little way back up the road. It was a perfect photograph. The winding mud road, the No.1 car, the forested hillside, the low clouds, the towering Coast Mountains, except, that it was a small bear, so small that I could hardly see it through the lens of the digital camera. I took some shots, knowing the bear wouldn't come out clearly, and walked back to the car. As I got to the car, I don't know why but I turned around. In the very spot where I'd been taking photos a few seconds before, a huge black bear was strolling casually across the road. I mean this thing was *huge*, it looked bigger than a Citroen 2CV. I held my breath, hoping the bear wouldn't notice me. It didn't. Like all bears it was on its way to the opticians. After that I gave up trying to photograph the bears.

Heavy rain followed me all the way down the Cassier Highway to Meziadin Junction, where there's a gas station and restaurant. I tanked-up with coffee and gas and contemplated whether to take the road to the coast. Highway 37A leaves the Cassier at Meziadin Junction and runs for 38 miles to the twin towns of Stewart and Hyder, on the coast. Hyder is in Alaska, at the very bottom end of the panhandle, Stewart is in British Columbia. These two small communities are a short distance apart, yet an international border separates them. There's just one bank in this little backwater, and it's in Stewart. As a result, although Hyder is in the United States they use Canadian money. Hyder phones also have the British Columbia area code, and Hyder children go to school in Stewart. The Stewart-Hyder scenario is the most pointed example of the border settlement between America and Canada, which gave half of Canada's western coastline to Alaska. Crazy map making, although it does keep plenty of customs and immigration officers in employment.

The scenery around Stewart and Hyder is often described as the most spectacular you'll find anywhere in the world. However, over the last month I'd overdosed on spectacular scenery, so I gave the side trip to Stewart-Hyder a miss. For me, the jewel in the crown was the Cassier Highway. Out of all the Highways I drove in the far north the Cassier was the best, both for its awesome scenery and real 'wilderness experience', not to mention the bears.

One hundred miles south of Meziadin Junction I came into the village of Kitwanga, which is the southern terminus of the Cassier Highway, where it meets the Yellowhead Highway. Before the coming of the white man and 'civilisation', the northwest, rich in food and other resources, had the greatest concentration of Native Americans on the continent. There were 72 distinct tribes stretching down from Alaska to what is now the lower 48 states. Kitwanga was the base of a fierce chieftain called Nekt, who ruled the Tsimshian tribe. Dear old Nekt used to make raids against the coastal Tlingit tribe for food, slaves, and control of lucrative trade routes. Nekt had a large collection of Tlingit scalps. He defended his fort at Kitwanga by hoisting huge logs up the hillside, which were then fastened with cedar ropes. When the war horn signaled an enemy attack, the logs were rolled down to crush the invaders. Like many weapons of war, the rolling logs weren't much of a success and in the early 1800s the fort at Kitwanga was destroyed by the Tlingits in a fierce battle that killed thousands. Today, Kitwanga is a retirement spot for white Canadians. Pretty bungalows with prim gardens and white picket fences dot the hillside. The bloody history of Kitwanga has been tidied-up into a tourist trap on the outskirts of the village that calls itself a National Historic Monument.

The Yellowhead Highway followed the River Skeena west. There was a lot of traffic; or at least, it seemed like a lot of traffic. For the first time in days I had to stay on the correct side of the road and keep an eye out for other vehicles. How tedious. Also, now that I was back in civilisation I thought it would be prudent to make Jamie the Love Doll less conspicuous. She found a place in the back of the car, hidden under a blanket. All that could be seen of her was one of her arms, which poked out from under the blanket and waved at passers-by.

After 50 miles I reached Terrace, which with a population of 20,000 was the first big town I'd seen since Fairbanks. What can you say about Terrace that hasn't already been said? Not much. The 90 mile drive from Terrace to Prince Rupert restored my spirits somewhat. The Yellowhead Highway clung to the steep banks of the Skeena River. A huge amount of water crashes down the broad river bed. My, this river sure was in a hurry to get somewhere. At points along the banks and on the gravel beds, tiny salmon fishermen could be seen casting their lines into the violent waters. Accompanying us was the single track line of the Canadian Pacific railroad.

The Skeena River reached a wide sea loch. Such was the violence of the waters coming down the river that even in the loch you could still see the current moving at a rapid rate of knots. On the south side of the loch were snow capped mountains. It looked like the west coast of Scotland. I could have been driving along Loch Duich. The Isle of Skye didn't lay at the end of this road, though, Prince Rupert did.

When I got to the sprawling town of Prince Rupert I drove straight down to the ferry terminal. A woman clerk in the booking hall gave me the same old story: all the ferries going south were booked solid for the next week. Booked solid? surely the tourist season in the north was almost over now? The woman clerk agreed and told me smoking wasn't allowed in the building. She said that they were on the last busy week before things quietened down for the winter. Everyone was returning south after their vacations and adventures in the north. However, a glimmer of hope emerged: standby space on a ferry leaving in two days time. She explained that standby meant you took a chance on the sailing. If other passengers didn't turn up, or cancelled their booking you might get on the ferry. She was very ambiguous about the chances of this. Sometimes all the standby passengers got on the ferry, sometimes none of them. I had to make a decision.

A number of people were lounging around the ferry terminal. Some of them had that 'look', the same look I had after sleeping in the *Yukon Queen*. There were hippies with backpacks, a mother with a screaming baby, some guys who looked like fishermen. I wondered where they were all heading and how long they had been waiting. I wouldn't have been surprised to see a skeleton in the corner of the booking hall.

If I hung around in Prince Rupert for two days it would cost me money. On the otherhand it was a good two day drive from here down to Vancouver, which would also cost me money. The British Columbia Ferries service from Prince Rupert stopped in Port Hardy, at the northern end of Vancouver Island, where I planned to spend the winter and write a literary masterpiece. It took 18 hours to make the voyage. I handed over my credit card and it took a hammering. The woman clerk explained that the money would be refunded if I didn't get on the ferry.

Prince Rupert looks out over an archipelago of islands and is ringed by mountains that tumble to the sea along a beautiful fjord-cut coastline. The location is pretty. The town itself is not that pretty. Charles Hays, President of the Canadian Pacific Railway, had a vision for Prince Rupert. Mr Hays hired a Boston landscape architectural firm which drew up plans for a model town. Victoria's best known architect was also commissioned to design a series of splendid hotels. By 1910 the City became incorporated with a population of 5,000. Unfortunately, a few years later Charles Hays went to England to secure more money for his project. In 1912 he returned to Canada on the maiden voyage of RMS Titanic and perished, taking with him most of his grand plans for Prince Rupert. What's left is a sprawl of houses and shops and industry and an incongruous sixteen storey skyscraper.

If history had been different, Skagway might have been Canada's most northern port. Now Prince Rupert takes this title. It also has the deepest harbour of any port in Canada and is the western terminus of the Canadian Pacific Railroad. Long freight trains line the harbour side. Cargo ships jostle for space with small fishing boats. This is a working town. If Mr Hays hadn't gone down with the Titanic it might have turned into a chintzy tourist trap. Prince Rupert wasn't very pretty, but it had character.

Prince Rupert is known as the 'Halibut Capital of the World'. It's also known as the unofficial City of Rainbows. That's because it pisses down here almost non-stop. They get nearly 100 inches of rain every year. British Columbians say you can tell if someone's from Prince Rupert because they'll have webbed hands and feet.

I examined my fingers and checked in for two nights at a nice hotel overlooking the harbour. My credit card took another hammering. It was worth it for the view from my room. I arranged a table by the window and retrieved my typewriter from the car. There, with a bottle of beer, I watched the comings and goings in the harbour and composed the last two Alaska Challenge bulletins. Bulletin No.23 was just to let everyone know that I got safely back from Prudhoe Bay. Bulletin No.24 was a thank-you to our company sponsors and everyone else who had been involved in the Alaska Challenge. I sucked on the beer bottle and wondered if anyone would be remotely interested in any of this. I was reassured, though, because during the last two months the 2CV Alaska Challenge web site had received thousands of hits. A fair number of Citroen enthusiasts, and other interested parties, from all around the world had followed our journey across North America. Ah, the wonders of modern technology.

For thousands of years the Tsimshian Indians had lived in this area. Then in 1834 the Hudson Bay Company built a fur trading fort 32 kilometres to the north of what is now Prince Rupert harbour. They named it Fort Simpson. Shortly after, the Tsimshian, about 2,500 in number, abandoned their winter villages around Prince Rupert and resettled in Fort Simpson. They wanted to take advantage of the trading opportunities brought by the white men.

Both the Tsimsheans and the white men grew rich from fur trading at Fort Simpson. Debauchery set in. In the 1850s, fur prices were much higher in Fort Victoria, down south on the tip of Vancouver Island. A 600 mile canoe trip got them down there, a long journey which satisfied the Tsimsheans nomadic urge and offered a chance to plunder other Indian villages along the coast. Fort Victoria also offered many attractions to the Indians, almost all of them demoralising. Many Tsimshean women made the trip down south, some as young as nine years old, to prostitute themselves in Victoria and the adjacent American territories. In the American territories liquor was freely available. Casks of rum were brought back up to Fort Simpson, where both the Indians and Hudson Bay employees held wild parties. On some days the entire Fort was drunk on rum.

I spent my two days in Prince Rupert bashing out stuff on my typer, hanging around in bars and drinking too much beer. There wasn't an awful lot else to do in Prince Rupert, unless you were an amateur meteorologist: it rained non-stop. It was still raining early on the morning of the third day, when I headed back to the ferry port with a hangover, hopeful of getting a passage south.

The ferry arrived at 7am. There were ten long lines of cars waiting to board. Us mugs on standby were in the tenth lane. There were about twenty cars in Lane 10 and I was midway in the queue. It took half an hour to load the first nine lanes of cars. The port workers walked around in sou'westers, walkie-talkies clamped to their face. Nothing happened for a while. The ferry tooted its horn, ready to depart. The port workers were besieged by the standby passengers. Everyone seemed to have a dire reason for getting on the ferry. They began waving us through. The first five cars, and then the second. Me and another guy in a red sports car were next. Red sports car was waved through the barrier, but then reversed back to the waiting lane. The ferry was full. I walked over to the booking hall to get my refund. Meanwhile, the ferry backed out into Prince Rupert harbour, turned and made its way south. It would reach Vancouver Island by late evening. It would take me two days to get there by car.

Once I'd got my refund sorted out I wasted no time and got straight back on the road, this time heading east on the Yellowhead Highway. The scenery between Prince Rupert and Terrace was just as stunning going in the opposite direction. I stopped in Terrace for breakfast. I also went to the local library for internet connection. I wanted to see if Tony had put up the final two bulletins I'd sent from Prince Rupert. He hadn't.

I carried on along the Yellowhead Highway and chewed-up the miles. At Kitwanga junction I felt the pull of the Cassier Highway. So far civilisation had been disappointing. The wilderness looked much more inviting. I resisted the urge and carried on until reaching the town of Smithers. I needed some cash and headed into town looking for a bank. There were lots of banks in Smithers, a small alpine-style town that reminded me of Switzerland. I produced my credit card and tried to draw cash on it: 'sorry, you've exceeded your limit', said the bank clerk. I tried the same thing at another bank, only to hear the same story. Well, che sara sara, I known for days now that my credit card was almost done, but I had emergency supplies, or so I thought. This was my personal bank account back in London, which should have had almost £800 in it. After some searching I found a hole in the wall that had the right symbols. I stuck my cash card into the slot. The ATM chewed it up. A cheery message flashed up on the screen: INSUFFICIENT FUNDS. PLEASE CONTACT YOUR BANK FOR DETAILS. After digging deep into my pocket I managed to come up with two dollars and forty eight cents in loose change. I was still in the far north and the car was low on fuel. Insufficient funds indeed.

My personal account had been with National Westminster Bank at London Bridge for more than ten years. Early in 1999, Jose and I opened up another account with them, for the 2CV Alaska Challenge. The bank account for the charity fund raising (the 'Alaska Appeal') was with another branch of the Nat West. I also wrote a letter to my bank manager giving details of The 2CV Alaska Challenge and saying that I would be away for a number of months that summer. The manager never replied. I was also in contact with Nat West's head office, trying to get sponsorship for the journey. All in all, National Westminster Bank were heavily involved in the financial side of the 2CV Alaska Challenge.

But, well, you know what banks are like. In August of 1999, the National Westminster Bank deemed my personal account 'inactive', because there'd been no money flowing through it since the end of June, which by funny coincidence was when Jose and I left for Rotterdam. Nat West charged me £200 excess borrowing charges, because my overdraft was now regarded as unauthorised borrowing.

As the weeks went by these charges kept increasing. I was also charged nearly £80 when that cash machine in Smithers chewed-up my card. Naturally enough, all these bank charges put me over my previous overdraft limit, which attracted even more charges, ad infinitum.

To be fair to Nat West, when I wrote to them later, explaining all this, they did waver some of the charges, but at that moment I was in northern British Columbia with just two dollars and forty eight cents in my pocket and I was mightily pissed off with the Nat West bank. However, my immediate concern was how to get some money..? Of course, Tony still owed me $2000 for the No.2 car! He could wire the money to me. Trouble being, Smithers didn't have a Western Union office. The nearest one was in Prince Rupert. I didn't want to go back on myself and decided to push on to Prince George, 230 miles further east along the Yellowhead Highway. I emptied the spare can of gas into the tank and headed east.

The alpine landscape gave way to typical Rocky Mountain scenery. The road followed the course of the Nechako and Endako Rivers. There was much activity along the Yellowhead Highway. Cars were parked along the roadside. People could be seen in the undergrowth. There were caravan encampments, tents and RVs gathered together. Signs said: 'BUYER', 'BEST PRICES PAID', and finally one that said: 'MUSHROOMS'. So, all these people were picking mushrooms, but such large numbers of them out here, in the middle of nowhere? I came to the conclusion that all this activity could only be in pursuit of hallucinogenic drugs: magic mushrooms. Later, I discovered that they were picking ordinary mushrooms, which is a multi-million dollar business in British Columbia.

By mid afternoon I'd left the mushroom pickers behind and found myself in Prince George. It seemed a different place to the town Jose and I had passed through many weeks before. It looked hard, gritty and unfriendly. It's funny how lack of money can change your perspective on things. I rang Tony. I hadn't spoken to him since we stayed at his house in Winnipeg. Tony sounded as though he was expecting to hear from me. We said 'hi' to each other and exchanged pleasantries. The sub text being that this was a 2000 dollar phone call, 2000 dollars that he owed me for the No.2 car and that I now desperately needed. I hadn't known Tony that long but I trusted him implicitly, otherwise I wouldn't have left Winnipeg without that two thousand bucks. Tony didn't let me down. He sounded like anyone who has to pay out a fairly large sum of money, disappointed, but he said he had the cash. There was a small problem though. Due to the time difference it was late afternoon in Winnipeg. The banks were just closing. There wouldn't be time to arrange the money transfer. It would have to be done in the morning. We exchanged more pleasantries and then hung up.

Ok, so I was down and out in Prince George, with less than five bucks on me, but with the knowledge that a tidy sum would soon be heading my way over the wires. Actually, Prince George seemed the right kind of place to find yourself down and out. This rough-edged place was carved from an endless spruce forest to become one of the biggest cities in British Columbia, with a population of 80,000. Pulp mills, kilns, planers, plywood plants, Prince George has got them all. If timber turns you on you'll have a lot of fun in this town.

Simon Fraser established a North West Trading Company post here in 1805, and named it Fort George in honour of the reigning George III, who was quite mad. As a commercial centre it quickly altered the lives of the local Carrier Sekani natives, who abandoned their semi-nomadic lifestyle in favour of a permanent settlement alongside the fort. Does this sound familiar? Well, unlike the scenario at Prince Rupert, the natives and white men at Prince George didn't get out of their heads on rum. This austerity still permeates the town. There ain't much to do in Prince George, except to take free tours around the big pulp mills and processing plants, where planks and piles of sawdust the size of small hills stretch almost as far as the eye can see.

I was too busy in Prince George to tour the pulp mills. A thorough search ensued. I looked through everything, my bags, my clothes, the car. Various loose change and bills added up to just over 12 dollars Canadian, 8 dollars American, 25 Dutch guilders, 200 hundred Belgium francs and 38 French francs. The Dutch, Belgium and French coins were useless, however, I did find somewhere that took American coins. At the end of it I had around sixteen Canadian dollars capital. A burger and chips cost me more than five dollars. I couldn't afford a packet of cigarettes. However, I had a large amount of hand-rolling tobacco that I'd bought in Holland. There was still 12 bottles of beer left over from my arctic emergency supplies. So, with a full belly provided by an American clown, puffing on hand-rolled Dutch cigarettes and drinking Alaskan beer I settled down for the night in a lay-by. The only other vehicle in the lay-by was an old beat-up pick-up truck hooked-up to a caravan. The owner was nowhere to be seen. A dog sheltered underneath the caravan. It was tied to a long piece of rope and looked ill and malnourished.

This night dossing in the car felt quite luxurious by previous standards. The lay-by on the Yellowhead Highway had a tourist information centre. The tourist office was closed-up for the winter season, but a standpipe supplied drinking water, and the weather was mild. Yeah gods, compared to roughing it up in the Arctic this could have been the Hilton Hotel. The only drawback being, that I was in a big town. Bears and wolves weren't the worry here, human predators were. In the wilderness the No.1 car had been an oddity that made people smile. Here in Prince George it was also a magnet for trouble. I'd already encountered a car full of drunken teenagers, who threw empty beer bottles at me as they drove by. Luckily, though, this was midweek and after midnight things quietened down a bit, except for the dog growling and whimpering. I demolished eight bottles of beer and had the best nights sleep ever in that car. No doubt helped by the knowledge that 2000 bucks were winging their way towards me. As I drifted off to sleep I promised myself that when the money arrived I would stay one night in a decent hotel and have an excellent meal.

Next morning at 9am sharp I was outside the Western Union office in downtown Prince George. I went through the rigmarole of filling out a 'receive money' form before being told that the money hadn't arrived yet. Well, it was nearly lunchtime in Winnipeg. Perhaps Tony planned to send the money during his work break. I went over to the main police station to tell them about the abandoned dog in the lay-by. Nearby was the Prince George Municipal Library. I had a wash in the toilets there and then used their free internet access to check on things in cyberspace. Surprise, surprise, the charity sponsorship form was not on the web site, nor were my final two bulletins. Two hours later I returned to the Western Union office and had to fill in another form before being told the same thing: no money had come through. I had less than ten dollars on me. The car was almost out of gas, so I couldn't go for a drive. I decided that some publicity would help kill the time and might buy me breakfast. I headed down to the offices of the *Prince George Citizen*. At the front desk I explained about the 2CV Alaska Challenge, told them the car was parked outside and lied that I really liked Prince George. Within 30 seconds I was in the newsroom being interviewed by a reporter.

The *Yukon Queen* and I had our picture taken outside the newspaper office. I was already big in the Yukon. Maybe I was also going to be big in BC as well? More importantly, maybe I'd get breakfast bought for me? No such luck: the reporter rushed off to cover something more important and left me with a *Prince George Citizen* biro. Oh well, at least this brush with the press had wasted a few hours.

Back at the Western Union office I filled in yet another 'receive money' form only to be told that the money still hadn't arrived. What was Tony doing? I thought about ringing him again. Long distance phone calls are expensive from call boxes and my phone card only had a few bucks left on it, so I decided to wait a bit longer. I visited the Western Union office again late in the afternoon, just before they closed. Still nothing from Tony. A sign in the office said: 'money within 24 hours', so I decided to wait until the morning.

Burger and chips again. As I chewed the emulsified fats I pondered on how a poverty diet can kill you. I was once more down to my last five bucks but felt pretty sure the two thousand would turn up in the morning, so I decided to blow the money on a beer before settling down for my second night in the lay-by.

A mile or so further down the highway there was a strip of hotels, gas stations and car dealers. I selected one of the cheaper looking hotels and found a large pub attached to it like a limpet. Things were quiet in the pub. I sat on a bar stool and nursed the only pint of beer I could afford. There was one other guy sitting on a stool. He looked in his early forties and smiled and joked with the barmaid. It appeared as though the guy had been on that bar stool a long time. He had the look of someone whose just had a good session with his mates, the mates have gone home and he was lingering, savouring the moment.

The guy's name was Ted, a smallish man with gingery, greying hair;

a life-long resident of Prince George who worked in the lumber business. Somehow this did not surprise me. Ted tried to slide a joke into every single sentence he uttered. I told him my story and played it up a bit: my woman abandoned me in Fairbanks, bears on the Cassier Highway, no room on the Prince Rupert ferry, running out of money, roughing it in Prince George... it worked, Ted sympathised and bought me beer until closing time. He then offered to put me up for the night at his place. I accepted the offer and wondered what his wife would think.

We staggered out into the car park. Ted gawped at the No.1 car and whistled. Hadn't he believed my story? I was somewhat surprised to see that Ted meant to drive home. I offered to drive him in my car. I felt a bit drunk, but Ted was three sheets to the wind. He waved my offer aside and told me to follow his pick-up truck. He only lived five blocks away; and so I followed him out of the car park and on to the main highway. It was drizzling and cold. There wasn't much traffic about.

It was a stupid thing to do. We could have walked back to his house in less than 15 minutes. It's just that I was taking awhile readjusting to civilisation. Back in the United Kingdom I never drunk drove. I had a push bike and would wobble back from pubs late at night on that. In Alaska things were slightly different. I soon discovered that in Fairbanks people thought nothing about getting hammered in a pub before driving home. The drink driving laws were pretty lax. If the police caught you doing it most times they'd just give you a verbal warning. They only prosecuted if you caused an accident. Of course, up in the Arctic and on the far north wilderness roads there were no laws at all. Up there it didn't seem at all strange to drink and drive. When you're on a dirt road thousands of miles from anywhere, and you haven't seen another vehicle for three days, what's the problem?

In British Columbia, though, they were pretty strict about drunk driving. I followed Ted for one block, then we turned off the main highway into a side road and straight into a police road block. A big cop wearing a rain cape waved a lantern to and fro. Ted pulled up beside him. Through my windscreen wipers I saw the cop lean down to the drivers window. He then waved Ted over to the side of the road, where there were three other cars. The cops were breatherlising the drivers. The big cop came over to me. I wasn't quite sure what the legal alcohol limit was in British Columbia, but I was certain I was way over it. The big cop paused for a moment to look at the No.1 car. I lifted up the window flap to answer his questions. As I spoke I tried to keep my breath in, so that he wouldn't smell the booze. He asked me for my driving licence. I gave him my international one. He asked me if the car was registered in BC. I pointed to the British licence plates. He asked me the make of the car. I told him it was a Citroen 2CV. The big cop pondered for a moment, then waved me through. I suppose he figured that the paperwork involved in booking me was going to be far too much trouble.

As I drove through the roadblock I passed Ted. We looked at each other through the rainy windows. I shrugged. There wasn't a lot I could do to help him. I drove on into the miserable night, where the lay-by beckoned.

The next morning found me outside the Western Union office, waiting for them to open. I'd got the 'receive money' form down to a fine art and filled it in within seconds. The girl checked on her computer screen. I held my breath. She smiled. The money had arrived. She gave me a voucher to take to a nearby bank, where two thousand crisp, clean Canadian dollars were counted out into my hand. It felt comparable to having sex.

I didn't hang around in Prince George, not even for breakfast. The two days here had made me feel claustrophobic. I headed south on BC Highway 97, through the Rocky Mountains, back down the Caribou gold rush trail. By lunchtime I reached Williams Lake. Williams lake seemed pleased to see me and so I decided to spend the night there. It was still a long drive to Vancouver and now, with the day half gone, I wouldn't have made it. Besides, I'd promised myself a bit of luxury after slumming it for two nights. I checked into the Days Inn, the same hotel Jose and I had stayed in weeks previously on the way up to Alaska; and believe it or not, they gave me the same room. I missed Jose and spent half an hour pondering on synchronicity before falling asleep.

The following day I hit the road early. At Cache Creek, BC Highway 97 ended and I picked-up Trans-Canada Highway 1. The Trans Can heads south here for Vancouver. It follows the route of the Fraser River, named after Simon Fraser who discovered it in 1808. Mr Fraser came west over the Rocky Mountains looking for an easy river route to the Pacific. He actually thought he was following the Columbia River. It took him months to make the journey down the river, guided by local Indians, pushing forward using ladders, ropes and improvised platforms to bypass rapids too treacherous for boats. It took him 35 days just to get down the Fraser River Canyon. This canyon, squeezed between the high ridges of the Cascade and Coast Mountains, was long regarded as impassable. To negotiate it the Trans-Canada Highway is forced to push through tunnels, hug the Fraser's banks, and at times cling perilously to rock ledges hundreds of feet above the swirling waters. Even someone such as I, who had overdosed on spectacular scenery, was impressed. Two railway lines also wind a tortuous route through the canyon. On one side of the river is the Canadian Pacific Railway, the first line to be built here in 1885, on the other side of the river is the Canadian National Railway line. It's a rather crazy example of the early competition between the railways in Canada.

The most spectacular part of the Fraser River Canyon is Hell's Gate. The 'cut' at Hell's Gate is almost 1000 feet long and at its narrowest point only 110 feet wide. The furious waters of the Fraser River pass through Hell's Gate at an awe-inspiring velocity of 3.9 million gallons per second. A deep, angry roar echoes around the surrounding mountains. If you stand close to the gorge you can feel the rocks vibrating.

At the south end of the Fraser River canyon is the small town of Yale. Back in the 1800s Yale was one of the largest cities in the northwest. It was gold, of course, that brought people here. First the Fraser River gold rush and then the Cariboo gold rush. Yale marked the start of the old Cariboo Wagon Road. Today, less than 200 people live here. The only remarkable thing I found about Yale is that it is one of the few places in this part of Canada where you can find a monument to the Chinese who helped forge this land.

The Chinese first came to North America after slavery was abolished in the United States. The Americans, looking for cheap labour, discovered that poor Chinese men from Guangdong and Fujian provinces could be convinced to move to the US to do the hard, back-breaking work that used to be done by African slaves. The Canadian railway companies followed suit and 17,000 Chinese men were recruited to work on the western section of the Canadian Pacific Railway. This was extremely difficult and dangerous work (for which the Chinese were paid half as much as white workers doing the same job). Tunnels needed to be blasted through the mountains and railway track had to be laid down high above the many rivers and gorges. This involved moving huge amounts of rock by hand and the Chinese began to be known as "coolies" (bitter strength). In all, over 700 Chinese men lost their lives building the railway. It is estimated that for every mile of track laid at least four Chinese died due to explosions, exposure, scurvy and malnutrition. There was no way to bury the dead so the bodies were simply left beside the tracks and covered with rocks and dirt. There is a famous photo of the driving of the Last Spike of the Canadian Pacific Railway. Suffice to say, there is not one Chinese face in that photo, despite the fact that the contribution of the Chinese men was invaluable and the railway could not have been built without their 'bitter strength'.

Ten miles south of Yale the Trans-Canada Highway left the mountains and rolled down into the broad and fertile Fraser River Valley. At the head of the valley lies the small town of Hope, known as the "Chainsaw Carving Capital of Canada". I stopped for gas and had a look around, to see if anyone was carving things with a chainsaw. No, it was pretty quiet. Hope is a main junction for those coming across the Rockies. Three different routes, Highway 1, Highway 5 and Highway 3, converge here to become one main road into the Fraser Valley and on to Vancouver, a two hour drive away. The five lane highway travelled through an increasingly populated landscape that merged into Canada's second biggest city. I was back in Vancouver after nine years, the place where I'd first got the idea to drive to Alaska.

Vancouver hadn't changed much in the intervening years, except for one thing: the traffic, which was now awful. I battled through the jams and took a look at some of my old haunts: my apartment on 12th Avenue, my favourite bar in Kitslano, the downtown area, and

Gastown. Gastown is where it all began for the City of Vancouver. The name comes from its most famous resident, 'Gassy Jack' Deighton, a retired riverboat captain who arrived on the shore of the Burrard Inlet in 1867. Jack had a penchant for whisky. Within 24 hours of arriving at the place that would be named after him, Gassy Jack built a salon and was doing business. His isolated saloon catered to the loggers and soon attracted other businesses to open in the area. Whisky galore brought murder and mayhem. However, when the Canadian Pacific Railroad proposed to build tracks to the Gastown area in 1884, property values tripled. Gastown was incorporated in 1886 as the township of Granville, (named after the head of the CPR) and shortly after was renamed Vancouver. Most towns in this part of the world were built upon gold. Vancouver is unusual because it was built upon whisky.

I spent the night in a hotel near the airport. The following day I headed down to the district of Tsawwassen, which is on a peninsular about 15 miles south of downtown Vancouver. Tsawwassen is a Salish Indian word which means "facing the sea". It's a difficult word to pronounce, drunk or sober. Unfortunately, the Tsawwassen Indians do spend a lot of their time drunk. Yup, it was the same old story here as in the rest of the northwest. As if unemployment, addiction, suicide and incarceration were not enough, the Indians in the Vancouver region have also been decimated by AIDS.

The touchy-feely Canadian Government is trying to help the Tsawwassen Indians by giving them self-government (the Indians are also exempt from income tax) and there's now around 300 Indians living on the Tsawwassen peninsular. Back in the 1950s they built the ferry terminal and port here without any consultation with the Indians, whose land it is. During the construction of the port the last remaining Long House was demolished (a Long House is the Indian equivalent of a church). These days, plans are afoot to build 5000 new homes right on Tsawwassen Indian's Reserve. These homes are for wealthy non-natives.

I'd arranged to stay for a few days in Tsawwassen with Pat, a Citroen buff who had been following the 2CV Alaska Challenge. I arrived on his wife's birthday. That evening the family gathered at the house for a celebratory dinner, to which I was also invited. However, I spent a lot of the evening out in their garden. This far south it was still summer and pleasant and warm. This wasn't the main attraction of the garden: Pat's house was nonsmoking. I smoked, in the garden. At the bottom end of the garden there was a tall wooden fence. On the other side of that fence lay America. This was the border, and yet another example of crazy map making in the Pacific northwest.

The border between Canada and the USA runs mostly in a dead straight line along the 49th parallel. This parallel bisects the southern end of the Tsawwassen peninsular. What's left on the US side of the border is a few square miles surrounded by sea, a place called Point Roberts. In the days when British Columbia prohibited liquor sales on Sundays, a large number of Canadians used to cross the border to get a drink in Point Roberts. Times have changed and today Point Roberts is mainly the preserve of welfare scroungers. It's a tiny place and there's nothing much there. If you live in this isolated and forgotten corner of the USA you can quite legitimately say you're unemployed and claim welfare, and thousands do.

On the border there is a US Customs Post. The customs officers manage to keep a serious face when they ask southbound travellers where they're heading. You can only give one answer: Point Roberts. Most people who arrive at this Customs Post do so after taking a wrong turn at the nearby BC Ferries terminal.

I knew where I was going, when, after two nights with Pat and his family, I drove the short distance to the ferry terminal and bought a one-way ticket to Vancouver Island.

Chapter 6 - Lotus Land

With a heart-stopping blast on her horn the *Queen of Saanich* slid away from the dockside and out into the choppy, grey waters. She is a large ferry that plies between Tsawwassen and Swartz Bay, on Vancouver Island. Tsawwassen is a short drive from Vancouver. Swartz Bay is a short drive from Victoria, the biggest city on Vancouver Island and the capital of British Columbia. The crossing takes a couple of hours and is British Columbia Ferries busiest route, with departures every two hours throughout the day. I figured you just needed to know that.

The stretch of water that separates the southern half of Vancouver Island from the mainland is called the Strait of Georgia. The first part of the voyage is across open sea, then you encounter the Gulf Islands and the ship begins weaving between them, sometimes passing within feet of sheer rock faces. Nicotine addicts get to see most of the beautiful scenery. Smoking is banned everywhere on the ferries, except on the cold, windy decks. The ships are also dry. BC Ferries will take you across to Vancouver Island, but they won't let you do it with a gin and tonic in your hand.

In the Strait of Georgia the 49th Parallel gets a bit confused. Ten miles offshore this dead straight line suddenly halts, then dives south through the Strait, zigzagging along the way before heading west again beneath the tip of Vancouver Island. This means that some of the Gulf Islands are in the US and some are in Canada. The ferry passes through US territorial waters for part of its journey. BC Ferries won't tell the Americans if you don't.

The Strait of Georgia is another example of the border dispute between Canada and the US. The 49th parallel was agreed as the border between the United States and the British territory (what would later become Canada) by the London Convention of 1818.

However, this border was only recognised as far as the Rocky Mountains. West of the Rockies was still an untamed wilderness and things were a bit vague as far as borders go.

When British and American fur traders began settling in the Pacific coastal region, and competition for the area's rich resources hotted up, the border became an issue. For years the claim to Vancouver Island was in dispute. The Americans wanted the border to be extended up to the 54th parallel, which would have given them all of Vancouver Island. However, in 1843 the British sponsored Hudson Bay Company established a colony on the southern tip of the Island called Fort Victoria. This colony became the centre of the coastal fur trade. British settlers arrived and began farming. Fort Victoria lay below the 49th parallel and thus the Americans claimed it was theirs. The Brits told them to bugger off and got Vancouver Island by virtue of the fact that possession in nine tenths of the law, the law in this case being the Oregon Treaty of 1846. The fact that Point Roberts remained as US territory shows just how hotly this part of the border was contested. Other flashpoints along the border were Maine-New Brunswick, on the Atlantic coast, and of course the Alaska border dispute. All in all, it took 120 years and five separate treaties before the modern day border between Canada and the United States was established.

It took Vancouver Island 360 million years to crawl up from Mexico to its present location. The Island is approximately 350 miles long by 70 miles wide and stretches along Canada's rugged Pacific coastline, sheltering British Columbia's lower mainland from the blustery rains and wind of the open sea. For a large number of visitors, however, Vancouver Island is just part of a longer journey. In the far north of the Island, 7 hours driving time from the south, lies the small town of Port Hardy. From here the ferry goes up to Prince Rupert, where you can connect with the Alaska Marine Highway system. If things had gone to plan I would have arrived on Vancouver Island at Port Hardy.

As it was, though, the *Queen of Saanich* paused for ten minutes outside the Swartz Bay ferry terminal. The crew were undergoing a lifeboat drill. I thought about another lifeboat drill, in the middle of the Atlantic Ocean, and wondered how the Captain and crew of the

Marie Anne were faring. Hurricane *Floyd* was presently battering the south east coast of the USA, including Savannah. Things were a little calmer in Swartz Bay. The passengers milled impatiently around the deck. It was the usual mixed bunch making the crossing that day: tourists, buisinessmen, truck drivers, and an awful lot of hippies.

There's nothing particularly remarkable about Swartz Bay. It's just a big, modern ferry terminal in a very pretty location at the northern tip of the Saanich peninsular. On the forty minute drive down to Victoria I noticed that the traffic on Vancouver Island was also a lot worse than it used to be. I got to Victoria in the early evening. It hadn't changed much in nine years, except that the Canadian Dental Association were holding their annual conference there and every hotel was booked solid. I had to drive half way back up the Saanich peninsular before I found a Days Inn that had a room free.

The next day I drove back to Victoria and strolled into the offices of the *Times Colonist*, the main daily newspaper on Vancouver Island. This brush with the press went beyond mere ego. I figured that some publicity on the Island would help me find work. Just about everyone read the *Times Colonist*. First, though, a photographer followed me out to the car park and asked for the dreaded roof shot. The *Times Colonist* wanted to get the full story of the Alaska Challenge. However, the journalist who'd been assigned to interview me was tied-up on another job. They told me he'd be back in an hour, and if I wouldn't mind waiting... I apologised and said that I was in a bit of a hurry, which wasn't really true. Fact is, by that time I had grown blasé about the press. The *Times Colonist* ran the piece the next day. There wasn't an awful lot of text, but there was a nice big picture of me, looking like a right pratt as I stood up through the roof of the car.

After securing a bit of publicity for myself I headed north. My destination was Campbell River, 160 miles further up the Island. John and Heather Fuller lived in Campbell River. John told me he was one of only three people on Vancouver Island who owned a Citroen 2CV. He'd followed the progress of The 2CV Alaska Challenge and invited me to stay at his home, which was brave of him, since we'd never met before. The fact that I was a fellow 2CV buff was good enough for him, and vice versa.

Almost all of the 750,000 population of Vancouver Island live in and around the city of Victoria. The rest of the inhabitants are strung out along the east coast of the island as far as Campbell River. The far north of the island, the interior and the west coast are one vast mountainous wilderness with a few isolated settlements. There is just one main highway, the Island Highway, which runs from Victoria all the way up the east coast to Port Hardy. Last time round I never left Victoria city limits. Now, I felt quite excited at the prospect of the drive up to Campbell River.

After driving wilderness highways in the far north one's expectations are high. The Island Highway was a bit of a let down. The first ten miles or so out of Victoria are through an ugly urban sprawl with the obligatory gas stations, billboards and fast food restaurants. Then the road enters dense forest and begins a steep climb. This is the Malahat Drive, which inevitably takes you up to Malahat Summit. There is a lay-by at the top. I pulled in to take a look at the magnificent view across the Saanich Inlet and the Gulf Islands.

That's about as far as it went with regard to magnificent views on the Island Highway. After the Malahat Summit the road wound steeply down and hugged the coastal lowlands. I passed through small towns called Duncan, Ladysmith and Cassidy. There were lots of people hitchhiking along the highway. Indians, hippies, folks who couldn't spare a dime. Seventy miles north of Victoria I encountered Nanaimo, the second biggest city on the Island. North of Nanaimo it is more sparsely populated, the settlements further apart. Places like Parksville and Fanny Bay have a distinctly colonial feel to them, with prim, English-style bungalows, cosy pubs and seaside shops selling buckets and spades.

Campbell River is a small town, and guess what, it sits at the mouth of the Campbell River. The town faces Quadra Island, just across the narrow Discovery Passage, and has a pretty little harbour. Campbell River is known as 'The Salmon Capital of the World'. It would have been a very pleasant place if it weren't for the fact that it ponged. Just north of the town there is a huge pulp mill. The milling and pulping of wood produces a very unpleasant odour. When the wind was blowing in the wrong direction this odour settled over the town. Unfortunately, the wind was nearly always blowing in the wrong direction.

The first thing I noticed in John's driveway was a gleaming white Citroen 2CV. The vehicle was in immaculate condition, just like John Pengelly's one in Toronto. The *Yukon Queen* looked a sorry state in comparison. John and Heather didn't seem to mind and made me most welcome. They were both in their 50s and liked to enjoy life. The house sat on a hillside overlooking the sea. John had a telescope set-up on the large veranda at the back of the house. It was a hobby of his to watch the cruise ships plying up and down the Discovery Passage. One hundred years previously this had been the main route to the Klondike gold fields. Such were the numbers trying to get a passage north that old rust buckets were brought out of retirement. These ships often carried more than their registered number of passengers, who had to endure cramped, cold conditions and sea sickness during the two week voyage up from Vancouver and Seattle. At the end of that voyage lay Skagway, otherwise known as 'hell on earth'.

The respite at John and Heather's house gave me a chance to lavish some badly needed TLC on the *Yukon Queen*. The stuff she was carrying hadn't been touched since loading it in London all those months ago. Now the contents of the *Yukon Queen* filled half of a Vancouver Island front lawn. John and I stood back in amazement: how the hell had all that fitted into the car? Somehow it had: a spare engine, gear box, suspension arms, etc, etc. All this junk had been carted around North America for more than 10,000 miles. The only spares required were a couple of bulbs and a couple of spark plugs, not to mention one spare tyre. I inspected the damage sustained when I jacked up the car in Haines. It wasn't too bad, just a split in the bodywork. For the umpteenth time I found myself amazed that the car had survived the last two months.

John knew a bit about mechanics. He gave the *Yukon Queen* a service and oiled the wheel bearings. Meanwhile, I replaced the broken headlamp and thoroughly cleaned the bodywork. Then I drove the car round to a local garage and got them to weld the broken exhaust pipe back together. At the end of it all the *Yukon Queen* was back to her old self. She'd aged a bit, and taken some hard knocks along the road, but she was still feisty and raring to go. John offered to take the spare parts off my hands. 2CV spares aren't easy to come by in North America. I declined his offer. Somehow the *Yukon Queen* wouldn't seem complete without her load, and it took me more than two hours to load it all back on board. Who knows, I might just need an engine, gearbox, suspension arms, etc, etc.

I stayed with John and Heather for three days. During this time I asked around Campbell River to see if there was any work going. Nope, nothing, not even in the smelly pulp mill which employed half the town. John had warned me about the depressed economy in Campbell River and said the best chance of finding work was down in Victoria; so, in a revitalised *Yukon Queen* I headed south again.

Vancouver Island has the most temperate climate in Canada. It was partly this fact that made me decide not to spend a subzero winter in Fairbanks. Now, in mid September, I had the roof down on the car and managed to get a suntan. I also managed to get the radio working again. Mellow music accompanied our drive south. Jamie was relaxed, although very silent. It was all rather pleasant, except that my funds were low and I needed to find employment of some kind.
Half way back down to Victoria I came across the little town of Qualicum Beach. The Chamber of Commerce describes the town thus: "Qualicum Beach is to the artist of today what Stratford-on-Avon was to the era of Shakespeare". Huh?! The grand claims to fame made by these small towns in the middle of nowhere never ceased to bring a smile to my face, speaking of course as someone who is big in the Yukon.

I decided to resist the charms of Qualicum Beach and just for fun I turned off the Island Highway and took Highway 4 west across the mountains. Highway 4 goes to the only settlements on the remote west coast: Ucluelet and Tofino, two very small towns that are a short distance apart. The scenery along Highway 4 is spectacular, and includes Cathedral Grove, a patch of forest that contains some of the biggest and most ancient redwood trees in North America. After passing through Cathedral Grove I arrived in Port Alberni, which belying its name sits inland in the mountains. Thing is, in this part of the island the dividing ridge of towering mountains have had a nervous breakdown. Port Alberni is connected to the west coast by a wide inlet which is more than forty miles long. This sea approach to

Port Alberni is, needless to say, spectacular. I was in a car, though, and Port Alberni didn't live up to it's promise. It is a somewhat dreary and run-down working town. Ah ha, work! I asked around and soon discovered that Port Alberni has some of the highest unemployment on the island. It made Campbell River seem positively delightful.

That mountainous nervous breakdown has not only connected Port Alberni to the west coast, it's also allowed the sea to invade other parts of this central region. The result is a myriad of coves, inlets and islands, many of them still uncharted to this day. The sixty mile drive from Port Alberni to the west coast town of Ucluelet is Wonderful. Ucluelet is not very wonderful. A depressed economy and a government ban on salmon fishing have turned it into a bit of a ghost town. The end-of-the-road outpost of Tofino, twenty six miles further up the coast, seemed a much better prospect. Tofino (population 1,100) was once a haven for American draft dodgers and live-off-the-land hippies, many of whom still reside here. The town sits at the end of a spit of land, with the ocean on one side and inlets and islands on the other side. Very pretty. Most tourists go to Tofino to watch the whales or to watch the storms.

The atrocious weather makes you realise why very few people live on the west coast of Vancouver Island. The mountainous waves, screaming winds and stair rod-like rains that pummel this part of the coast from November to March make you strongly aware that nature is firmly in charge in these parts. Tofino has cashed-in on its climate and in the low season hotels offer discount rates for storm watchers. One hostelry even pipes the sound of the howling wind and nearby crashing waves into its dining room. Even in September the weather was grotty and I got soaking wet during the ten minutes or so that it took me to walk around and explore Tofino. After that I faced the prospect of spending another night in the car. I found a car park on the outskirts of town, and, with the Pacific rollers doing their thang just on the other side of a sand dune, I had one of the coldest and most uncomfortable night's sleep I've ever had in that car.

The next morning the rain followed me out of Tofino and back into the interior. Port Alberni still looked very depressed as I drove through on my way to the eastern side of the island. Near Cathedral

Grove I got caught in a stretch of roadworks. It was a long wait. The rain had eased up so I decided to stretch my legs and have a cigarette. Immediately behind me was a large, beat-up pick-up truck. The driver got out to take a look at the *Yukon Queen*. I found myself facing a stocky man, medium height who looked to be in his 50s. He had a flowing white beard and long silvery hair. A cliché hippy; not at all surprising: there are zillions of them in this part of the world.

The man introduced himself as 'Cat' and said that he'd been on a business trip to Ucluelet. He really loved the *Yukon Queen* and walked around admiring her. I told him I was an intrepid adventurer. Cat told me he was a web site designer. He seemed like a nice guy. Our little chat didn't develop much further, though, because we were cleared to pass through the roadworks and the traffic began moving again.

Victoria was much as I'd left it six days previously. I drove around for a bit, as you do. The city didn't strike me as a very uplifting place. I would have to live here as well as work here; and I smoked. The wave of political correctness which was engulfing North America at that time had already reached Victoria and the district of Saanich, where there was a total ban on smoking in public places, including bars and public parks. Strict fines were imposed on anyone who broke the ban. Put that in your pipe and smoke it; or maybe not.

Yes, we all know that smoking is a filthy habit which will kill you, it's just that I'm one of those bloody minded people who don't like being dictated to. If 'authority' says I can't do a certain thing I'll usually do it, just for the hell of it. Thus, my decision to base myself in the district of Cowichan, where the smoking ban hadn't yet reached, was based on solid principles and not a severe addiction to nicotine.

Forty minutes drive north of Victoria, back up the Island Highway, lay the town of Duncan, the administrative centre of the Cowichan district, where lots of folks have yellow fingers and a hacking cough. The architecture in downtown Duncan is cliché wild west, with a single track railway line running straight through the centre of town, complete with a station that could have come out of *The Adventures of Jesse James*. As well as cowboys you've also got your injuns' and there are totem poles all around town. I liked Duncan and spent the night sleeping in a lay-by on the outskirts of town.

The next day I explored the Cowichan district - 'Cowichan' is the name of the First Nations folk who have lived in this area for thousands of years. Duncan is on the Cowichan River, which six or so miles to the east leads into Cowichan Bay and the sea. To the west of Duncan it's a 35 mile drive up into the mountains to Lake Cowichan, a very long, large lake with crystal clear water. The tarmac roads runs out here at a little village called Youbou, half way along the north shore of the lake. If you want to go further west along the lake you have to use logging roads. I used them for about five miles until coming to a National Park camping ground. It was a very pretty spot; remote, but not too remote, and there were water taps and picnic tables. Of course at that time of year, late summer, the camping ground was deserted. Perfect, and so we spent the best part of a week living there. Just me, Jamie and the bears. I had an inflatable mattress and slept on one of the picnic tables. The mild weather made things easy and I managed some excellent night's sleep. Every day Jamie and I would go for a swim in the lake. This was bathtime, and despite the fact that the waters came from snow and ice on the mountains they were surprisingly warm. The village of Youbou lay just down the road, to get supplies, or to spend time in the bar there. All in all, it was very pleasant living by the lake for a while. To begin with the bears were the only worry, because I'd hear them moving around at night while I slept on the picnic table. After a while though, when it became apparent that they weren't going to bother me, I was glad of the bears company.

It was an idyllic respite after all those months of hard travelling, but it couldn't last long. Early October arrived and sent Summer packing. The nights were getting chilly. I still hadn't found any paid work, despite frequent trips down to Victoria. Work or no work, I needed a roof over my head. Trouble is, roofs are so expensive. It would have been nice to rent somewhere near Lake Cowichan. I didn't have the funds for a long term let, what with a month's deposit, a months rent up front and all that lark, which left me with short term lets, holiday accommodation, hotels and the like. There wasn't much going in the Lake Cowichan area. Duncan seemed a better prospect. However, although I found the town interesting it was not the sort of place where I'd like to live. Instead I moved further east to Cowichan Bay, where I paid for a month up front in the Wessex Inn. Ouch!

The Wessex Inn is a modern, two storey structure in mock tudor style, situated just outside Cowichan Bay village. My spacious room contained a very large bed and a kitchen and from the balcony you just about had a view of the bay. Not a bad place to live. The room also had a table that I used as a desk. It was now the 5th of October and the first time since the 28th of July, when the *Marie Anne* docked in Savannah, that I found myself sleeping in the same bed, the same place for more than a few nights. Some sort of home at last, and even if it was still semi-permanent it sure beat the hell out of crashing on people's sofas, or having their spare room for a night or two.

Pretty little Cowichan Bay now had a famous resident; or at least, he was famous in his own hotel room. White men first arrived in these parts in 1848. Ten years later the first hotel cum general store opened, right here in Cowichan Bay. The town of Duncan came into being when the railroad from Victoria was built in 1886. After that the Cowichan district developed rapidly; that is, it developed rapidly for the white men. For the Cowichan Indians it was the same old story as elsewhere in North America: the white men brought death and the destruction of the Indian's way of life. All those totem poles that one sees in modern day Duncan (there's nearly 80 of them) are called the 'Totem Pole Project' and are part of a "mission to share and to build the pride of First Peoples through education, art, and traditional weaving, beading, spinning…" The reality is that quite often the Indians are too drunk or stoned for 'weaving, beading, spinning' and unemployment is rife.

To give the Canadians their due, the Cowichan are one of the few tribes that weren't carted off to a reservation. They still live on the same land that their ancestors have inhabited for thousands of years. Many of then can be found in the area between Cowichan Bay and Duncan. They live in houses that are mostly squalid and run-down. The Indians rarely came into Cowichan Bay village. They could be found in Duncan, often blind drunk. I encountered the Indians mostly on the six mile drive from Cowichan Bay to Duncan. The road crosses the Cowichan River a number of times and you'd find the Indians fishing from the bridges. The Indians nearly always had a sullen air about them, and who can blame them?

I hadn't brought any fishing rods with me. However, amongst all the junk in the car I did have my manual typewriter, an old Imperial 80 on which I'd written eight very avant-garde and very bad novels that no one wanted to read or publish. My typer took pride of place on the desk in my hotel room. And there I sat, smoking cigarettes and gazing through the balcony window at the half view of the bay. For a moment I contemplated starting my book about the Alaska Challenge but dismissed the idea. My little adventure didn't seem to be over yet. I could sense that I was still on some sort of a journey. Besides, I was almost stone broke and earning money had to take priority over writing a book which might never get published.

Thinking about the book did give me an idea, though. The Alaska Challenge bulletins had been much enjoyed by the Citroen buffs, or so they told me. There were 24 bulletins, running to around 10,000 words. Ten thousand words is not an awful lot, yet with the accompanying photographs it would make a booklet which I could flog and hopefully make some money out of. Fired-up by the idea, I immediately began putting together a publishing proposal. I thought the booklet would sell, and the great thing was that I still had the *Yukon Queen*. I could use the car as a marketing tool for the booklet, and even flog the booklets directly from the boot. Sitting there in that hotel in Cowichan Bay it seemed like a great idea. I just needed to find a publisher.

Sparks flew off my old Imperial 80 as I started bashing out various drafts of the publishing proposal. I went through the Cowichan District Yellow Pages and identified two publishers who I thought might be interested in the Alaska Challenge booklet. Once I was satisfied with the publishing proposal I posted it off to them.

Cowichan Bay village is just a line of mostly wooden buildings along a road that runs between the base of a small cliff and the bay. Such is this narrow strip of land that most of the buildings hang out into the bay on stilts. It's all very picture postcardish. There's a small harbour used by the fishing boats, and further along the waterfront a small marina and hotel complex. The harbour and the marina summed-up the economy of Cowichan Bay: fishing and tourism. The local pub, also hanging out into the bay on stilts, is called *The Lobster Pot*. I used to pop in there now and again for a beer, and sometimes haddock and chips. The haddock was excellent.

After hanging out in the *Lobster Pot* for a bit it didn't take me long to realise that the economy of Cowichan Bay was very depressed, almost manically so. Every week a village meeting was held in the pub. The main agenda was always the local economy. Fishing meant mostly salmon, and the salmon stocks had been ravaged that year by a virus. The fishermen were all broke. The marina, hotels and knick-knack shops in Cowichan Bay relied for most of their income on rich Americans who sailed their flashy boats up to the east coast of Vancouver Island. However, the Americans weren't coming in the numbers they used to, preferring instead to explore the coasts of Washington and Oregon. This left the tourist industry in Cowichan Bay stone broke. The biggest topic of debate in the *Lobster Pot* was the big new marina, which they were trying to get a government grant to build. This debate became quite heated because the village split between two factions: those who tried to earn a living in Cowichan Bay, and those who had retired there because of its scenic location. The big new marina would completely ruin the view of the waterfront. The big new marina would also hopefully entice back those rich Americans. At times the residents of Cowichan Bay almost came to blows over the issue.

Out of all the places I could have chosen to call home, Cowichan Bay in particular, and Vancouver Island in general, were probably among the worst unemployment black spots in North America - I probably would have had more luck finding work in Point Roberts. My hopes of earning a buck or two began to hinge almost entirely on the 2CV Alaska Challenge booklet. After my first week at the Wessex Inn I rang the two publishers. Both of them had received my publishing proposal. The first publisher said that he hadn't had a chance to look at the Alaska Challenge web site yet and didn't sound particularly interested in the project. The other publisher said that he'd seen the web site, liked the idea of a booklet and could I come over and see him.

The publisher's name was Tim Peterson and he lived in a small hamlet about 10 miles from Duncan. Tim was in his 50s, a bit eccentric with ruffled clothes and a small, undisciplined beard. I already knew a bit about Tim, because he wrote a weekly column for the local newspaper. His house lay surrounded by trees and was reached by a narrow track. Tim ran his business from home. In his office I was heartened to see a printing press and piles of fresh, new books. We ran through the booklet idea, than I took Tim outside and showed him the *Yukon Queen*. This sealed the deal: Tim just loved the car, and also my plan to use it as a marketing tool to sell the booklet. The problem was, Tim ran a very small business. He could only take on one project at a time, and at that moment he was still publishing a local history book. He told me the Alaska Challenge booklet would follow. I tried to intimate just how broke I was. Tim was sympathetic and said that he'd get the local history book put to bed as soon as possible. I knew it would be both embarrassing and a waste of time to ask for an advance against sales of the booklet.

I left Tim's house disheartened and still penniless. I just had to hang in there somehow until the booklet started rolling off the presses. In the meantime I needed some kind of a break. It came during my second week at the Wessex Inn. Early one evening there was a knock at my door. At first I didn't recognise the caller, then I twigged: it was Cat, the hippy I'd met more than a fortnight ago on the road back from Tofino. Cat looked his usual scruffy self. I made him a cup of coffee while he had a good look round my hotel room. Cat told me that he lived nearby and had seen the *Yukon Queen* in the hotel car park. He asked me what my plans were. I explained my circumstances. Cat explained that he had a business proposition for me. He was somewhat cagey about it and told me to meet him the following day, at a restaurant in Duncan. He was meeting one of his clients there at midday and would see me afterwards.

Cat left me in a euphoric mood. I walked down to the *Lobster Pot* for a celebratory haddock and chips and looked skywards to that place where lucky breaks come from. By the following lunchtime I'd calmed down somewhat; after all, I didn't know this guy and had no idea what business he might put my way. All I knew was that Cat designed web sites. I saw him in the restaurant, sitting with his client. I was somehow surprised that the client looked normal. Cat now appeared business-like. His long, silvery hair had been brushed back into a ponytail. His beard looked like it had been trimmed. He wore a pair of smart trousers, a brown bomber jacket and carried an attaché case. The client left and Cat signalled for me to come over. I sat across the table from him and suggested that we have a beer. Cat said that he liked to keep a clear head during meetings and coffee would be better. Yes, very business-like.

Cat's web site design business was called Web & E-Data Services, or WEED for short. He and his business partner had just launched a venture called 'Better Boats', a web site with classified ads for buying and selling boats and associated equipment. At that time I knew next to nothing about web sites and wondered how on earth I could fit into it all. Cat said that my job would have two strands. The first, promoting Web & E-Data Services. The second, drumming-up business for Better Boats by going round the hundreds of marinas on the east coast of Vancouver Island. Cat saw the *Yukon Queen* as an essential part of both strands. It was such an unusual car, and the publicity I'd received on Vancouver Island courtesy of the *Times Colonist* meant that now I wasn't just big in the Yukon. Rob Godfrey and the *Yukon Queen* were a good sales tool. The car would carry banner ads for Better Boats. I asked what sort of salary I could expect. Cat explained that it all depended on how much business I brought in. I told him I would think about it and let him know in the morning.

It was basically a sales job, and in my experience sales jobs always suck. However, at that moment in time I didn't have any better offers. Also, the work sounded like fun. Within five minutes of leaving that restaurant I'd made up my mind that I would be selling WEED and Better Boats. My theory being, that even if the money was lousy at least it would tied me over until the Alaska Challenge booklet emerged from Tim's press. It's funny how your thought processes work, isn't it.

The next morning I rang Cat and told him we had a deal. He sounded pleased and gave me his address, telling me to come over and see him. Cat's place lay only a few miles away, on the high ground overlooking Cowichan Bay. I expected to discover a nice house amongst all the retirement homes up there on the hillside. Instead I found a run-down single storey dwelling sitting on a plot of land overgrown with weeds. It looked similar to the houses the Indians occupied down on the Cowichan River. Hmm, so this was the home of Web & E-Data Services.

A somewhat startled and rather pretty young woman answered my knock on the door. She introduced herself as Suz and said that Cat had been called out and would be back shortly. The interior of the house was in much the same condition as its exterior. There was a walk through kitchen/lounge and two bedrooms and a bathroom, all separated by cheap plyboard walls. At one end of the lounge were Cat's desk and computers. At the other end the kitchen table, where Suz prepared some herbs. I sat in the middle of the lounge, on a dusty old sofa, and felt very awkward as I met Suz's pleasant smiles.

We heard a crunch of gravel on the driveway; the slamming of a car door. Cat made a grand entrance. He looked a little bit more windswept than when I had seen him the previous day: Hi Suz, Hi Rob! He plumped himself down at the desk and lit-up a bedraggled cigarette. Our all important business meeting began in a haze of exotic smoke.

Despite an ambiguous salary, the Better Boats part of my new job looked quite pleasant. What's so difficult about driving up and down the coast and visiting the marinas? The Web & E-Data Services lark was a little bit harder, since at that time I knew naff all about building web sites. I asked Cat to give me some idea of just what web site design and hosting entailed: "Hey, Rob, just tell them they need a web site for their business and my WEED is the best on the island, ok".

Suz gave us smiles and coffee as Cat printed me out some business cards. I was now an Associate Director of WEED, and the Sales Manager of Better Boats. Hey, I was going up in the world.

I was feeling somewhat dizzy and lightheaded when I left Cat's house and giggled all the way back to Cowichan Bay. It sure seemed a beautiful day and I thought that all this web site stuff could be a wonderful money spinner. This was 1999, and although internet use had become well established in North America it was still a relatively new phenomenon in other parts of the world. The Dot Com bubble had not yet burst and the internet seemed to have limitless possibilities.

The omens were good because the 2CV Alaska Challenge had been an internet based project. E-mail played a huge part in getting the thing organised. The Alaska Challenge bulletins were one of the earliest travelogues on the net (now it's old hat). The charity fund raising was done entirely via the internet; the first time this had been attempted in the UK. The karma felt right, here on Vancouver Island, because once again I was involved in internet stuff, this time enabling me to earn some money.

But in reality the final two Alaska Challenge bulletins were never put on the web site; nor was the charity donation form: the fund raising had been a total disaster. This was partly due to the fact that I knew nothing about web sites and had to put the Alaska Challenge site in the hands of someone else. Not a good resume for the Associate Director of WEED.

That evening I received a phone call. The caller described himself as Cat's business partner and said his name was Jack. Jack wanted to meet me and we arranged it for the following morning, in the village coffee shop. Jack turned out to be another cosmic character, in his early sixties, medium build with longish brown hair, an ear ring and a penetrating glance. We sat outside the café in the sunshine and talked about lay lines and reincarnation. After Jack had finished sussing me out he told me that he was a gold prospector in eastern Canada and had done 'a bit of this and a bit of that'. He'd bought a house on the hill overlooking the bay, where he and his wife lived for part of the year. Jack said that shortly they were going to move to Cowichan Bay permanently. Eastern Canada was too cold in the winter.

I took to Jack straight away: a genuinely nice guy, and obviously the financial backing behind Better Boats. Jack, too, thought that the buying and selling of boats online was a good idea. We talked about Cat. We talked about the bedraggled cigarettes that Cat smoked. Jack asked me if I took drugs. I told him quite honestly that the only drugs I took were nicotine and alcohol. Jack seemed relieved and went on to talk about the healing properties of pyramids.

I drove into Duncan to get the car measured-up for the Better Boats banners. The guy in the sign shop was somewhat amused by the *Yukon Queen* and admired the skill that had gone into the banners she carried. Citroen 2CVs have lots of curvy bits, which doesn't make life easy for a sign writer. I told this sign writer the usual stuff about the Alaska Challenge and gave him one of our publicity blurbs. Next, I went to an electrical goods store and bought myself a mobile phone. At one hundred and forty bucks I could not really afford it and it made a huge dent in my budget. However, the Associate Director of WEED, not to mention the Sales Manager of Better Boats, needed a mobile phone. I also bought myself an executive retractable biro and a ruler.

Another business meeting was arranged at Cat's house. Jack turned up, too. The room filled with exotic smoke and we discussed our sales strategy for Better Boats. I suggested that we print out some full colour publicity blurbs, to pin up on marina noticeboards, instead of the black and white ones we'd been using thus far. I also suggested that we should use a little anchor as the company logo. Cat and Jack seemed impressed by my business acumen. I made notes with my retractable biro as Cat's attention span grew shorter and shorter. Eventually he became confused and had trouble following the conversation. Jack and I looked at each other. Jack rolled his eyes. We went outside for a cigarette. Suz didn't allow tobacco smoking in the house.

I threw myself into my new responsibilities. Most fun of all was Better Boats. October on Vancouver Island brought warm and sunny weather and so I had the roof down on the car. The marina noticeboards were always my first port of call, and later, when I got back to my hotel room, I'd ring the private advertisers and try to persuade them to advertise online with Better Boats. These classified ads were only one half of the operation. The other half consisted of the businesses that took banner ads on Better Boats. Every marina had a chandlers and a boat builder. It was my job to call in on them and explain about the joys of advertising their business on Better Boats. Talking to these business owners, and indeed the boat owners, was always a bit tricky, because the Sales Manager of Better Boats knew naff all about boats.

And let's not forget the Associate Director of Web & E-Data Services, who had a much less scenic and more tedious job; basic sales work. At least Better Boats did provide some kind of service that was needed. As for WEED, I'd turn up uninvited at a business and try to persuade them that a web site would boast their sales tremendously, would make them rich beyond their wildest dreams and would make them incredibly attractive to the opposite sex. It didn't really matter what type of business they were involved in, anything from fun parks to funeral parlours. In fact, one of my more interesting calls was to a taxidermist on the Island Highway. Surrounded by stuffed moose and owls and snakes I almost persuaded the guy that he needed a web site.

After a few weeks of driving and telephoning and obtaining a suntan, I had not made a single sale. Cat did not seem too worried about this: "Hey Rob! it takes time", but all that driving and telephoning was costing me money, and my funds were running ever lower. One day, when Cat was particularly confused, I asked him for some wages. He gave me twenty dollars to cover my petrol expenses. It was the only money I ever got out of him.

For a number of weeks now I'd been living on the kindness of family and friends back in England. There's only so much money you can borrow, though, and Cat was right: this sales lark did take time, and felt akin to getting blood out of a stone. Everyone on Vancouver Island seemed to be strapped for cash. Getting them to sign on that infamous dotted line was often like going five rounds with Mike Tyson. Meanwhile, a financial crisis loomed. Jack wasn't much help, and explained that the only true wealth is wisdom. He suggested that I try the power of crystals.

Instead, I went to see Cat, to ask for some wages again. Cat had just got back from a trip to the wilderness part of the island. His bombsite garden now had a caravan parked in it. His house filled with pleasant, smiling young people who all seemed to be busy. It was harvest time, the harvest being marijuana. Cat sat at his desk. He held a bedraggled plant in his hand and examined it with a magnifying glass. "Hey Rob! come take a look". The young people smiled pleasantly at me. Cat passed over the magnifying glass and showed me the THC on the plant. THC stands for tetrahydrocannabinol, which is a right mouthful and is the little crystals on the leaves and stalks of the marijuana plant. It's the THC which makes you high. British

Columbia produces some of the most potent pot in the world, with THC levels as high as 30%, compared to pot produced in other regions which can have a THC level as low as a few percent. Growing and selling marijuana is illegal of course, and it's estimated that British Columbia's annual pot production is worth as much as 4 billion dollars. The authorities attitude towards pot is more liberal these days, yet if you're caught cultivating the stuff you can still face huge fines and imprisonment. That's why Vancouver Island's such a popular place when it comes to growing marijuana plants: the huge, unpopulated wilderness and all those lonely island outposts means that you can raise a crop with very little chance of being caught; and a large number of people do raise a crop. This is one reason why they call Vancouver Island 'Lotus Land'. My question about a wage got lost in the clouds of exotic smoke.

When I woke up in the next morning I had a cup of tea and then drove over to see Tim Peterson. I needed to get the Alaska Challenge booklet rolling. I needed to earn some money. Tim wasn't around. His secretary told me that he would be getting in touch real soon, that the booklet was still very much a goer. I left Tim's place somewhat buoyed-up if not somewhat frustrated. It was Halloween and time for witches and goblins and trick-or-treat, and pumpkins, huge bloody pumpkins. The faces carved on the pumpkins seemed to me mocking me as I drove back to the Wessex Inn.

So far, the only benefit I'd received from being in business partnership with Cat came from the use of his laptop computer, a pretty good machine that didn't actually belong to Cat. A complicated story lay behind the ownership of the laptop, and as far as I could make out, it once belonged to an ex-business partner of Cat's. The ex-business partner had got behind with the rent at Cat's place and run into financial difficulties. He'd left the laptop with Cat to cover the money he owed, which one day he would pay back; or something like that. I felt tempted to ask Cat if the ex-business partner was an Englishman, since after almost a month I still hadn't earned a single cent out of WEED and Better Boats.

But I did have use of the laptop, which enabled me to do a preliminary production job on the Alaska Challenge booklet, and to draft-up some marketing strategies. I just needed Tim to publish the damn thing, so that I could make my million bucks and live happily ever after. I e-mailed Tim my preliminary booklet production, and then rang him for a chat. He said that he thought we could make some money out of the booklet, but I'd have to wait just a little bit longer. Problem being, I didn't have time to spare. I had less than a week left at the Wessex Inn and hardly any money in the pot. It was decision time again, and I decided to cling on a little bit longer. It was the prospect of being published, rather than the prospect of making any money out of Cat's web site stuff, that made me stay on Vancouver Island.

I needed some funds, though, and my last ditch option was to sell something. The only two things of value I possessed were the *Yukon Queen* and my digital camera. The camera would have to go, and with a heavy heart I made the drive down to Victoria to try and get the best price for it. The camera had been a Christmas present from my Mother. I felt beastly about selling the damn thing. I consoled myself with the fact that if I sold it to a pawnbroker I could always buy it back later, once the million dollars started rolling in from the booklet.

That camera had been used to take thousands of pictures during the Alaska Challenge. It had been a trusty workhorse. The pawnbroker who paid me $600 for the camera didn't know all this of course. Whoopee, I was flush again! although acutely conscious that the six hundred bucks might have to last me a very long time. My little bit of luxury at the Wessex Inn had almost come to an end. I needed to find somewhere else to live, but I knew that a month's rent up front, plus a deposit, would wipe out most of the six hundred bucks, leaving me stone broke again. Cat came up with the solution: I could live in the caravan in his garden. Summer was now definitely over and the infamous monsoon season had started in British Columbia. I didn't fancy the prospect of living in a caravan at this time of year; really, though, I had no choice in the matter, if I wanted to remain on Vancouver Island, and I'd already decided to do just that.

I made the most of my final night in that big, warm, comfortable bed at the Wessex Inn. The next morning I packed everything into the car and drove the short distance up to Cat's house. Cat tapped away on his computer - "Hey Rob! howya doing". He'd forgotten about me taking up residence in his caravan. After a while, though, his brain synapses started kicking into gear. The battered caravan sat out front of the house. It needed to be moved round to the side, where it could be hooked-up to mains electricity and plumbing. The rain poured down. It didn't help to lift Cat's somewhat confused state of mind as he backed-up his truck to the caravan. For a man in his 50s who did a lot of drugs, Cat was incredibly strong and he hitched-up the caravan to the truck before I could even get there to lend a hand. The caravan had been parked under a small tree and as Cat towed it away some branches smashed one of the roof lights. Cat didn't notice and within five minutes the caravan was re-positioned by the side of the house. Cat connected-up the electricity supply but never got round to sorting out the plumbing.

Ah, home sweet home, a medium sized caravan, rather old and run-down but reasonably clean. At one end were two seat sofas facing each other, which could be turned into a big bed. Above the sofas a hammock, which is where I slept, and used the seat sofas to store my possessions. At the other end of the caravan lurked the cooking area, with a small sink and gas stove, and a closet-type toilet, which I couldn't use because it wasn't hooked into the plumbing. Adjacent to the cooking area was a small table with sofa seats either side. I used this as my desk and office area.

The first thing I noticed about the caravan was the strange smell inside. After exploring the drawers and cupboards, and discovering the remains of bedraggled plants, it became apparent what caused the smell. The caravan had been used to transport the marijuana harvest from the wilderness to Cat's house. I found those bedraggled plant remains in the most peculiar places, but never managed to find them all. Thus, the sweet smell of Mary always pervaded the caravan, but alas, not the sweet smell of success.

I began drinking. Vancouver Island's mild climate is great for the grape and in recent years there's been a renaissance in the wine industry. The locally produced gut rot is dirt cheap. I used to buy it in big gallon jugs. I think the reason I hit the gut rot was twofold: firstly, it was still not happening for me on Vancouver Island and I now found myself short of money and living in a grotty caravan in the pouring rain. Secondly, the Alaska Challenge had been one hell of an experience and now I finally came back down to earth, with a resounding thump. Reality? Help!

Reality was my immediate neighbours. It soon became obvious that Cat and Suz were going through a rocky time in their relationship. No doubt the shortage of money helped matters along. The atmosphere was tense. This, and the constant smell of pot, which made me feel nauseous, meant that I avoided the house as much as possible. I cooked meals for myself in the caravan and used to take my ablutions in the toilet and shower room down at the marina. The only time I ventured into the house was to fill up the caravan's water container, and of course to discuss business matters.

The pouring rain put a bit of a dampener on the Better Boats side of things. There'd been no sign of Jack for weeks. Rumour had it that he'd gone back to eastern Canada for a bit; and as far as the WEED side of things went, I still hadn't secured a single sale for Web & E-Data Services. Cat, too, didn't have any luck in securing web site design work. He started working for a builder friend of his, as a labourer. This didn't seem to ease the strained relationship between him and Suz and I could often hear their rows from the caravan.

The wine helped, it helped make that caravan seem more bearable. With the gas stove lit to provide warmth, and with just the light above my desk switched on and the constant rain pattering on the roof, it was rather cosy. At the end of an evening the fug from my cigarette smoke even managed to dispel the smell of the marijuana plants. Of course, the roof light leaked badly, solved by means of a bucket to catch the streams of water. Cat's garden had been turned into a quagmire by the weather, and there wasn't much I could do about the mud which got inside the caravan, or indeed the damp which permeated everything. I used to sleep soundly in my hammock, though. The wine saw to that.

Sometimes, when the weather was particularly bad, I wouldn't even venture out, except for more wine. I spent many days in that caravan, with the laptop computer, teaching myself all about web site design. The laptop contained the software that Cat used for Web & E-Data Services. I found that I immediately took to HTML and within a short time began building my own web sites. HTML stands for Hyper Text Mark-up Language. It's the programming code that a web browser reads in order to show a web page on your screen. Basic HTML is a bit like a recipe, a recipe which tells your web browser what the ingredients of a web page are and how to assemble them. It was 1999 when I sat in that caravan and things have moved on a bit since then, with more sophisticated types of HTML and Java script, etc. However, the basic principles of web site design stay the same. The only difficult bit is keeping up with all the new innovations.

I could now build web sites but WEED still floundered like a proverbial dying duck. I asked Cat if his builder friend also had a job for me. Cat shook his beard. The builder friend's business was strapped for cash and he employed Cat more as a favour rather than because he needed extra labour. I rang Tim Peterson again to see if anything had happened yet with the booklet. Tim apologised for being out of touch and said he was still going to publish the booklet; there'd been problems with the local history book that presently occupied his printing press and this was holding-up everything else. Tim promised that he'd get in touch as soon as he had a clear run to do the booklet.

Just when it seemed that things couldn't get any worse, Suz left Cat and went to live with her mother. I came back one evening to find Cat sitting at my desk in the caravan, drinking my gut rot wine and mumbling into his beard. Cat rarely called on me in the caravan and when I found him there I knew straight away that something was wrong. "Hey Rob! let's get hammered". Cat was already well hammered on the gut rot wine, and this on top of the vast quantity of pot he smoked. He dragged me along to a nearby Chinese restaurant. The pot pacified Cat. The alcohol made him very aggressive. Things got a tad hairy in the restaurant, particularly when Cat tried to punch out one the waiters. I really don't know what caused him to attack the waiter; but there again, I was also smashed out of my brains on gut rot wine.

A rough bar just off the Island Highway became our next port of call. I found myself playing a game of pool with Cat. I thought it would be a smart move to let him win, which wasn't difficult, since I was trying to hit two white balls. Cat took five bucks off me and then challenged a nearby Indian to a game, this time for fifty bucks. The Indian took the bet and did not speak a word throughout the game, in which he beat Cat by a narrow margin. Cat made some less than flattering remarks about the Cowichan Tribe. The Indian took off his hat, which always marked the start of a fight. Other Indians in the bar began gathering round. I started feeling a bit nervous. Cat seemed quite relaxed and stood up to his full height, facing the Indians. I've never met anyone, before or since, who's 50-something and as strong and fit as Cat. The Indians were no fools and when Cat did finally hand over the fifty bucks they backed-off.

After that evening I did my best to avoid Cat altogether. Sometimes, though, I couldn't escape him. Often, when Cat was really hammered, he would start telling me his Vietnam stories, and the story he kept telling over and over again was about how his best buddy got blown away by the Viet Cong. It wasn't just a memory for Cat, he could see the flowing brain matter right there in front of his face. Ten thousand young Canadian men fought in the US armed forces during the Vietnam War. At the same time up to 60,000 American draft-dodgers and 12,000 army deserters found refuge in Canada (Jimmy Carter's first act as president in 1977 was to grant them an amnesty). Canadian pot is as potent as war memories.

Cat's brother came to stay for a while, a regular looking guy and a recovering alcoholic, so it must have been great fun for him to be around Cat and I and the empty gallon jugs of wine. However, his presence did have a moderating effect on Cat's alcohol consumption: the two brothers went on a pot binge that lasted for a number of days. I hardly saw them during this period. They rarely left the house, which was fine by me, since at least I knew that I wouldn't have to deal with Cat's recent aggressive behaviour.

And so the days rolled by and the rain poured down and I continued to desperately seek work. With Christmas on the horizon holly picking became the big thing. I went to a number of holly farms and told them I was an experienced holly picker who had picked holly all over the world. They would take my name, address and number, telling me they'd get back to me. They never did. The depressed economy on Vancouver Island meant that large numbers of people applied for the seasonal holly picking jobs, and it mattered not if you had an Olympic Medal for holly picking.

After two weeks Suz returned. She and Cat had very loud sex, then Cat's brother was dispatched back to his home on the mainland. Cat sobered-up but continued smoking huge amounts of pot. We were all still broke. It now looked like things were back to normal, whatever that was. The seasonal holly picking had planted the seed of an idea in my head, an idea that would turn around our bad luck and make us very rich indeed. I sat in the caravan, drank gut rot and worked out the details of an idea that was so simple, so brilliant that it could only be a work of genius: WEED would do web sites for special occasions - birthdays, weddings, anniversaries and the like. The internet was still in its early days. A lot of people had access to the net, yet few of them had any idea of how to build web sites. WEED would do it for them. We couldn't lose. I did some calculations and worked out that every single day on Vancouver Island at least two thousand people were celebrating their birthday. There were correspondingly large numbers of people having weddings, anniversaries, etc; and of course, that was without the annual celebrations like Christmas, Easter, Mother's Day, Father's day, and all the rest of it. As the rain hammered against the roof of the caravan, and I started hitting my second litre of gut rot, I came up with a name for the venture: 'Wacky Web Sites', and this is part of the publicity blurb I wrote:

Do you want to give a friend, relation or loved one something truly original, something unique to them, something you'll be remembered for?

Wacky web sites could be the solution to your problem!

With a Wacky Web Site you can mark the special occasion of a friend, relation or loved one by giving them their very own web site on the Internet. This web site will contain photos, text and graphics that are unique to them. You can put whatever you want on the web site. Remember, there are no rules on the World Wide Web, it's a wacky place, anything goes!

All I had to do now was hit Cat with the idea. I put my designs on to a floppy disk, jumped from the caravan, slipped over in the mud and then ran to the house. I discovered Suz crashed out on the sofa, puffing on a bedraggled cigarette. Cat sat at his desk, staring intently at the computer screen. The computer was turned off. My sudden entrance and enthusiasm stirred them both. I quickly explained my idea and Cat was impressed: "Hey Rob, Wacky Web Sites!" Suz, too, got caught-up in the excitement and managed to get up off the sofa. We all felt that this was it, the money earner we'd been looking for.

Cat's concentration level at that moment in time couldn't handle looking through my detailed statistics of how many birthdays, weddings, anniversaries, etc, were celebrated every single day, and how we only needed to get a tiny percentage of this market to make a fortune. "Hey Rob, Wacky Web Sites!" Cat said that he'd look through the details in the morning. Suz offered me her joint, and by way of celebration I took it.

The next morning I got up early; well, if you call 10am early. I had a gut rot and Mary hangover. There was no sign of life from the house. Still fired-up by the Wacky Web Sites idea, I drove into Duncan to find a printer. Wacky Web Sites felt like our saviour and in order for it to work we needed publicity. None of us had the funds to take out adverts in the press, so instead I would get publicity flyers printed and deliver them by hand all over Vancouver Island (Vancouver Island is the same size as England). I found a printer who did me a really good deal on the publicity flyers. Even the printer was impressed by the Wacky Web Sites idea. It was an omen. I had hundreds and hundreds of flyers printed.

When I got back to the house at lunchtime, Cat and Suz had finally stirred. Cat looked through the information on my floppy disk and seemed very impressed: "Hey Rob, Wacky Web Sites!" Suz made coffee and rolled joints. The potency of Lotus Land pot was such that after half an hour we were all completely stoned and unable to talk properly. Cat and Suz staggered into the bedroom. They were celebrating their reunion by having huge amounts of sex. I staggered back through the rain to the caravan. Ok, if Cat and Suz were unable to launch Wacky Web Sites I'd do it myself. I had so much faith in my idea, felt so confident in its successful outcome, was so smashed out of my brains, that I didn't see Wacky Web Sites for what it was: Custer's last stand.

I did it myself, in the pouring rain. I delivered hundreds and hundreds of flyers to homes in and around Duncan. I then drove down to Victoria and spent days doing the same. The real killer was the architecture in this part of the world. Many of the homes are built with the living space raised above ground level and a half sunk basement. This meant that to reach the front door you had to climb up a long flight of steps to a veranda. Sounds easy, huh? Not if you're doing it hundreds of times a day, carrying a huge weight of leaflets and in the pouring rain. After two days the muscles on the back of my legs were screaming in pain and I had developed a very bad chest infection. Even Cat commented on it one evening: "Hey Rob! what's with the funny walk?" But the gut rot kept me going and after one week I had delivered every single leaflet to what I estimated was more than one thousand homes on Vancouver Island.

I'd done it, and now it became just a matter of waiting for Wacky Web Site orders to come flooding in. This near to Christmas my timing was perfect. But the orders didn't come flooding in; in fact, not one single order arrived. I went back to the printers in Duncan and got hundreds more leaflets printed. The printer was very impressed at the success of Wacky Web Sites. I handed over another fifty dollars. My chest infection had given me a fever and I was dripping with sweat. Once again the gut rot wine came to the rescue and I went back out into the pouring rain and delivered the leaflets.

I spent the next two days laying in my hammock, recovering. The caravan with its leaking skylight felt like a prison. I had no food in and the gas bottle had run out. I didn't have the energy to leave the caravan and get supplies. Being extremely ill sapped all my strength. I began having hallucinations.

After a while the drumming on the caravan's roof stopped and I was no longer bothered by the wolves. I emerged into the world again and went to see Cat: "Hey Rob! where ya been?" Still not one single order for a Wacky Web Site had arrived; and besides, even if a customer had phoned or e-mailed, Cat and Suz were always way too stoned to deal with enquiries. This didn't help my cause, because the six hundred bucks I'd got for the digital camera were running dangerously low. Perhaps the fever still gripped me, for I now contemplated selling the only thing of value I had left: the *Yukon Queen*. I drove down to Victoria, where I knew a car dealer called Scott, one of the handful of people on Vancouver Island who owned a 2CV. He used it as a publicity tool for his car dealership and it carried banner ads and he kept it parked out front of his downtown lot.

Scott commented on my funny walk and my fever ravaged face. I told him I wanted to sell the *Yukon Queen*, the most famous Citroen 2CV in North America. I would accept ten thousand dollars for her, nothing less. Scott told me that business was slow and he just didn't have that sort of money; besides, he already had a 2CV and didn't really need another, however famous it might be. He added that his cousin, a Citroen buff, might be interested in the car. We exchanged details and I headed back up to Cowichan Bay.

At the start of the Malahat Drive, just ten or so miles from Victoria's urban sprawl, I saw thousands of seagulls filling the sky. There were eagles as well. I knew what was attracting them: the Goldstream salmon run, which is one of the most famous salmon runs in the Pacific northwest. The Goldstream salmon run usually starts in October but got off to a slow start that year because of a virus that had killed many of the fish. Now, though, in mid November it was in full swing. Chum, coho and chinook salmon enter the Goldstream River via the Finlayson Arm from the Pacific Ocean, to return to where they were born three or four years previously, to spawn and then die. The Goldstream River is more of a stream than a river, only four or five feet across in places, with shallow, fast running waters.

I parked up the *Yukon Queen* and then walked over to watch one of nature's most amazing spectacles. The small stream was absolutely choked with salmon. The male fish had grown big, strong teeth and hooked jaws, which they used to fight for mating rights with the female salmon, wounding each other severely. The female salmon die after laying their eggs. The male salmon are not far behind them. Many die of exhaustion or fighting wounds before they even get to the mating process. It was an orgy of death, and the gulls and eagles feed upon the carcasses. At night, bears, raccoon and otters also join in the feeding frenzy.

I stood there and watched this vicious cycle of birth and death and it made me think of the futility and stupidity of my own situation. Bloody hell, I'd just been to Victoria, where I'd been trying to sell the *Yukon Queen*! What ever was I doing?! I made-up my mind there and then that the time had come to leave Vancouver Island. I was broke and had dug myself into a hole that seemed impossible to get out of, but somehow I would head back to eastern Canada, and somehow I would get the *Yukon Queen* back across the Atlantic to England. I had no idea how I would do this, but thought I'd cross that hurdle later. First priority was to leave Lotus Land and the gut rot behind and get back on the road again, heading east.

Once the decision had been made I felt a huge weight lifted from my shoulders. I felt free again. On the drive up to Cowichan Bay I was singing. When I got back to the caravan I inflated Jamie the Love Doll and she took her usual place on the front passenger seat. Cat staggered out the house and found it rather amusing: "Hey Rob, that's the sex doll!". He didn't find it so amusing when I told him I was leaving Vancouver Island. He immediately reclaimed the laptop computer, no doubt thinking that I was going to make off with it. We then shared a glass or two of gut rot wine and wished each other well. I would spend the night in the caravan and leave in the morning. Cat was leaving later that night for another trip to the wilderness part of the island. We wouldn't see each other again. Our business partnership was over. Our friendship managed to survive a little bit longer.

Next morning the *Yukon Queen* bombed south down the Island Highway. As I passed through all the places that had been a part of my life for the last few months I felt no regrets whatsoever. It had been interesting. It had just about bankrupted me. It had been another slice of life. When I got to the ferry terminal at Swartz Bay it even stopped raining. November had now almost run its course. I boarded the ferry and didn't think for a moment that I was going to attempt to cross Canada with the onset of winter, with hardly any money and in an old, beat-up 2CV; probably the most famous Citroen 2CV in North America.

Chapter 7 - A Retreat In The Snow

After two and a half months at sea on Vancouver Island I became a landlubber again. I drove off the ferry at Tsawwassen and thought about calling in to see Pat. During my early days on Vancouver Island I'd stayed in touch with him by e-mail. Pat and his wife didn't know about my failed business partnership with Cat and the gallon jugs of wine. I looked at the leaden sky and tapped my empty pocket. I figured they wouldn't want me turning up on their doorstep, and besides, I had to get across to eastern Canada as soon as possible. My plan was to reach Montreal and then take a cargo ship back across the Atlantic. The fact that I didn't have enough money for the petrol to take the *Yukon Queen* 3000 miles / 4850km to Montreal, or enough money to ship me and the car back across the Atlantic, didn't bother me: I would figure that one out when it came to it. My immediate concern was to get the *Yukon Queen* over the Rocky Mountains and on to the prairies. I had friends and allies on the prairies.

The traffic was awful on the Trans-Can Highway leading out of Vancouver. It was a typical November day: cold, wet and miserable. The *Yukon Queen* had hauled her load more than 10,000 miles to get to Vancouver Island, and what with all that driving up and down the island, she had easily clocked-up another 10,000 miles, most of them in torrential rain and with no mechanical problems whatsoever. Now the *Yukon Queen* was facing what was probably her final challenge on our little jaunt around North America: crossing the Rocky Mountains in winter road conditions. Was I asking too much of her?

By late afternoon we reached the small town of Hope, at the head of the Fraser River Valley. As before, I looked around the "Chainsaw Carving Capital of Canada" to see if anyone was carving things with a chainsaw. Nope, it was pretty quiet, and getting dark with heavy rain. I tanked-up with gas and winced at the price. I now had to decide which route to take. From the town of Hope there are three routes across the mountains: you can stay on Trans-Canada Highway

1, which makes a somewhat twisty and tortuous journey through the Rockies; or you can take Highway 5, which is a newly built toll motorway, known as the Sky Highway, because, well, it literally goes straight up into the sky; or you can take Highway 3, which is the southern route across the Rockies via Princeton and Nelson. Before leaving Vancouver Island everyone advised me to take this southern route, because the weather conditions would be less severe. On the approach to the main highway junction in Hope there are huge indicator boards which inform the weary traveller of road conditions on the three routes across the mountains. The bulletin for Highway 3 said that there were no reported problems. The bulletins for Highway 1 and Highway 5 mentioned the word 'snow' quite a lot, which sounded rather jolly.

In order to save on petrol costs I wanted to take the most direct route east, and I also wanted to make Calgary a port of call. This sort of ruled out Highway 3, leaving me the choice of Highway 1 or Highway 5. Oh well, in for a penny in for a pound: at the main junction in Hope you are warned of the steep gradients on Highway 5, and I would have to pay a toll. However, it would still work out cheaper, petrol-wise, than the tortuous route which Highway 1 took. Ever since making the decision to leave Vancouver Island and head east I'd become an avid watcher of the weather forecasts: winter was late in coming to Canada that year. I would take the risk and the highway into the sky.

Highway 5 didn't muck around and headed straight up into the mountains. The gradient wasn't too bad to begin with and I was on a very well built road, three lanes in either direction, four lanes on the steeper parts. I was somewhat surprised at the lack of traffic on the Sky Highway. I seemed to be the only driver making the journey up into the mountains. The construction of the highway was a major engineering feat and it seemed a pity that folks in these parts didn't appreciate it. Maybe it was the ten dollar toll that put them off?

Although night had fallen, the moon was showing off and I could see the spectacular scenery all around me. My ears began popping. There were also lots of signs that kept blathering on about snow chains. Snow chains? I was carrying a spare gearbox, five spare tyres, suspension arms, etc, etc, but I didn't have any snow chains. And then we hit the snow; just a light dusting at first, that grew thicker and thicker as we climbed upwards. The highway began to get really beastly and I had to change down into second gear to make the incline. The *Yukon Queen* was slipping and sliding all over the road. It was lucky there was no other traffic about. Jamie was very silent.

Somehow we got to the toll plaza, 35 miles up from Hope and in the middle of nowhere. I handed over my frozen ten bucks and asked what conditions were like further up the highway. The pleasant young lady in the toll booth welcomed me to Canada, which confused me somewhat. She told me that I'd just been through the worst stretch. Further up, the highway was mostly clear of snow, although there'd been reports of black ice. I asked her why there was very little traffic on the road. She said that the Sky Highway had only recently been built and people didn't know about it yet. Didn't know about it? It was a bloody six lane motorway running through the mountains!

Seventy miles up from Hope we came to Merritt, which is the only settlement along the 120 mile length of the Sky Highway. Considering its location, Merritt is quite a large town and is a main transportation hub. From here you can take connector highways to the Okanagan valley in the east and the Trans-Canada Highway in the west. Pretty exciting, huh; and I was rather excited to see that even though we were higher up in the mountains the snow had not yet settled on the road. It didn't last long: on the final 50 mile stretch to Kamloops the moon did a disappearing act and it began snowing. The *Yukon Queen* was slipping and sliding again, and this time I also had to deal with appalling visibility. It wasn't much fun, and now the lack of traffic on the road was a major worry: if the *Yukon Queen* got stuck in the snow I could well find myself stranded in a remote part of the mountains. "People didn't know about it yet", indeed!

We made it, though, we made it to Kamloops where we rejoined Trans-Canada Highway 1 and a little slice of civilisation. It had taken me nearly six hours to drive the 120 miles up the Sky Highway. I felt so exhausted by the ordeal that despite my lack of funds I checked into a hotel for the night. Before falling into a deep sleep I vowed that I would never again attempt these mountain roads in darkness.

With that in mind, the next morning I got up at first light. There in Kamloops I was only half way across the Rocky Mountains. If all went well, by nightfall I would be in Calgary, first stop on the prairies. I tried to forget that from Calgary it was still 2320 miles / 3740km to Montreal. That's twelve tanks of fuel for a Citroen 2CV. I tried to forget how much each tank of fuel would cost.

A light dusting of snow lay on the ground, yet the day was clear and mild and driving conditions were good as I bowled along eastwards. I was now on exactly the same route that Jose and I had taken back in the summer, but going in the opposite direction. I passed through Salmon Arm and then Revelstoke, where pretty white flakes began to fall from the heavens. On the climb up to the Rogers Pass a strong wind began whipping the snow, causing blizzard conditions. The road was narrow, with just one lane in each direction. I crawled along at 10 miles per hour, all the lights on the car blazing. After a few miles of battling through the atrocious weather I slid to a halt by a gang of workers who were trying to clear the road. We were all encountering the first heavy snowfall of winter in the Canadian Rockies. I had half a mind to turn back to Revelstoke, fearing that I'd never make it over the pass in these conditions. However, the road gang made me feel more secure: at least there were people about if anything untoward happened. Besides, now that winter had finally arrived in the Rockies it seemed unlikely that the snow would let-up in the near future. I could be spending a very long time in Revelstoke.

I asked the road gang how far it was to the top of the pass: about two miles. I told the gang that I was going to attempt the drive up there. One of them said that the *Yukon Queen* would never make it. I replied that if she did make it at least I knew that I could slide down the other side of the pass. I don't think they heard me. Everyone was muffled-up against the blizzard conditions.

It may surprise some readers just how well Citroen 2CVs cope in the snow. There are two main reasons for this. Firstly, the 2CV has front wheel drive, which gives it better traction. Secondly, the tyres on a 2CV are very narrow, which means less tyre contact with the snow and ice, which means less chance of tyre slip. 2CVs are also very light cars. You'll see big four-wheel drives stuck in snow drifts that a 2CV will easily pass through. Of course, that road gang wouldn't have known all this, because Citroen 2CVs were never sold in North America.

I still pushed my luck, though, as the *Yukon Queen* crawled up the Rogers Pass in first gear and barely doing five miles an hour. It didn't matter, as long as I could keep the car moving; and keep moving she did.

At the summit of the Rogers Pass there is a gas station. As I appeared through the driving snow some people came out to take a look. They couldn't believe that my little car had made it up there in such atrocious weather. It was one of those moments when I really regretted selling my digital camera. The *Yukon Queen*, the top of the Rogers Pass, blizzard conditions, it would have made a wonderful picture.

I didn't hang around. I wanted to be across the Rockies by dusk, snow or no snow. Actually, going down the other side of the Rogers Pass proved to be even hairier than climbing up it. The problem now was not to keep the car moving, but trying to stop it moving too fast. I barely used the accelerator, just lots of *very* gentle braking. I only hit the crash barriers once. I was becoming quite adept at this driving in the snow lark. Jamie, of course, was very silent.

We passed through Golden, where back in the summer the brakes had failed on the car and Jose crashed. Well, it added a bit of excitement to the Alaska Challenge bulletins. I looked around at the winter wonderland it had now become and wondered what Jose would make of it all. I didn't have time to wonder for long, because there was one more steep climb to overcome before I could slide down the eastern flanks of the mountains and on to the prairies. This was Kicking Horse Pass, which is the British Columbia–Alberta border. At 5,338 feet it's also the highest point on the Canadian Pacific Railway. The railway was built here in 1911; the Trans-Canada Highway didn't dare to venture through until the 1960s; but you know all this anyway.

Kicking Horse Pass seemed a breeze compared to the Rogers Pass, mainly because the wind had calmed down and the snow was much lighter. I even paused at the lay-by there, where Jose and I had stopped in the summer. The Alaska Challenge bulletin No.14 has a photograph taken at this exact same spot in August. Damn, if only I had the digital camera.

East of Kicking Horse Pass it's literally downhill all the way, made easier because the weather wasn't quite so beastly. When I got to Banff at dusk I was ahead of the bad weather. It was freezing cold but the streets were clear of the white stuff. The streets weren't clear of people, though. Banff is a big winter resort and at this time of year it's packed with folks who are there for the skiing in the mountains. It was quite a shock to suddenly find myself in such a bustling place. I'd had quite enough of skiing in the Rockies with the *Yukon Queen* and didn't want to hang around for long. I went into a restaurant and made a call to Adina, in Calgary. The mouth-watering smell of food, the sight of happy holidaymakers stuffing themselves and the heat in the place made me realise just how cold, hungry and broke I was.

Adina, of course, was the Head Of Marketing at Vitacorp, one of the company sponsors of the 2CV Alaska Challenge. When Jose and I passed through Calgary in the summer, Adina and her boss, Andrew, had been wonderful hosts. I'd been e-mailing with Adina ever since. She knew I'd been living on Vancouver Island, knew I was heading back east and knew that I needed a place to stay in Calgary. Adina was a sweetie, because despite the fact that we'd only meet a few times and hardly knew each other, she readily agreed to let me stay at her place. I suppose that's what comes of being big in the Yukon.

From Banff to Calgary it's a fifty mile drive across the undulating prairies, and I kept one step ahead of the snow. I told everyone I met that it was coming. I arrived in Calgary at eight o'clock in the evening. As before, it felt very strange to be back in this city where so much had happened to me as a young man. Adina's apartment was in downtown Calgary, and she really proved to be a sweetie, because despite the fact that I was unshaven, shivering and starving she welcomed me with open arms. After my two day ordeal crossing the Rocky Mountains I thought I'd treat myself to a steak and a belly full of beer; screw the expense. Later, I had an incredibly comfortable night's sleep on Adina's sofa. The next morning, Adina told me that I was welcome to stay another night, no doubt relieved that Rob Godfrey, wild man of the arctic, hadn't drunk all her whisky and bitten the head off her cat. It would have been nice to hide from the world for a while, and Adina's sofa was certainly very inviting. However, the journey that had started more than five months previously was still sweeping me along, and I could sense that it was rapidly coming to some sort of conclusion.

The snow followed me across the prairies. When I arrived in Regina I heard that back in Calgary they were now experiencing blizzard conditions. It hadn't reached Regina yet, although the temperature was subzero. This meant that I couldn't sleep in the car, because freezing to death is such an unpleasant way to die, so reluctantly I spent some of my meagre resources on a hotel room. I awoke to find myself on the front of a Christmas card. Time to run ahead of the snow again. As I made my way back to the Trans-Canada Highway I came to a set of lights that were turning red. The car was moving at only 20 miles an hour. I braked and nothing happened. We were sliding across sheet ice, straight across the junction, where a crossing car had to swerve to avoid me and a truck had to brake violently. Luckily for me, the truck's wheels held the ice and it managed to stop, just inches from me. It had been a very close shave, and reminded me that after crossing the Rocky Mountains I had perhaps become a bit too blasé about driving in snow and ice.

A day's hard driving enabled me to get ahead of the snow again. I reached Winnipeg at eight in the evening. "It's coming, it's coming!" I told Tony, who enquired about weather conditions further west and who had agreed to put me up for a few nights. Tony apologised for not putting the charity sponsorship form and my two final bulletins up on the Alaska Challenge web site. I told him not to worry about it. By that time I was beyond caring. However, the atmosphere between us was somewhat strained. The *Yukon Queen* and the No.2 car had a more emotional reunion. It seemed strange to see them together again, and brought back all those summer memories, when we had lots of money in the bank.

I was now stone broke. I could not afford the petrol for the next leg of the journey east. A phone call to England secured me a little bit more money. However, it wasn't enough to get me and the *Yukon Queen* to Montreal, let alone for that cargo ship across the Atlantic. Hmm, what does 'moi' do now? I suppose I could have become a male prostitute and hung around on street corners in the hope of selling my body, but it was so damn cold in Winnipeg, and besides, my teeth still badly needed the attention of a dentist. There was only one other option: with a very heavy heart I knew that I would have to sell the *Yukon Queen*.

Daybreak found Winnipeg subzero but snowless. I drove over to the Winnipeg Motor Museum and introduced myself to the guy who managed the place. He had a face a bit like a transit van and was very interested in the *Yukon Queen*, the first Citroen 2CV to be driven up to the Arctic Ocean in Alaska. I showed him some of the press cuttings and we agreed it would make a lovely display in the museum. I mentioned a price of 10,000 dollars for the *Yukon Queen*. The manager said that it was the low season and the museum was receiving very few visitors and he just didn't have that sort of money in the pot. He offered one thousand dollars. I refused, saying it had to be 10,000 bucks or nothing; for "probably the most famous Citroen 2CV in North America". The manager agreed that the No.1 car was worth 10,000 bucks, but he just didn't have ten grand. He gave me the number of a classic car collector who lived in Winnipeg, saying that he might be interested.

The classic car collector went by the name of John Anderson and I found him waiting for me outside his house. John was in his early 40s, with short, dark hair and a somewhat roguish look about him. He earned his crust as a currency speculator and was very, very rich. He showed me some of the classic cars in his cavernous garage. Yup, seriously rich. John immediately took to the *Yukon Queen* and the story behind her. He walked around the car and whistled, then offered me 10,000 bucks, cash, which he could pay me within the hour, after going to the bank. That's when I made my big mistake: I hesitated. John seemed so keen to buy the car that I thought I might be able to get more than ten thousand for her. I told John that I was selling the car very reluctantly and would let him know in the morning.

In anticipation of at least 10,000 bucks soon to be filling my pockets, I left Tony's basement and checked into a suite on the 11th floor of the Sheraton Hotel, one of the best and most expensive hotels in Winnipeg. It swallowed up nearly all the money I'd just received from England, but I knew that in the morning I'd sell the car and be in funds again; quite a lot of funds. I suppose I could have checked into a cheaper hotel, or stayed in Tony's basement. It's just that by this time I'd been slumming it for so many months that I figured I had earned myself a bit of luxury, in the shape of a suite on the 11th floor of the Sheraton Hotel.

Next morning I stretched out in a luxurious king size bed. Outside it was subzero again, but the white stuff still hadn't arrived. I rang John Anderson. A woman answered the phone and told me that John had gone away on business and wouldn't be back for a number of weeks. I asked if she had a contact number for him. She said she didn't. I drove round to John's house. He wasn't there; he really had left town, and I was left in the lurch: without any money and without a buyer for the car.

I left the Sheraton Hotel and went back to Tony's basement. Things were even more strained between us. It was obvious that I had outstayed my welcome. I needed to sell the car, and fast. Tony's wife said that she knew of someone who just might be interested in the car. Phone calls were made. The 'someone' turned out to be a woman named Lesley, and yes, she was interested and told me to come over and see her.

Lesley's business lay in the run-down part of central Winnipeg. She owned one of the old warehouses there and on the ground floor a curiosity shop called Volantis Flying Fish. The shop had a wonderful name and inside an even more wonderful display of extremely curious items. Lesley was a slim, attractive women in her fifties. She wore purple John Lennon-type specs and chain-smoked cigarettes. Lesley and I clicked right away. I knew she was going to be the next owner of the *Yukon Queen*. It was fate, destiny, or what have you. She was exactly the right sort of person for the car.

We sat in her office and chatted for a while. I showed Lesley some of the newspaper cuttings and told her the story of the Alaska Challenge. An attractive young girl made us coffee. The young girl lived upstairs, in one of the upper storeys of the warehouse. Apparently it was some sort of commune and lots of people lived up there. I was big in the Yukon, and maybe that's why Lesley and the girl asked me if I wanted to move in and be part of the commune. I thought about letting it all hang out for a while. It certainly would be fun. However, at that moment the temperature outside hovered at 15 below freezing. If the commune had been in Barbados I might have accepted the offer; but not in Winnipeg, not in the winter.

Lesley and I went out to have a look at the car. Fate had already decreed that Lesley was to be its next owner. She fell in love with the car as soon as she laid eyes on it. We went for a test drive. Lesley had never driven anything like the *Yukon Queen* before and to begin with found the gear lever difficult. She soon got the hang of it, though, and was bombing around downtown Winnipeg as though she were on the streets of Paris. We screeched to a halt back outside Volantis Flying Fish. Lesley could not afford to pay 10,000 dollars for the *Yukon Queen*; in fact, she couldn't really afford to pay anything for the car. Business was slow and she was short of cash. Quite honestly, I would have given the car to her for nothing, because of the karma: Lesley and the *Yukon Queen* were made for each other. However, stone broke and stranded in the middle of Canada, I had to be realistic about things. Eventually, Lesley and I settled on a price of 2000 dollars. This money was supposed to buy a new computer for her business, but Lesley said that she just had to have the car and could always get the computer at a later date. We shook hands on the deal, with a proviso: one day I would return for the car, and would buy it back from Lesley. I'd sworn that somehow I would get the *Yukon Queen* back to England. Lesley becoming the temporary owner of the car was that 'somehow'. As I drove away from Volantis Flying Fish I began figuring out how I was going to get the money and return to Winnipeg for the car.

In the meantime, we agreed that I would pick-up the payment for the car the following day. Lesley gave me a cheque to take to her bank for cash. She rang the bank to let them know about me and the cheque. I got the cash without any difficulty. That was on a Friday morning. We also agreed that the huge amount of spare parts the *Yukon Queen* carried would be left with Tony. Tony seemed quite happy with this arrangement, since it would give him spares for the No.2 car, and if Lesley ever needed spare parts, Tony's house was not far away. I spent the Saturday transferring all the parts to Tony's garage and getting the *Yukon Queen* ready for her new owner. Then I checked back into the Sheraton Hotel. The *Yukon Queen* would be formally handed over to Lesley at 10am the following morning; but not before I did some publicity with the car. I rang the *Winnipeg Sun* and was put through to a reporter called Tammy. After I'd explained the story behind the car, Tammy said that she'd bring a photographer and meet us outside Volantis Flying Fish the next morning. I just couldn't resist it: my final piece of publicity in North America with the *Yukon Queen*.

On that Sunday morning in Winnipeg it was 14 degrees below freezing and a keen wind seemed determined to make it even colder. Lesley was somewhat annoyed when Tammy and her photographer showed-up. However, when I explained that the publicity would be good for her business, Lesley soon got into the swing of it. The two of us had our picture taken with the *Yukon Queen* outside Volantis Flying Fish. We didn't linger on the photo shoot because of the weather. Tammy had already got most of the story from me the previous evening and she and the photographer left, saying that the piece would appear in the next day's *Winnipeg Sun*. I handed over the car keys to Lesley and walked back to my hotel, which was just a short distance away. I'm not sure if the tears in my eyes were due to the subzero temperatures or the fact that I'd just sold the *Yukon Queen*.

On the Monday I checked out of the Sheraton Hotel for the final time. The staff had got to know me, and the *Yukon Queen*. Where's the car? they asked. Well, being without the *Yukon Queen* certainly came as a shock to the system. My worldly possessions were now carried in a rucksack and a huge suitcase. Amongst other things, the huge suitcase contained my very big and very heavy typewriter. I took the typer on a taxi ride to the station. It was only two blocks away and I had a ticket to Toronto.

The train left Winnipeg right on time at ten to two in the afternoon. It's a 34 hour journey to Toronto. Most people don't seem to mind travelling in sardine cans at 30,000 feet above the ground, and as a result there weren't many passengers heading to Toronto on the rails. Smoking was not allowed anywhere on the train. However, you cannot entirely stub out human foibles and back then, on long distance trains in Canada, you could usually smoke in the restaurant car, at the discretion of the conductor. Our conductor was a conductress, a jolly young girl called Julie who was quite happy to let us puff away; and so a small group of us, hardened smokers one and all, spent most of the journey drinking beer and wine in the restaurant car. In fact, I never slept at all during that 34 hour party.

As we travelled through the endless province of Ontario the snow managed to catch up with the train. The winter wonderland outside the windows added to the jolly atmosphere in the restaurant car. Amongst our group there was a hippy. He looked to be in his late forties, with a beard and long, black, straggling hair that hadn't been washed for many a moon. Likewise, his fingernails were black and hadn't been cut for ages. They were like talons. The hippy chain-smoked cigarettes and never spoke a word to any of us. He was completely lost in his own thoughts. Every now and then his face broke into a smile. Sometimes he laughed very loudly. We all wondered just what was going through his head. However, despite his appearance and strange habits, the fellow was always very courteous and no one minded him being there with us.

At the longer station stops we would get off the train to stretch our legs, and yes, have a smoke. During one of these stops I managed to have a conversation with the hippy. He told me his name was John. He'd come from British Columbia and was heading back to spend the winter in Toronto. John didn't reveal much more about himself and for some reason he really took to me. Maybe it was my rotten teeth. After that he began talking to the crowd in the restaurant car and even bought us drinks. We were all surprised to see that he paid for the drinks with a gold credit card.

The train arrived in Toronto at nine thirty on the Tuesday evening, 29th November. John asked me what my plans were. I told him I was on my way to Montreal and planned to spend the night in a hotel. John said that he was going to stay at a friend's place, and I would also be able to stay there. It seemed a rather jolly idea, that is until we took a taxi from the station to one of the more salubrious districts of Toronto. The taxi dropped us on a street corner. John headed off down the crowded sidewalk and I followed, lugging that huge suitcase along, as well as my rucksack. Lots of people on the sidewalk called greetings to John. They didn't look like the sort of people you'd introduce your mother to. Why hadn't the taxi dropped us off right outside the friend's house? Why was John leading me along the sidewalk? I didn't like the look of it and called out to John to stop. He carried on going. I shouted out to him that I had changed my mind and would stay in a hotel instead. John shrugged and disappeared into the crowd. The dangerous dudes eyed me curiously. I was in trouble here; I could sense it. Luckily, at that moment a taxi was passing and I managed to hail it. It took me back to the downtown area, where I spent the night in a hotel. This incident in Toronto was a sharp reminder of just what a protecting influence the *Yukon Queen* had been. In future I would have to be more careful.

I got to Montreal the following afternoon after five and a half hours on a train. Canada certainly is a very big country. Montreal was wonderful: gem of the St. Lawrence, the Paris of North America, *la Ville aux cent clochers* – Montreal was founded by French explorers more than 350 years ago, thus making it one of the oldest cities in North America. Political correctness hadn't reached this far yet. The snow had, and it was bloody freezing. Without any consideration of the cost I checked into a plush downtown hotel. The 2000 bucks which Lesley had paid me for the *Yukon Queen* were really taking a hammering, but I didn't care, I'd already made-up my mind about what I was going to do. I needed ten thousand dollars to buy back the *Yukon Queen*, cover all my expenses and ship her across the Atlantic to England. The only way I could get such a large sum of money was to either steal it or win it. My anxiety attacks and claustrophobia wouldn't take to prison life, so my only option was to win the money. Amongst other things, Montreal is known for its world class casino. I would go there and win the ten thousand dollars.

With this plan in mind, how fast I spent Lesley's two thousand dollars became irrelevant. However, I did need to have some stake money, and the more the merrier. That plush hotel was costing me an awful lot of money so after two nights I moved into a cheaper hotel near the station; and there, in a small, depressing room in an icy city, I worked out my plan. Well, it was quite simple, really: I'd play the roulette table, do or die. I didn't want to rush into things, though, and spent a number of days just getting familiarised with the casino.

The Casino de Montreal is situated on Isle Notre-Dame, across from Montreal's Old Port. It's a modern, curvy building of steel and glass and is a landmark in its own right. Spread over the five floors of the casino there are 2,750 slot machines, 112 gaming tables and numerous other devices, such as bingo and electronic horse-racing tracks, all designed to make the porous punter part with their money. Unlike the casinos in Las Vegas, which are windowless and smell like hamster cages, the Casino de Montreal is light and airy and is an uplifting building to be in.

On the evening of my fifth day in Montreal I got dressed-up. Well, I put on an old tie and brushed my hair. I had a date with Destiny. I had one thousand dollars in my pocket. Luck be a lady tonight. I took a taxi to the casino and strode confidentially through the front doors. After one champagne cognac in the bar I went to the high rollers roulette table, 20 bucks minimum bet, and took my place. I eyed the other gamblers, but it wasn't much like a James Bond movie. There were two batty old ladies, a Chinese man who looked like he ran the local take-away and a slightly bemused American who seemed to have got there by mistake. They all had one thing in common though: they could afford to lose a minimum of twenty bucks every minute or so.

The croupier was an attractive young blonde. Her blue eyes smiled at me. I put fifty dollars on red and won. I let my winnings ride on red and won again. Hey, this was easy. I spread two hundred bucks around the numbers and seemed to come out on top again. Everything I'd won so far was placed on black. I lost. A waiter placed a complimentary drink at my side. I came to the conclusion that I was being too timid. This was all or nothing, man. I put five hundred dollars on black. It won. I put one thousand dollars on red. It won. I spread two thousand dollars around the higher numbers and came out on top again. I now had more than five thousand dollars. People began to gather round and watch. Luck was a lady indeed. Things were going my way. Five thousand bucks seemed a small fortune to me, but I needed ten thousand to be able to reclaim the *Yukon Queen* and ship her back to England. I was going to win the ten thousand. It was fate, destiny. The run of good luck that had been a feature of the Alaska Challenge was going to hold. I could feel it in my bones. I put all of the five thousand bucks on black. Everyone held their breath. The attractive young croupier spun the wheel. The ball tinkled. It spat out red. From the moment I sat down at that roulette table it had taken me less than eight minutes to lose everything I had.

Using the spare change left in my pocket, I took a bus back to my hotel room and felt very depressed. I didn't really care about losing the money. I did care about losing the *Yukon Queen*, a car which had been my faithful companion throughout one of the biggest adventures of my life. The next morning I walked the icy sidewalks and sold my mobile phone, my boots and some other items and managed to scrape together enough money for a cheap flight across the Atlantic. I was still reeling from losing the *Yukon Queen*, and now my heart was to be broken again: I couldn't afford excess baggage charges and so I had to let go of my old Imperial 80 typewriter, my fifth limb. As I made my way to the airport I carried just the rucksack. My typer, and most of my other possessions, were left behind in that huge suitcase in a hotel room in Montreal.

Flights to London were beyond my means. Air Transit, though, were doing an incredible deal on flights to Paris: $170 one-way. It was the lull before Christmas, their planes were empty and they needed to fill seats. A blind drunk intrepid adventurer filled one of their seats, because my anxiety attacks have always meant that flying is a big no-no. I can only step on a plane after having an awful lot to drink. Fortunately, the flight from Montreal's Mirabel airport was delayed by four hours, which allowed plenty of time for filling hollow legs.

I don't remember much of the eight hour flight to Paris. I was in a drunken slumber. When I came to the plane was touching down at Charles de Gaulle airport. It was lunchtime. My anxiety attacks are triggered by situations where I feel trapped and not in control, so underground railways are also a big no-no for me. However, I was still slightly drunk and so managed to get from the airport to the Gare du Nord. I didn't have enough funds for the train back to England. Jose came to the rescue with an emergency money wire. Thankfully it came through later that afternoon and I picked up 500 lovely French francs at a post office near the Gare du Nord. I planned to take a Eurostar back to England, using the newly opened Channel Tunnel. However, the fare was very expensive and there were no discounts for intrepid adventurers. I had no choice but to take a train up to Calais and then a ferry across the Channel. I arrived in Calais late in the evening. I should have been on the midnight ferry to England, but fell asleep in the departure lounge. I think it was a combination of the after effects of all that alcohol and a tremendous upsurge of emotion and weariness, now that the big adventure was almost over.

It was just me and the lorry drivers and a Force 6 gale that made the crossing in the wee hours of the morning. I arrived in storm-lashed Dover at just after 6am on the 6th December, to discover that there was a warrant out for my arrest for non-payment of fines resulting from not having a tv licence.

But that's another story.

Epilogue

Limousin, France, April 2004

Things never felt the same for me after the Alaska Challenge. I was 36-years-old when the *Marie Anne* sailed from Rotterdam and the journey to Alaska began. Perhaps I left my youth behind in that hotel room in Montreal, along with most of my other possessions? although I did pass my 40th birthday while living in a cowshed in middle-of-nowhere France, where I completed this book, so it doesn't seem like I've given in to the comfy chair and carpet slippers just yet.

It took me six months to pay off all the debts that resulted from my little jaunt to North America. It seemed a small price to pay for being the holder of such a wonderfully naff record: the first man to drive a Citroen 2CV up to the Arctic Ocean in Alaska. And others were not far behind me: the following summer a group of Dutch people took five 2CVs up the Dalton Highway to Prudhoe Bay, and they made it there and back. Incredible cars, and between 1948 and 1990, when they ceased manufacture, more than six and a half million 2CVs rolled off the production line, making them the most popular Citroen ever. I figured you just needed to know that.

Jose and I remained friends. She even planned to join me on my next jaunt, the Paris to Peking Challenge, and this time we wouldn't be driving a 2CV, but a Traction Avant, one of the really old Citroens that were much favoured by the French Resistance during the war. However, at the time of writing my dream of driving an old Citroen around China is still waiting to happen; in otherwords, I'm still trying to get sponsorship money. As for Jose, two years after the Alaska Challenge she moved back to Holland. We still keep in touch.

And the car, that wonderful little car, I never did go back to North America and reclaim her. The cares and worries of everyday life saw to that. However, in 2002 I attempted to find out what had become of the *Yukon Queen*. I tried contacting Lesley but got no response. Tony told me that she had sold her business and left Winnipeg. He didn't know her whereabouts. No one seemed to know her whereabouts. I posted messages on the internet, on Citroen buff's message boards, asking if anyone had seen the *Yukon Queen*. Within a few days I was told that there'd been sightings of her in Vancouver. It was definitely the *Yukon Queen* because she still carried the banners of our company sponsors. Shortly after this, Tony told me that he'd got word that Lesley had relocated to the west coast.

It seemed quite fitting that the *Yukon Queen* should find a home in Vancouver, the place where it all began.

end

More books by Rob Godfrey can be found at:
www.robgodfrey.com

Printed in Great Britain
by Amazon

72246012R00149